Cage & Aviary
BIRDS

CU00324438

Cage & Aviary
BIRDS

Richard Mark Martin

illustrated by Malcolm Ellis

COLLINS 8 GRAFTON STREET, LONDON

William Collins Sons & Co Ltd
London · Glasgow · Sydney · Auckland
Toronto · Johannesburg

This edition published by William Collins Sons & Co Ltd.
1980
Reprinted 1984, 1986
© 1980 Equinox (Oxford) Ltd
All rights reserved

ISBN 0 00 219238 1
Planned and produced by
Equinox (Oxford) Ltd, Littlegate House, St Ebbe's Street,
Oxford
Filmset by Keyspools Ltd., Colborne, Lancs
Colour reproduction by Art Color Offset, Rome
Printed by Brepols, Turnhout, Belgium

No part of this publication may be reproduced, stored
in a retrieval system or transmitted, in any form, or
by any means, electronic, mechanical, photocopying,
recording or otherwise, without the prior permission
of the copyright holders.

CONTENTS

PREFACE	5
THE BIRD	7
A HISTORY OF BIRDKEEPING	12
CHOOSING A BIRD	19
HOUSING	24
FEEDING	34
GENERAL MANAGEMENT	40
BREEDING	47
TREATING SICK BIRDS	53
CANARIES	60
BUDGERIGARS	74
SEEDEATERS	95
PARROTS	156
SOFTBILLS	196
GLOSSARY	248
BIBLIOGRAPHY	249
INDEX	251

PREFACE

Keeping cagebirds is a wonderful pastime with a long history and a universal appeal. It is an absorbing, highly satisfying and rewarding interest that can be enjoyed by people of all ages and from all walks of life. Cagebirds have many advantages over other animals as pets and there is an enormous variety of birds to choose from with characters every bit as varied as their looks. They may be divided into five main groups which are all embraced within the pages of this comprehensive guide which has been written with the minimum of jargon and using the help of many color illustrations thoroughly to cover all aspects of the subject. It contains all the beginner needs to know about cagebirds and much of great value to the experienced fancier. It begins by outlining briefly what a bird is and how it differs from other kinds of animal, tracing it back to the prehistoric *Archaeopteryx*, explaining how its body works and the kind of life the main types lead that the reader may better understand them. The history of birdkeeping is discussed and then the relative merits of the kinds that are available, with advice on how to make a wise choice, followed by chapters dealing with their housing, feeding and general management. Despite excellent advice birds still occasionally become sick, so there is a chapter on how to recognize the symptoms of sickness and effectively treat it.

The main part of the book devotes a separate chapter to each of the main bird groups: Canaries, Budgerigars, Seedeaters, Parrots and Softbills, and deals with them in depth. The magnificent color plates accompanying each section are designed to aid speedy and accurate indentification and depict hundreds of popular species and varieties with concise and pertinent information about each bird placed close by for quick reference.

Bird keeping and breeding and the sale, import and export of birds are all strictly governed by law. In many countries export of rare species is banned in order to conserve wild stocks and the keeping of certain species prohibited. In Britain it is an offence to sell birds of indigenous species that are not genuinely aviary bred and close-ringed. United Kingdom legislation, as set out in the Protection of Birds Act, 1954, and its amendments, and EEC wildlife and countryside laws and import controls are always likely to be revised. Up-to-date information on British legislation is available from the Department of the Environment. All who intend to purchase birds, except from recognized dealers, should be aware of current legislation.

THE BIRD

CHAPTER 1: THE BIRD

During the late Paleozoic Era (between 250 and 300 million years ago) the early reptiles diverged into various streams and began to develop new modes of life. Many of these — including the dinosaurs — were doomed to extinction, others survived to become modern reptiles, but two were to throw off the shackles of a cold-blooded life, with all the limitations which it imposes, and emerge as the most successful forms of modern life: mammals and birds. Both are warm-blooded and have a reptilian ancestry but there the similarity ends.

Mammals had their heyday some 50 million years ago and since then have been on a gradual decline. Birds, on the other hand, are on the crest of an evolutionary wave: comprising nearly 9,000 species — over double that of mammals — they also show a fantastic diversity, mobility and versatility. They range in size from the tiny Bee Hummingbird *Mellisuga helenae* 63 mm (2½ in) long including an outsized bill to the towering flightless Ostrich *Struthio camelus*, all of 244 cm (8 ft) tall. While the prototype mammals modified their forms and developed fur and insulation from their inherited scales, the emerging birds developed them into feathers (also insulatory), and the two lines went their separate ways.

The birds' mastery of the air no doubt kept pace with the perfection of their feathering: probably progressing from simple jumps to gravity-assisted glides to powered glides and so, eventually, to controlled flight. Even so it has taken them millions of years of evolution to perfect their conquest of the skies. There is more to flight than simply feathers — as many "birdmen" of the past have discovered to their cost. Feathers form the body-covering we see but beneath is an astonishing anatomy consisting of a highly specialized musculature and a unique skeleton. The forelimbs have undergone the most far-reaching changes in becoming the actual organs of flight — the wings — providing both lift and propulsion through the air. These are powered by immensely strong muscles which are anchored to the strengthened keel of an enlarged breastbone. The tail in many guises performs a wide variety of stabilising and directional functions, and tends to harness the power of the wings.

The shape of a bird's wing — basically convex above, concave below, with a thick leading edge and a thin

7

THE BIRD

trailing edge — has never been bettered by aerodynamic experts. The rigid flight feathers emanate from the forearm and the three digits of the "hand." Covering the remainder of the body is a plumage consisting of sometimes highly colored, sometimes camouflaged contour feathers (which protect and streamline) and an underlying system of down feathers (which insulate). Feathers are amazingly elaborate products of epidermis, comprised almost exclusively of keratin, they are therefore extremely strong, sound and light. Each feather is made up of a series of interlocking barbs and barbules which the bird keeps in good order by preening. Molting, which enables a bird completely to renew its plumage at least once a year, is nearly always a progressive and symmetrical process so that throughout its duration — which takes some weeks — the bird can continue to function normally.

Apart from the benefits afforded by their plumage and power of flight — which combine to make birds the most widespread and mobile of all animals — they also display many other interesting features. Egg-laying, seen to be a severe disadvantage in mammals, has been turned to the advantage of birds, and they have overcome the drawbacks of nest-building, egg-laying, incubation and rearing their sometimes altricial (helpless) young in a way that reptiles and mammals have found impossible. This is certainly due in part to their high mobility. Mammals are somewhat encumbered by having to carry about unborn young and then protect them for long periods once they are born. The big advantage of this system is that it produces relatively small numbers of high quality young, but birds, by retaining the egg-laying method of reptiles and infusing it with their own brand of warm-bloodedness, achieve the best of both worlds. Thanks to their rapid growth rate and quickly gained independence, many birds are able to rear three clutches of sturdy youngsters each year. Food can be transported over long distances from wherever it is plentiful, and their outstanding powers of migration coupled to stupendous endurance mean that they are able to follow the most favorable climates around the world, utilising them to the full.

From the earliest known bird, Archaeopteryx, which emerged some 150 million years ago, the Class Aves has come a long way. Birds are now to be found living virtually all over the world, having claimed habitats as

Archaeopteryx, which lived some 150 million years ago shows how birds evolved from reptiles.

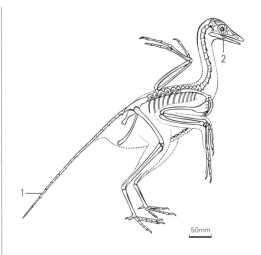

50mm

1 Reptile-like tail
2 Toothed jaws

dissimilar as oceans, mountain-tops, deserts, jungles, lakes, rivers and polar ice-caps. They have followed in the wake of man and benefited from some of his activities, though many species have suffered cruelly at his hand as well. Diversity of habitat naturally means a wide variety of different diets as well, and among birds can be found all manner of herbivores, carnivores, insectivores, frugivores (fruit-eaters), nectivores and, indeed, omnivores. Perhaps most important of all are the vast legions of seedeaters (which occupy a large portion of this book) and invertebrate-feeders (often called softbills) ; it is perhaps to these two types of diet that birds are best suited.

   The digestive system of birds is remarkably efficient, it satisfies the demands made on it by a high metabolic rate and a vigorous lifestyle. Energy is needed to fuel the powerful wing muscles which are able to propel some birds halfway round the world twice a year on migration, maintaining at the same time a high body temperature. A warm body is also essential to the efficient functioning of a high metabolism and effective nervous system. The jittery, wary demeanour of many

9

THE BIRD

birds is further indication of this and all part of their defensive mechanism against predators, which number other birds among them. The actual structure of birds is first and foremostly governed by the demands of flight, this can readily be seen even in the skeletons of flightless varieties — which have lost the power of flight rather than never had it. Apart from the enlarged breastbone, the other most striking modifications are the formation of the very bones themselves, which are hollow, and the manner in which the shoulder, vertebrae and pelvic girdle have become fused, so forming a featherweight but amazingly strong body-case. Such limitations result in a considerable degree of standardization, although the basic body plan does vary sufficiently to accommodate the secondary demands made upon it by diet and an individual life-style.

Just to skip casually through the illustrations of any comprehensive bird book shows something of the remarkable extent to which birds have adapted and moulded a basic shape to suit all possible ecological niches. The search for food is the greatest single pressure on a bird's behavior, and all other desires and instincts are fitted around this motivating force. The shape of the horny bill — which has replaced teeth — illustrates the variety of diets birds have turned to in their search to avoid competition and make use of all available sources of supply: the hooked, flesh-tearing bills of birds of prey; the delicate probing bills of waders; the stout, conical bills of seed-crackers; the dagger-like bills of herons; the chisel-like bills of woodpeckers; and the spatulate bills of ducks are just a few examples of this adaptive radiation. Some species, such as pelicans and flamingos, have solved feeding problems in their own highly distinctive and individualistic ways but it is all part of the same process. To an ornithologist, the shape of a bird's bill immediately tells him a lot about its owner. The wings, which might be scimitar-shaped like those of a swift or falcon, or, at the other extreme, broad like those of a vulture, are further clues. Feet, too, provide firm indications of a bird's lifestyle: they might be webbed like a duck's, broad-toed like a loon's, long-toed like a lily-trotter's, needle-taloned like an eagle's, or the more standard gripping and perching foot of most passerines.

Songbirds are members of the Order Passeriformes,

and birdsong which so delights the human ear is one reason for the popularity of certain species as cage-birds. Biologically it performs a very different function, as do the calls of many other birds which can hardly be described as songs. The calls of birds fundamentally constitute a language; if we accept that a bird does not give voice solely for its own gratification then it *must* intend its utterance to be heard by something else: language in its most basic vocal form — the conveying of information. It might be along the lines of: "Beware, an enemy is approaching," "Keep out, this is my territory," "Feed me," "I like you," "Follow me and I'll show you food," "Keep together" etc: the language is obviously comprehensive enough to deal with all eventualities. Besides vocal expression there are also the visual languages of gesture, display, ornamentation and color. The displays of birds are extraordinary in both their effect and beauty. One normally thinks of courtship displays but there are also others dealing with intimidation, aggression and submission. The bright colors and plumage eccentricities of many male birds are an essential part of courting a mate or mates; while the drab garb of most females and young has the opposite purpose — camouflage.

Language, then, is an essential part of any society, and birds are generally social animals. Many con-gregate in huge flocks not only for safety reasons but also to capitalize on localized food abundancies. A healthy flock is a healthy bird is a healthy species. Some, like seabirds, even breed communally while others become very territorial, reverting to a co-operative life after the breeding season is over. Most migratory species travel in company with their fellows or even with members of different species.

Before concentrating on bird-*keeping*, it will be useful briefly to explain classification. Linnaeus, the great 18th-century Swedish naturalist, was the father of the binominal system which categorizes animals and plants into classes, orders, families, genera, species and subspecies (when necessary, intermediary groups such as subfamilies are interpolated between these primary categories). A sufficiently unique species will constitute a species genus and family all of its own: the Sunbittern *Eurypyga helias*, occasionally seen in zoos, is a good example, being the sole member of the Eurypygidae. Accepting that an animal (or plant) is a biological entity, the binominal system sets down its position relevant to other animals, and represents a clear international language. Unfortunately there is a modern trend to "update" scientific names and re-classify, which is very confusing.

The theory behind the binominal system is that each species has at least two names: a generic one which allies it to a family, followed by a specific one, which is its own personal label, and frequently descriptive. When two or more members of the same species differ enough to warrant individual assessment, a third or subspecific name is added on, and this is where disagreement often creeps in. "Lumpers" like to eliminate subspecies wherever possible while "Split-ters" will recognize even a slight deviation as a separate subspecies or race; I tend to "slump" somewhere in the middle.

The importance of the binominal system can be easily illustrated: the confusion which surrounds the Red Hooded Siskin *Carduelis cucullatus* is a fitting example — sometimes it is called simply the Hooded Siskin, and if its scientific name is not also included, a reader might wrongly assume that the species being referred to is *Carduelis magellanicus* (which is more properly called the Hooded Siskin): as can be seen, the two are related but quite different. Many of the scientific names stem from classical Greek, but they are nowadays always latinized.

CHAPTER 2: A HISTORY OF BIRDKEEPING

Over 3,000 years before the birth of Christ man had already begun to tame certain types of wild birds, going on to breed them and so turn their virtues to his own ends. As long ago as 2600 BC descendants of the wild Rock Dove *Columba livia* were already domesticated; indeed the pigeon was probably the very first domesti-cated animal. In the early Near East cultures the dove was regarded as sacred; to the Syrian Goddess Astarte it was a symbol of fertility; the Grecian Goddess of Desire, Aphrodite, sanctified it; and later the Romans associated it with Venus. Later still the dove was protected by the Islamic religion in most Mohammedan countries; and we still regard it as the symbol of Peace.

But, far from being merely symbolic, the pigeon was also highly functional, and indeed still is today. As a source of fresh meat it was highly esteemed, and its abundant feathers could be used for bedding. When its phenomenal "homing" ability was realized it was swiftly put to good use: messages were transmitted by pigeons in Ancient Egypt. This activity was developed by the Greeks and Romans, and regular pigeon-posts became commonplace throughout much of the Middle East. During the 6th century — when the Saxons conquered England — pigeons were kept on ordinary farmsteads in specially made cotes; later they became a feature of many prosperous estates.

The sport of pigeon-racing also grew out of the discovery of this astonishing ability — which enables pigeons to find their way home across land *and* water they have never seen before. It is not a phenomenon unique to pigeons, of course: many birds employ the same or a similar sense when on migration. It has now been proved that birds navigate by means of the earth's magnetic field, stars and solar system. Pigeon-racing was a logical human progression from simple message carrying, and now pigeons are bred solely for their speed and stamina. It enjoys enormous popularity in many parts of the world, and in Britain at least, there is scarcely a village or town which does not have its band of ardent followers and its clusters of lofts or cotes. It represents one of the earliest forms of bird-keeping as a hobby.

Likewise, during the 2nd and 3rd millennium BC, the Red Junglefowl *Gallus gallus* was being domesticated in India and China. By Greek and Roman times the manipulation of new "breeds" was already well underway. But birds have been kept solely on account of their visual beauty, interest or exquisite songs for a long, long time. Alexander the Great (356–323 BC) is reputed to have introduced the Indian Ring-necked Parakeet *Psittacula krameri* to Greece, and more recently the same species was kept by Indian princes in marvellous aviaries and tended by specially employed servants.

The first real cagebird, that is a wild bird tamed to live *and breed* in a cage for aesthetic rather than utilitarian reasons, was the now familiar and much loved Canary *Serinus canaria*. This was the first bird to become entirely conditioned to a caged life. It is a robust finch from the Canary Islands, Madeira and the Azores and is usually said to have first come to the attention of prospective bird-fanciers early during the 17th century, when a ship bound for Livorno (Leghorn) on the west coast of Italy was wrecked near the Isle of Elba. On this ship were apparently large numbers of Canaries, which

HISTORY OF BIRDKEEPING

escaped from their burst cage and populated Elba. However, this story may well be somewhat apocryphal, and the truth may yet show that Canaries had been bred in, and exported from, Germany for most of the 16th century.

For roughly four centuries the Canary, by virtue of its intrinsic beauty; sweet, musical and versatile song; and peaceful nature, remained the most popular cagebird until it was to some extent superseded by the Budgerigar *Melopsittacus undulatus* which John Gould, the celebrated English naturalist, author and artist brought home from Australia in 1840. He little realized the scale of the craze he was about to start. Gradually these Budgerigars (so called from the aboriginal betchery — good, and gah — food) spread across Europe, breeding well and gaining in popularity all the while. Strangely enough, it is not known for sure when they "invaded" America, but it was most likely during the reign of Queen Victoria. That the Budgie has much to its credit is very obvious: it is beautifully (and now variously) colored, vivacious and friendly with a distinct if not outstanding ability to mimic the human voice.

Before the Budgerigar became universally known, a small pigeon called the Barbary Dove *Streptopelia "risoria"* had achieved a measure of popularity. A more recent appearance is that of the "Java Dove" which is a pale mutation of the Barbary Dove. These tame doves are easy to keep, will breed in quite a small cage, and are ideal subjects for the beginner.

The conquest of the high seas by mariners opened up the world and brought to light a fantastic array of new species to excite all contemporary naturalists. Parrots most of all fired the imagination of medieval animal-lovers. To European eyes at least they must have been an astonishing spectacle; no wonder strange stories grew up about far-off lands. Returning sailors boosted their egos and tales by sporting tame parrots on their shoulders, which amazed their audiences by mimicking their masters, and displaying the appealing features which people still find so attractive today.

A long time was still to elapse before the widespread importation of exotic birds was possible; until then, bird-fanciers caught and tamed the songbirds which lived wild in their own neighborhoods and housed them usually in small wicker cages. The Linnet *Carduelis cannabina* is the best known example of this

14

HISTORY OF BIRDKEEPING

in Europe, while in America, cardinals were popular, as were bulbuls in the Middle East. Wicker cages were supplemented with ornate metal ones in the 19th century — which were little better for the birds. Some of the older zoos still possess fine examples of early cage designs but they are of more interest to the architect than to the practising aviculturist!

This century, aviculture gathered momentum, as did the whole science of animal husbandry. To meet the heavy demands for new and exciting stock, professional animal collecting flourished, especially between the two world wars. Today, with the increase of concern for the world's natural resources, this trade is somewhat frowned upon. But at that time zoos and wealthy private collectors were energetically expanding their menageries, and the days of the shoddy animal show, which prospered in Victorian times, were rightly numbered. Now, even though the most naive animal-keeper would willingly admit that present-day techniques are still to be much improved, we can be justly proud of the great advances which have swept through the profession, clearing out much dead wood and many old-fashioned ideas and prejudices.

Since the upsurge of interest in tropical birds by aviculturists living in cooler climates, there have been three main areas of supply: South East Asia, equatorial Africa and various parts of northern South America. The arduous sea voyages which expeditions to such parts of the globe entailed meant that while large animals stood a reasonable chance of survival, small and extremely delicate birds were an entirely different matter. The development of refrigeration and of highly nutritious dried foods, such as those designed for human babies, greatly aided the in-transit maintenance of fruit- and nectar-feeders etc. But it took the ascent of international high-speed air cargo really to make the wholesale importation of such birds as tanagers, flycatchers, sunbirds, hummingbirds and even finches from remote lands economically viable.

Most famous collections of birds were, and still are, to be found in North America and Europe, and the practice of keeping a pet bird or two in a cage for its pleasurable company has developed on the one hand into a serious science, and on the other, into a large, well-organized, thriving, international hobby.

There are very few types of birds which at some time

HISTORY OF BIRDKEEPING

or another have not been subjected to the cage and aviary treatment. But by no means are all well-suited, and over the years the most favorable varieties have been defined and bred intensively — providing many varieties, hybrids and domestic clines. In the past these birds have usually tended to be seedeaters such as parrots and finches simply because they were the easiest to acquire and cater for. The years of effort, breeding and thought that have gone into the keeping of these "hardbills" is evident even today insofar as these types are still by far the most common and popular. The extensive keeping of "softbills" is a very recent development, and the successful breeding of them more recent still; there is more to learn about this branch of aviculture than any other.

Captive-bred strains of common European birds such as the Greenfinch *Chloris chloris* and the Bullfinch *Pyrrhula pyrrhula* are so well established that they breed almost at the drop of a hat, while wild-taken birds of the same species (were it legal) would certainly be much more reluctant. Softbills, lacking the years of aviary-conditioning, breed less reliably and readily. Perhaps, before too long, results will improve and become more predictable, but it is also possible that softbills being by nature more delicate and sensitive to environmental changes are simply less suited to a captive existence than the tougher hardbills.

The keeping of Budgerigars well illustrates the change in aviculture from its chancy beginnings to its present-day sophistication. Budgerigars were first bred on a large scale in Belgium and France; Holland following suit quickly. Large Budgie studs were maintained in these countries — one at Toulouse in southern France usually kept in stock some 100,000 birds! The market was thus well and truly flooded, prices dropped to negligible proportions, enabling even the very poorest classes to own them as pets. On top of this, large quantities of wild-caught birds began to be imported into Britain from Australia, so much so that most of the world's high-quality stock now emanates from Britain.

In a wild state, color variances from the norm, or freaks of any kind, seldom survive to breed, although wild yellow Budgies are occasionally seen among the usual green ones. However, by selective breeding in captivity — where the unusual can be protected rather than persecuted as it would be in the wild — and a

Topography of a bird:
1 Lesser wing coverts
2 Alula
3 Middle wing coverts
4 Primary coverts
5 Primaries
6 Secondaries
7 Greater wing coverts
8 Tertiaries
9 Retrices or tail feathers
10 Upper tail coverts
11 Primaries
12 Rump
13 Secondaries
14 Tertiaries
15 Greater coverts
16 Scapulars
17 Mantle
18 Lesser coverts
19 Hind neck
20 Nape
21 Crown
22 Orbital ring
23 Superciliary
24 Forehead
25 Lores
26 Upper mandible
27 Lower mandible
28 Chin
29 Ear coverts
30 Moustachial stripe
31 Throat
32 Side of neck
33 Upper breast
34 Lower breast
35 Middle coverts
36 Alula
37 Side
38 Belly
39 Primary coverts
40 Flank
41 Thigh
42 Tarsus
43 Extent of remiges
44 Under tail coverts
45 Cere

HISTORY OF BIRDKEEPING

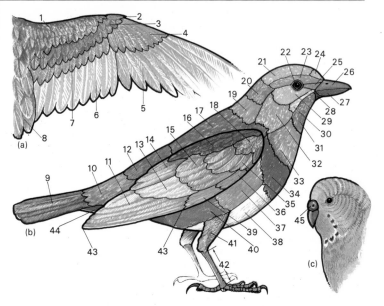

knowledge of genetics, it is now possible to breed Budgies of almost every color. A blue Budgie might be as unnatural as a green flamingo, and only with a goodly amount of tongue in cheek can really be called a Budgerigar at all. However, to any enthusiast this is of no account, and more and more the Budgie-fancy exists as a tool for the serious breeder to demonstrate his own particular skill. In the meantime, the pet Budgie, while lacking some of the exaggerated "features" of the "ideal," goes gaily and chirpily along, evidently enjoying his own life and greatly enlivening that of his owner.

Undoubtedly the practice of showing birds and the spread of this activity around the world has greatly united and promoted the cagebird movement. Shows draw people of like mind together, enable them to compare their work, discuss new techniques and, as important as anything, provide healthy competition. A large cagebird show is the focal point and shop-window of the entire hobby, covering every aspect of the fancy with the possible exception of professional public collections such as those maintained by zoos.

HISTORY OF BIRDKEEPING

Although a cagebird show is primarily directed at the most popular breeds such as the Budgie, Canary, Zebra Finch *Poephila guttata* and Bengalese Finch (a domesticated form of the Sharp-tailed Munia *Lonchura striata auticauda*), there are many other categories, catering for all tastes. The "Foreign" is one of the most exciting and here, instead of the birds conforming to a standard which is prone to continual "improvement" or change as fashion decrees, the Foreign class endeavours to show natural species — the only criteria being perfect form, health and feather. Obviously, as on any such broad-based platform, individual taste and even rarity value must inevitably play a large part, and the judging of such classes is a highly subjective business — whereas the judging of, say, a Gloster Canary ought to be quite the opposite.

There is a fine line (sometimes so fine as to be almost invisible) between the perfectly reasonable, responsible and humane practice of keeping certain birds in cages and aviaries and the same practice when applied to other types. Extremes as always are obvious : no-one could possibly object to a pet Budgie in a living-room, and surely everyone can see the total unsuitability of an Andean Condor *Vultur gryphus* in a similar environment! Towards the center the position inevitably becomes more obscure and opinionated. Experience is by far the best yardstick, but this *must* be tempered with sensitivity and vision on the part of the human individual. For example, the Barn Swallow *Hirundo rustica*, although to the uninitiated eye looking like just another cagebird, is as unsuited to a caged life as an insectivorous bat, simply because of its highly specialized method of feeding, which is designed to catch flying insects on the wing. An even better example is the Swift, *Apus apus*, which lives virtually its whole life airborne.

Aviculture now performs a more useful and important function than had hitherto been imagined : increasingly it is being used and regarded as a conservation tool. Already several species have been saved through captive propagation, and more are currently being subjected to specialist breeding programs. There is little doubt that if aviculture in today's form had existed earlier quite a few extinct species, such as the Passenger Pigeon *Ectopistes migratoria*, the Carolina Parakeet *Conuropsis carolinensis* and even the famous Dodo *Raphus cucullatus* (a

CHOOSING A BIRD

large flightless pigeon), would still be alive today.

Great efforts are now being made to ensure that as many replacement birds as possible are bred so as to reduce future demands on wild populations. The conclusion of these efforts should be complete self-sufficiency for the protected true wild species — if you like, a self-perpetuating zoo-bank. It is the only ideal worth aiming at because the international movement of wild birds may be curtailed or restricted at any time. While breeding their birds is the moral duty of all bird-keepers, much of value and scientific worth may at the same time be gained from simple experiments and detailed observation.

In this Guide we are primarily concerned with the typical cage and aviary species, therefore all other forms of bird-keeping, such as those involved in falconry, the cult of ornamental waterfowl, gamebird farming and even the diversified breeding of weird pigeons (which are often so cruelly misshapen as to look like grotesque caricatures) have to be largely ignored.

The future of pure aviculture lies in the advancing field of animal husbandry and nature conservation. The individual disciplines will rightly determine their own particular ends. But everyone, no matter on what scale they operate, can contribute something of real value to this absorbing vocation. The opportunity is real enough, and specialization is becoming increasingly desirable. Hopefully, the days of rambling haphazard collections are past, as is the worshipping of size for its own sake. A small collection concentrating on just one or two groups of animals, and managed by a small band of devotees, can achieve far more than many large, highly-fragmented collections run by motley bands of Jacks Of All Trades.

CHAPTER 3: CHOOSING A BIRD

Before choosing a bird, you must first of all decide why you want one. There are many different reasons: it may simply be for companionship — perhaps the most common of all — or it may be a serious interest in aviculture; the desire to own a lively and intelligent pet or simply to enhance one's home or garden. Once you have analyzed your reasons your choice must be influenced by considerations of cost, availability, feeding and housing requirements. No bird must be acquired at a whim. It is a decision which requires

CHOOSING A BIRD

plenty of thought and commonsense. Most pets rely on their human owners entirely, and a bird in a cage is more dependent than most. It is not able to bark like a dog to attract your attention, and it is prevented from fending for itself as a cat might. Only the person involved knows why he wants to keep a bird or birds, but beginners especially need help to recognize the *type* of bird best suited to his own particular needs.

If companionship is the driving force then it is difficult to better the Budgerigar; it is lively, friendly, talkative, easy to look after, cheap and lives contentedly in a small cage. But the Budgie is not the only parrot-like bird worthy of consideration, there is a variety of others which the slightly more ambitious can consider: the Amazon parrots *Amazona* spp. are frequently kept singly as pets, as is the African Gray *Psittacus erithacus* (the best talking parrot), and to a lesser extent the cockatoos *Cacatoe* spp. and macaws *Ara* spp. It should be pointed out however that one of the Budgie's biggest advantages is its domesticity — all the others are true wild species, lacking its generations of conditioning, and their acquisition as pets, to be kept singly with no provision for their procreation, is quickly becoming irresponsible. To keep them in pairs in aviaries is quite a different matter and entirely desirable. A possible compromise would be to consider keeping a pair of smaller birds in a cage which could still be housed in a living-room quite comfortably; there are a number of varieties which lend themselves to this method of management. Among other parrot-like birds certain types of lovebirds *Agapornis* spp. will breed happily in quite a small cage, ideally this ought to be at least 1,067 mm ($3\frac{1}{2}$ ft) long $\times$ 475 mm ($1\frac{1}{2}$ ft) deep $\times$ 610 mm (2 ft) high. But the birds best suited to this form of housing are some of the small finches. The Zebra Finch springs to mind and is ideal, as is the Bengalese. The Java Sparrow *Padda oryzivora* is perhaps better off in a small colony, but there is a domesticated white form which lives contentedly and will even breed in a small cage. It should be noted here that new fanciers in America are prohibited from acquiring Java Sparrows as they represent a possible hazard to grain crops in the south. An absolute beginner would be well advised to gain experience on some of these tough hardbills before moving on to the more demanding ones and softbills etc.

A Canary, especially a Roller, offers not only

companionship but a melodious and beautiful song as well. Along with the Budgie, the Canary must be high on the list of anyone seeking a vivacious avian room-mate. Excellence of song is also a feature of certain softbills which are frequently kept as cagebirds. The Shama *Copsychus malabaricus* from the Oriental Region is reputed to be the finest songster in the world but is a large, long-tailed bird better off in an aviary. The Pekin Robin *Leiothrix lutea*, also from the Far East, is another glorious songster, considerably smaller and far more suitable. Softbills of whatever kind, however, demand a greater degree of care and expertise than most seedeaters, and are only to be considered by those who have already had some previous experience of bird-keeping. A seedeater is not automatically a finch, and some of the tiny seedeating doves, such as the Barbary, or even the delightful Diamond Dove *Geopelia cuneata* from Australia, are well worth considering for a living-room environment.

The Greater Hill Mynah *Gracula religiosa* from South East Asia is a softbill and is extremely popular as a cagebird solely on account of its quite phenomenal powers of mimicry. It is almost invariably housed by itself in a small inadequate cage, and has sadly become a victim of its own cleverness. Even by softbill standards the mynahs are exceptionally messy in all their habits: scattering their sticky food all over the cage, splashing their water far and wide, and fouling every conceivable nook and cranny. Mynahs are mentally alive, gregarious, social and highly active birds, and the near cruelty of condemning one to a solitary caged existence is illustrated by the habit they sometimes adopt of literally biting the hand that feeds them. Unlike a parrot — which is more intelligent — a mynah rarely forms a really close bond with a human-being. Housed in a spacious planted aviary, a mynah is immediately transformed into a charming and amusing pet. As with most birds, they should be kept in pairs whenever possible but it must be said that this might seriously retard their willingness to talk.

Apart from a few exceptions already mentioned, birds really are best regarded as subjects for aviculture and not as pets. Aviculture, of course, takes many forms but, by definition, breeding has to be an intrinsic part of all branches. That is not to say that many wild birds will not live relatively happily in a small cage, but in a spacious planted aviary their appeal is increased

CHOOSING A BIRD

beyond measure. For ease of management, if nothing else, aviary life is preferable; a Pekin Robin, for instance, in a small cage relies utterly on its owner for every detail of its life (a deficient owner results in a deficient bird), but the same bird in an outside aviary, while still needing a great deal of care and attention, will find a portion of its own food (including valuable trace elements), it will keep itself cleaner, take advantage of the sunshine and rain, and will be much more likely to breed — all these factors naturally increasing the pleasure the owner derives from the bird. Serious breeders of domesticated birds such as Canaries and Budgies often prefer to keep their stock under totally controlled conditions — where, for instance, the risk of disease is minimized. It must be remembered that such aviculturists are experts in their particular fields and know *exactly* the requirements of their stock.

Once your birds have been purchased and housed, the expenses they entail greatly decrease. A few birds can be kept for a fraction of what a large dog costs. Seedeaters are the most economical of all because their food is non-perishable and can be bought in bulk. Most softbills demand constant supplies of expensive fresh fruit and an insectile mix (see Chapter 5) or livefood such as maggots and mealworms which is difficult to obtain and keep. There are various om-nivores, like the jays and magpies, which will consume a wide variety of household scraps etc but such food should be regarded only as an addition to an otherwise balanced softbill diet. The cost of the actual birds is a different story and in these days of inflation, severe quarantine regulations (and therefore charges), in-creased transport bills and tightened export restrictions in many countries of origin, one can expect to pay a considerable sum for even quite an ordinary foreign bird. And prices increase steeply the more ambitious one becomes. Facts such as these, quite apart from the moral issue, make concerted captive-breeding pro-grams sound sense.

Assuming that you have decided on the type of bird best suited to your own taste and lifestyle, it is necessary to know how to go about acquiring it. It is *always* best to seek the personal advice of someone more experienced than yourself — at any stage of your hobby. If you know of no-one personally, visit a local zoo, bird-garden or private aviculturist. Enthusiasts are normally only too willing to talk about their love, and as they are able to offer *localized* advice which qualifies the more general hints which is the best a book can hope to offer, they are especially valuable as providers of information. It is also sound advice to join a local cagebird society or a national one specializing in the birds of your own choice; subscribe to specialist magazines and buy regularly one of the large-circulation journals which are usually packed with tips and informative articles.

If possible always collect your birds personally from reputable sources so that you can inspect them before purchase. It is usually advisable to buy birds bred in the current year because they will settle down so much better in a new environment; in the case of Budgies, Bengalese and Zebra Finches these should wear a closed, stamped ring of the year in question. Buying birds by mail order is an occupation fraught with danger and disappointment, despite the fact that many birds travel very well. National carrier services are usually efficient but the strain of using them regularly for delicate livestock is neither guaranteed to increase your lifespan or that of your birds! Wherever you decide to obtain your birds (and this can be a Hobson's choice determined by whosoever happens to have the type of bird you want) the same standards of inspection should apply. Also take into account the time of the year because it is not advisable either to import or move adult wild birds, even a short distance, to new quarters in unfavorable weather conditions or during a period of molt (usually after the breeding season), when a bird's natural resistance is hardest taxed. Whenever possible it is always best to seek out young, captive-bred stock, the ancestry of which you can investigate. The search for your ideal bird(s) might take you to a dealer, a fellow enthusiast or even a zoo; wherever it is have a good look at *all* the birds, the sort of food they are offered, the general hygiene and the quality of the accommodation.

Acclimatization is a job for experts, but basically it means conditioning a newly-imported bird from one environment to an entirely new one. In its usual form this applies to temperature, and a bird, over a number of weeks, is gradually weaned from a higher ambient temperature to a lower one until it is hardy enough to take its place outside.

Usually you will acquire your birds from premises in

HOUSING

your own country, and once you know what to look for, an unhealthy bird and a slipshod establishment are unmistakable. A bird in good health is a picture of alertness and looks crisp and freshly groomed. Above all, beware of listless, sulky-looking birds, and if they are housed in a communal aviary watch quietly for a while to make sure that your proposed bird is neither a bully nor a weakling. There are obvious faults to guard against such as missing or deformed toes, scaly legs (a sign of old age), blocked or discharging nasal passages, poor feathering and dull eyes.

Choosing show birds, as opposed to pet or aviary birds, is a highly-skilled business and demands much knowledge about the particular breed or variety you are interested in – such knowledge comes only from study and experience: visiting shows and collections, talking to experts and joining a specialist club. The color plates in this book show various "ideals" and provide a good starting point for anyone undecided about his own personal avian preferences.

CHAPTER 4 : HOUSING

The correct housing of birds is a subject almost as complex as the birds themselves. It is also one on which most experts disagree or at least have their own pet theories. This is understandable but it does make the subject very complicated for the newcomer or in-experienced amateur. Theoretically, most species (some might even say *individuals*) should or could have a cage designed specifically for them. This is a valid if impracticable view which has its antithesis in the totally inadequate and monotonous housing which is still all too prevalent in both private and public collections.

A beginner contemplating buying a cage or aviary is confronted by a mass of conflicting literature, dia-grams, designs, materials, advice and ideas — not to mention all the different equipment and appliances. Always remember that there is no reason why your housing need be inadequate or unattractive even if it might always be better. It is best to avoid revolutionary concepts until one has the experience rationally to weigh up their good and bad points. There are plenty of well-tested designs on the market, and it should not be beyond any reasonably competent handyman to build, if not design, his own aviary or fit out his own birdroom. This is certainly the most rewarding form of housing

Above: Wire cage suitable for budgerigars and canaries, with glass surround. Use in conjunction with stand for living-room.
Below: Box-cage suitable for all small finches.

and if well executed certainly the best for the birds, because the peculiarities of each proposed occupant, as well as all the local environmental and geographic conditions — which of course vary considerably even from garden to garden — can all be taken into account.

The illustrations depict a range of basic designs which are the kind most frequently encountered. Accepting that you can never have a perfect cage, the illustrated designs may all be considered as quite satisfactory. At best they are a compromise of such factors as size, weight, cost, fashion and ornamentation, with the needs of the birds not always top of the list. For instance the type of cage often sold for mynahs is quite unsuitable since it is far too small. These birds need a cage at least $2 \times 2 \times 4$ ft long ($600 \times 600 \times 1,200$ mm) but they are messy birds and better kept outdoors. The Hill Mynah, especially, should be regarded as an aviary bird and, if it must be kept inside, should have access to a roomy flight area.

Many birds live long lives and apparently thrive in certain styles of cages, but as often as not this is due

HOUSING

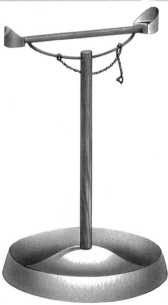

T-stand suitable for large macaws and cockatoos. Birds can be shackled by chain. Food and water are provided in the receptacles on either end of the perch.

more to their agreeable natures than to any specific merits of the cage itself. The most successful cages are those designed with Budgerigars and Canaries in mind: these birds are fairly easy to please because of their generations of conditioning. A cage suitable for a Canary is also ideal for other small finches. But with the exception of these and some other popular cagebirds, it is best to remember that a caged life is always unnatural, and one which needs sympathetic and compassionate human management. Parrots are nearly always kept singly, in a variety of weldmesh cages. Some individuals appear to live quite happily while others of exactly the same species are pictures of abject misery. This is usually a reflection on their owners: a parrot has an active mind and an innate desire to gnaw, deprived of outlets for these natural functions it can rapidly go downhill. A pet parrot demands much thought and initiative on the part of its owner, boring routines should be avoided, as should boring diets, and whenever possible the parrot should be allowed out of its cage, if only to sit on the top of it — a liberty many thoroughly enjoy. There is no doubt that cagebirds of

HOUSING

all kinds come to regard their cages as their own private territories, usually returning eagerly to feed, drink, roost or seek sanctuary. A parrot needs to exercise its wings occasionally, and a large one, like a macaw, unless kept on a T-stand — which incidentally permits the long tail to be kept in perfect order — has to be allowed out of its cage from time to time so that it can clamber about and exercise both mind and body. It is only due to their destructive habits that many parrots have to be caged at all.

Having considered the preferences of the birds themselves, the most important thing to remember about any form of housing concerns feeding and cleaning — the latter is a task which must be done regularly to avoid disease and unpleasant odors. Most small cages are well designed in this respect, they have a small hand-sized door, usually fitted with a self-closing spring, which need be used only seldom because food trays and drinking receptacles should always be fitted so that they can be attended to from outside. Cage floors should always be an easily removed sliding tray, beneath which there must be a second base to retain the birds while the tray is being cleaned and its litter renewed.

Specialist birdrooms are essential to the serious breeder of Canaries and Budgerigars; and they come in as many configurations as there are breeders! Their basic form usually consists of tiers of small cages, similar to the box type used for pet birds, but provision is made for these to be enlarged or for the birds to be moved about and segregated by the use of sliding panels. Quite often birdrooms also include a large communal flight, with or without outside quarters, where young, show or non-breeding stock may be housed. In this way one can end up with an effective and completely self-contained aviary system, which should also include a service and food storage preparation area. One of the advantages of this kind of set-up is that it can be altered or extended at will, providing plenty of scope for the maturing and imaginative owner.

As aviaries are often erected for purely aesthetic reasons, it is a gratifying bonus that for the breeding of the vast majority of birds they are also by far the best option. There is no limit to their design or usefulness, and if well landscaped they can be a constant source of delight in themselves. There are, of course, many

HOUSING

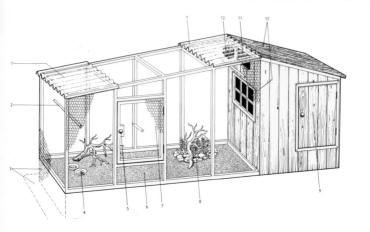

pitfalls to avoid: an aviary which pleases the eye of a human will not necessarily please that of the bird which has to live in it. The aviary illustrated on this page shows a good standard aviary which incorporates many desirable features, and which is suitable for a wide range of softbills, finches and other seedeaters. Note particularly the attached shed which is desirable in most temperate climates for all but the largest and most robust of aviary birds. The translucent covering over the ends of the outer flight is essential in all climatic conditions. Parrot-like species, because of their destructive habits, demand slightly different treatment; an aviary such as that described above can be crudely converted for parrots by concealing exposed woodwork beneath some form of tough metal, fitting larger and harder perches and by forgetting all about plants and shrubs! A heavier gauge of wire-netting, even to the extent of chain-link, is necessary for the larger parrots, like macaws. Netting of 25 mm (1 in) gauge is sufficient for all medium-sized birds, but for finches, which would be able to squeeze through that, a gauge of 6.5 mm ($\frac{1}{4}$ in) is ideal.

Many parrot and parakeet breeders house their pairs (breeding parakeets should not be housed communally) in series of long, narrow flights abutting each other which have the benefit of the lowest possible initial cost, economy of space and ease of main-

Aviaries should incorporate translucent covering (1) over main perches (2) which should be high and widely spaced. Netting (3) to extend 500 mm/ 20 in below ground and 400 mm/16 in outwards to deter burrowing animals. Water dish (4) can be located outside but food is better positioned in shed. Small doors (5) to deter escape with catch (6) operated from both sides. Floors (7) can be raked sand, soil or concrete. Low perches and cover (8) are desirable. Shelter should have door (9) with internal porch, windows but with roof solid and opaque (10). Bird access should be high except for ground birds such as quail which need ground access (11). Nesting sites (12) should be under cover.

tenance. They are also better for the birds as they provide both cover and, because of companions on either side, mental diversion. The birds are able to exercise their wings in proper flight, disturbance is kept to a minimum for there is a solid shed running along the rear of the flights which means that viewing is restricted to the narrow frontage. The floors are normally of concrete or sand because it is a hopeless task trying to keep turf alive and clean in a parrot aviary due largely to the caustic nature of their droppings. Ideally, even a pet parrot should have a custom-built aviary and not a converted finch or softbill one. These are best built from angle-iron or tubular metal, and the mesh should always be fixed to the *inside* of the uprights and cross-pieces — indeed, for reasons of hygiene, this is so in *all* aviaries.

Outdoor aviaries need to be sited intelligently. You must protect your birds from prevailing winds, and also make sure that they do not blow into the shed via the pop-holes: a draught is much more dangerous to a bird than a wind. Full advantage must be taken of all avilable sunshine but at the same time it is a grave mistake to neglect facilities for shade; even tropical birds detest prolonged exposure to direct sunshine. Avoid exposed positions and if possible do not site an aviary directly beneath trees because of the heavy drips which form during rain, the problems resulting from mildew, and possible contamination from wild birds roosting above the aviary. Take care to keep the aviary away from unnecessary disturbances such as roads, passers-by and dustbins. The design and construction of aviaries must take into account the threat of predators — cats, rats, foxes etc — and this is most easily done by burying the wire-netting beneath the ground and then turning it outwards. Cats are an ever-present problem, and one which is hard to combat. They pose their biggest threat at night by prowling around and clambering over the aviaries — this can easily cause night-fright with fatal consequences. Panicking birds can die from injuries sustained when exploding from their perches and crashing into the aviary walls or roof, or by being unable to find their roosting sites again and becoming exhausted; of course should it be raining or very cold, death is almost ensured. There are plenty of human predators about too, some of whom specialize in bird theft; so it is advisable never to advertize the presence of your valuable stock — keep it a well-

HOUSING

guarded secret known only to trusted friends. A burglar alarm in the birdroom is essential, if only for your peace of mind; always keep doors securely padlocked, and never have windows without a protective metal grill. For the birds' sake too, windows should have small mesh grills so that they may be opened with safety in warm weather. An intercom of the type used to link nurseries with living-rooms also has obvious advantages.

For some species extra heat in the winter is desirable, and I would always recommend the installation of electricity; even if for no reason other than the provision of a hospital cage — which is a cage designed to be heated to a temperature of 28–32°C (85–90°F) at short notice. Some aviculturists prefer to have their hospital cage in a separate room, but an electric light, *operated by a dimmer switch*, is still invaluable, if only to allow you the pleasure of a dull winter's evening in the company of your birds. It also has many other functions: enabling you to extend feeding periods, and, turned down, can be used as a nightlight to settle in new stock. In a birdroom or aviary-annex, electricity is by far the most efficient and safest (if expensive) form of heating. Stoves and similar heat sources are dangerous for reasons of fire-risk, dirt and poisonous fumes. Electric storage-heaters are ideal, as are ordinary tubular heaters. It is quite likely that artificial heating will not be needed, unless the weather is particularly severe, but it is always best to have a source on stand-by. The majority of birds are remarkably tough, and a cold snap can be positively beneficial. Damp, draughts and sudden extremes of heat and cold are the killers which you have to guard against. Most birds require little more than a sound, well-insulated and draughtproof shed into which they can retire whenever *they* want; trapdoors or pop-holes must be available for shutting stock inside (or out) when considered necessary. Hardiness in birds is best illustrated by the large group of humming birds. Many experienced aviculturists insist that these deceptively frail-looking and delicate birds thrive in outside aviaries even in the depths of winter, given, of course, that there are always dry, warm, inside quarters available. I have myself seen hummingbirds willingly buzzing round snowflakes, appearing thoroughly to enjoy the experience! Frosty, cold weather is one of nature's ways of controlling disease; and in a large collection the

Perches made of machined dowelling are slotted into a wire cage and held in place by tension or screwed into a box cage.

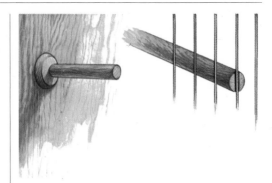

higher mortality of stock in mild, damp winters compared to the lower rate in so-called "hard" winters is very evident.

It is not possible to give meaningful measurements for aviaries because so much depends on available space and finance, personal preferences and the numbers of birds and varieties required. However, there are a few important guidelines to be borne in mind. Birds can never have too much space in which to fly or move about; the problems usually arise in making the most of restricted areas. Plants and shrubs, however desirable for shelter, nesting sites and visual appeal, must be kept within reasonable bounds and not allowed to monopolize the flight. The best way of managing this is to keep the tops pruned so as to allow a flight area beneath the aviary roof, the shrubs can then bush out lower down. Perches are a very important consideration: they must suit the birds using them in quantity, style and situation. It can be as bad to have too many as too few; generally speaking, the smaller the bird, the larger the amount of twiggy perches it requires. There should always be a variety of thicknesses so that the feet are forced to exercise. Some medium to large birds prefer an open, uncluttered flying space with a few well-chosen and firmly fixed perches at either end or in the corners of their aviary. Perches in cage *and* aviary should always be attached firmly. Mating invariably takes place on a perch, and if it twists or moves about violently it can unbalance the birds, resulting in infertile eggs.

Parrot-like birds again demand special consideration. We have already ruled out the possibility of

HOUSING

growing shrubs in their aviaries, but they make other claims as well. Parakeets enjoy flying: so, incidentally, do cockatoos and macaws, and ideally they should be given a fairly long flight path, but the "true" parrots, although they are capable flyers, much prefer to climb and clamber about, and never fly anywhere if they can avoid it. I have seen some get themselves into all sorts of impossible situations simply through this reluctance. Therefore, any aviary housing parrots should be amply supplied with fresh branches — those from fruit trees are especially suitable. The birds should be able to climb easily to feeding and drinking points, the ground, nest boxes and pop-holes etc. The floor of parrot aviaries (and this includes those for Budgerigars) is best spread to a depth of about 152 mm (6 in) with gravel or sand — which can then be raked over daily to preserve a healthy, fresh, clean and neat appearance. Turf in parrot cages tends to get soiled and covered with "grated" perches due to the destructive bills which are forever at work. The perches in any turfed aviary, no matter what species of birds inhabit it, should always be sited directly over soil, gravel or concrete — so that this can be hoed or otherwise cleaned regularly. I consider grass to be by far the best ground covering for all outside aviaries housing finches, softbills etc. It not only looks good but is also to a large extent self-cleaning, providing that the cage is not overcrowded. The floors of aviary sheds are best made of concrete or some other vermin-proof material, so that birds shut in at night will be perfectly safe; there is no reason why this should not be covered by a layer of peat, sawdust or sand.

The choice of plants for growing in aviaries is a wide one. Evergreens are most suitable because they provide shelter throughout the year and are often rapid and bushy growers. Cotoneasters, lavender, broom, gorse, escallonia and the vigorous heathers are all worth considering. Various herbaceous plants such as phlox, golden rod and asters are immensely useful for cover, nesting sites and material; insects are also attracted to them and this can only be good for your birds. Ivy and Russian vine are useful for covering walls or exposed wire-netting. This vine is an exceptionally rapid growing plant.

Pools landscaped into an aviary are both useful and decorative, they are also superior to dishes for bathing and drinking purposes. Better too small than too large, but most important is the depth and gradient: an ample

depth of water for all small passerines is 13 mm ($\frac{1}{2}$ in) ;
25–50 mm (1–2 in) is sufficient for most others ; only
true water and wading birds require ponds. The sides of
the pool should be of a gradual inclination and
roughened so that they are not too slippery. Surrounds
are more a matter of personal preference but I think that
a circle of rocks and gravel is best, thus avoiding muddy
water and ensuring speedy drainage when cleaning
out. A pool which is too large is dangerous for the birds,
and wasteful of water and effort. A small well-designed
pool is easy to clean out every second or third day, and
can with ease be filled from a kettle in icy conditions.

Nestboxes and breeding are discussed in Chapter 7
but it should be remembered that they are also much
used for roosting purposes. Many passerine birds like
to roost in holes and crannies which might otherwise
be lacking in an aviary ; make sure that there are some
suitable ones available. Some birds, barbets in particular, will perish overnight if not allowed to roost in a
cosy hole ; they will excavate their own if given a
suitable upright log but obviously need a few days in
which to do this. Parrots too require a couple of sturdy
boxes as permanent fixtures ; some species will even
spend much of the day inside them, and they do
become "homes" in the true sense of the word —
providing a base for resting, sleeping, breeding, hiding
and even feeding.

As with cages, one of the most important design
features of aviaries concerns their servicing. Provision
ought to be made for easy and safe access into the
aviary itself or shed-annex — this is best effected by
incorporating a safety-porch, which will enable you to
manoeuvre brushes and buckets inside without letting
the birds out. Doors should never be the full height of
the aviary or wider than the minimum to allow you a
swift, smooth entrance. Water on tap is a boon
appreciated by all aviculturists, although whenever
possible try to use fresh rainwater for drinking
purposes. Regarding cleaning, small cages need daily
attention but outdoor aviaries can be left slightly longer
as they are to a small extent self-cleaning and, of
course, there is more space per bird ; even so, perches,
pools and the ground beneath perches need regular
cleaning. On no account must water be allowed to
become stagnant or fouled. Periodic disinfection of
cage and aviary is a wise precaution. Outside this can
be conveniently accomplished with a mild solution

FEEDING

administered by a watering-can. Exposed timber should be treated annually with a wood preservative, while cages and the interior of birdrooms should likewise be smartened up each year with a coat of white emulsion, which is harmless to the birds. Perhaps the single most useful tip which I have discovered regarding maintenance of cage and aviary is simply that a little regular cleaning is far easier and more effective than a horrendous "springclean" every few weeks. In short, establish an easy routine which can be undertaken every day with the minimum of effort and fluster; synchronize this with feeding time and the birds too will benefit as they also like some kind of reassuring routine.

CHAPTER 5 : FEEDING

The diets you feed to your birds are certainly the most important part of their entire husbandry. They can turn a poor bird into a resplendent one but, if bad, have quite the opposite effect. Not to put too fine a point on it, you can kill or prolong the lives of your birds by the type of food you feed them. Diets must always be well thought out and balanced, and not allowed to become boring. Care must be taken to ensure that the occasional titbits and vital trace elements (which, in the long term, are as important as the bulk ingredients) are supplied in sufficient quantities, variety and at the right times.

Fundamentally, avicultural diets fall into three main categories (excluding carnivorous birds) — the same categories which help us to separate the birds themselves — hardbills (seedeaters), softbills (fruit and insect eaters) and nectar-feeders. Of course, just one step beyond this over-simplified classification and there are hundreds of important and confusing variations. Seedeaters, for example, include such diverse types as parrots, finches, quail and pigeons, and interspecifically these divisions differ widely. The term "softbill" embraces an astonishing conglomeration of birds from flycatchers to toucans, and kingfishers to starlings which, collectively, consume an extremely complex range of foods. Further to complicate matters, there are all the birds which cut right across our neat categories and almost succeed in making a mockery of the whole concept. Some parrots are nectar-feeders, and all eat large quantities of fruit; so do many finches, which also consume vast amounts of insects. There are pigeons which live exclusively on

FEEDING

fruit, softbills which eat seeds, and hummingbirds which could accurately be regarded as insectivores! However, the classification remains and is both necessary to our understanding of cagebirds, and an essential stepping-stone or, more fittingly, starting-block to the beginner. But always remember that most birds are opportunists — this is where their strength lies — and basically are best regarded as *omnivores*. It is impossible to duplicate a bird's wild diet, which is usually an amalgam of many small items gleaned from over a wide area during the course of the whole day, and artificial diets are always a case of substitution and compromise.

The bulk of the birds in this Guide, as explained in Chapter 2, are seedeaters since these are by far the commonest type of cagebird and it is on these birds that this chapter concentrates; all other diets are discussed where appropriate in the second part of the book.

The seeds on which they are fed in captivity once again fall into three main categories. Finches, doves, quail and small parrots such as lovebirds and the Budgerigar mostly eat either millet (white and yellow panicum) or canary seed or both. Medium to large parrots eat sunflower seeds and peanuts, although pine-nuts have recently emerged as a competitor and many parrot-fanciers (and parrots) now prefer them although their supply is irregular. The larger pigeons (together with such birds as pheasants and waterfowl, which fall outside the scope of this book) eat the bulkier grains: wheat, barley and maize; supplementing these grains are some very useful manufactured foods, called "turkey pellets" of various kinds, which have been designed for the poultry trade but which have also revolutionized the keeping of gallinaceous birds. Their by-products, the so-called "starter crumbs," also have many uses in aviculture, especially when hand-feeding "difficult" young birds. By and large, however, we must concentrate on the first of these hardbill categories, while acquainting ourselves with the others as well.

It can be seen from a glance at the accompanying table that the food value of the "bulk seeds" — millet, canary, wheat and possibly oats — compare favorably with each other, and are quite different from that of the "extras" such as hemp and niger. Some do similar jobs but a bird might, for example, dislike niger although it

FEEDING

Food Values of Seeds Fed to Birds

		Percentage of Carbo-		
Seed	Fats	hydrates	Proteins	Minerals
large white millet	4	60	11	3
small yellow millet	4	63	11	3
canary	6	55	14	2
sunflower minus hull	41	20	24	3
sunflower plus hull	26	21	16	29
pine nuts	47	12	31	3*
peanuts	47	19	26	2*
hemp	32	18	19	2
maw	40	12	17	6
niger	32	15	17	7
rape	40	10	19	4
linseed	34	24	21	6
oats	5	56	11	2
wheat	2	70	11	2

* Estimated value

NB. The figures for the small 'finch seeds' are 'minus-hull values' (most finches discard the hull before consumption). As can be seen under the 'sunflower' entries, the mineral content is greatly increased when the seed is analysed complete, at the expense of the fat or oil content. Therefore, pigeons and other birds which swallow small complete seeds ingest a considerably higher percentage of minerals per seed than those listed in the table.

will eagerly consume hemp. It is reassuring to know that they fulfill a similar function. Indeed, between these two examples there is a considerable size difference and relatively large birds like parrots will refuse tiny seeds, so it is desirable to find an equivalent but larger seed. The fat-rich seeds — rape, maw, hemp and niger — have to be used with caution. Cagebirds live unnatural, sedentary lives and while, in winter particularly, they need the warmth fat provides, they tend to be overweight at the best of times and therefore the supply of these seeds must be strictly rationed and virtually abandoned in the summer; obese birds are poor breeders. The various kinds of millet together with canary, sunflower, pine-nuts, peanuts and wheat provide all the carbohydrates and most of the protein to satisfy seedeating birds housed in cage and aviary.

Niger, maw and linseed are high in minerals, and are correspondingly valuable. Minerals are essential for correct bone formation, and also play a major role during the molt and in the digestive process, as do the energy-giving carbohydrates.

The seeding heads of panicum millet, called sprays, are greatly favored by nearly all finches and small parrots. Given the chance, they will consume large amounts but often ignore it if it is doled out in a dish in the usual way; large white millet, which is only available loose, is preferred by many species. Some fanciers believe in "forcing" their birds to finish off all seeds before renewing their supply, others will blow off the old husks and replenish — effectively giving the birds more choice. Both methods are valid but I must express an inclination to the latter, particularly in mixed collections where it is all too easy for a timid or faddy bird to get overlooked or pushed out by its fellows. I prefer to mix in the supplementary seeds with the bulk foods so that they are encountered occasionally or through searching. The residues are checked daily. A pet bird or two is a different proposition, and the owner can afford to be much more exact in his estimation of the birds' needs and preferences, and closely monitor their progress. To feed a few birds it is possibly easiest, and almost as cheap, to buy one of the appropriate prepacked, ready-blended seed mixtures which contain nearly all nutritional requirements (the other essentials, grit, greenfood etc are discussed below). The enthusiast, however, will prefer to buy seeds in bulk and blend his own mixture taking into consideration his birds' whims (and his own), the weather and the season. All seeds should be top-quality and bought from a reputable source. They must be clean, shiny and fresh, that is to say, alive: it is the germ of seed which provides the goodness. To keep seed fresh it is best stored in a *dry* airtight jar or, if bought in bulk, in a mouse-proof container like a plastic dustbin, bread-crock or galvanised silo. Never leave seed in a paper sack or in a damp, musty atmosphere; it is perishable and valuable.

Some fanciers go to great lengths working out exact proportions of seed mixes but this practice is often negated by certain inconsistent factors inherent in the birds and the seeds themselves. It is safer to supply the basic seeds ad lib separately, mixing into each dish a small amount (ie a sprinkling) of the fat-rich and

FEEDING

mineral-high seeds, introducing the fatty ones in the autumn, and possibly oats before the breeding season.

Vitamins are essential elements and best given to finches and parrots in the form of greenfood, preferably fresh daily. Chickweed *Stellaria media* is of special importance, but Dandelion *Taraxacum officinale*, Groundsel *Senecio vulgaris*, Shepherd's Purse *Capsella bursa-pastoris*, sow thistles *Sonchus* spp. and many other herbs, grasses and wild plants are invaluable additions to a basic seed diet, especially during the breeding season (when much animal life and eggfood is also consumed, see Chapter 9). Lettuce and spinach among the cultivated crops are also immensely useful and much appreciated by the birds. Care must be taken to ensure that all wild and cultivated greens gathered from gardens, fields and roadsides are free of chemical sprays; in fact, it is always safest to wash them thoroughly. Vitamins A and D are the most important, and these can be introduced into seed mixes in the form of a few drops of cod-liver oil; they can also be added to drinking water in a concentrated form available from chemists.

Sprouted or germinated seed is also high in vitamins and constitutes a popular part of a balanced and varied diet. If seeds are soaked in cold water (renewed daily) for two or three days (this period may have to be doubled in the winter) they will begin to germinate, whereupon they should be washed in tepid water and allowed to dry before being offered to the birds. A conveyor-belt system can be easily instituted which provides a constant supply.

Even seedeaters like a certain amount of softbill food, and this is most conveniently supplied in one of the manufactured insectile mixtures such as "Sluis universal." But the serious softbill enthusiast can experiment with homemade recipes, of which there are infinite variations (see Chapter 13). Softbill diets are a very complex matter. The term covers such a wide range of dissimilar birds: insectivores, frugivores, omnivores and even nectarfeeders. Some softbills need diced fruit and vegetables as a basic food: those most commonly used are apples, sweet pears, bananas, oranges, figs, raisins, currants, grapes, tomatoes and carrots (grated or boiled). Carrot-water can be used to advantage as the moistening agent when making homemade insectivorous foods. For the real fruit-eaters — toucans and turacos etc — diced fruit garnished

Gravity fed water dispensers for cage and aviary. They can also be used for feeding nectar-feeders such as sunbirds.

with an insectile mixture and occasional helpings of animal and plant material is sufficient.

Insectivorous birds, many of which are not at all suitable for captivity, are the most demanding and delicate of all avicultural subjects. While it is possible to buy and breed various forms of insects (see below and Chapter 13), these are not practicable, economic or sufficient in themselves, invaluable though they are as components. All the larger insectivores, birds such as thrushes and babblers, have to be weaned on to an insectile mix, which may or may not include dried insect-life (see table on page 199). As I have already said, most birds are best regarded as omnivores with specific leanings. True omnivores, exemplified by the corvids, are easy to feed: they will take all sorts of soft fruit, meat, insectivorous food, seeds and nuts etc. Parrots, too, are mostly easy to feed, basically requiring sunflower, nuts, fruit and the larger supplementary seeds. In direct contrast are the diets of the nectar-feeders, which include some of the most specialized of all birds — hummingbirds, sunbirds and lorikeets being the most obvious — their somewhat tricky diets are described in Chapters 12 and 13.

Nectivorous birds are rather unusual in not requiring grit, which is essential to most other birds. It aids digestion and contains minerals necessary for egg-formation. Grit is best bought ready mineralized, the main ingredient is limestone or ground oystershell. Cuttlefish bone, as much a part of cage and aviary life as the seed-hopper, is indispensable in the breeding season and indeed should be available to finches and

GENERAL MANAGEMENT

parrots throughout the year as it is rich in calcium and salt and helps to stop beaks from overgrowing. Lime, too, is an excellent source of calcium, and this can also be provided in the form of a lump of old mortar.

Livefood is an element in the lives of most cagebirds, and the subject will be encountered throughout the book. There are four main sources. Maggots (larvae of the common blowfly) are very useful but no fun to breed; they are better bought, expensive as they are, from an angling shop or, if needed in large quantities, direct from a commercial breeder. Mealworms, too, are hard to breed successfully in sufficient amounts but it is worth trying since it is not a practice which will alienate your family and neighbours! A fruit-fly (*Drosophila*) culture (see page 196) is a cheap and simple thing to institute and maintain, and is of great value to any collection housing hummingbirds, sunbirds and small flycatchers. During the summer much wild livefood can be collected in many ways, and is of inestimable help in rearing the young of most species. But whether feeding adult or young birds, don't forget that variety really is the spice of life and always consider the possibility of something new.

CHAPTER 6: GENERAL MANAGEMENT

The need for correct management begins from the moment you get your birds. There are many details concerning management which, although they may appear trivial, affect not only their health and longevity but also your enjoyment of them and your effectiveness as a keeper. The majority of "exotic" cagebirds are acquired from dealers, while pet and exhibition birds — Budgerigars, Canaries and the commoner finches and parrots — usually come from compatriot breeders. In either case, major (primary) acclimatization by the new owner is unnecessary as it will already have been undertaken by the importer. Secondary acclimatization, although important, is a much simpler procedure. Acclimatization is usually taken to mean the mechanical conditioning of an animal from one accustomed milieu to a completely new one over a period of a month or two. Most often this entails the ambient temperature being reduced by degrees, and is simple enough in itself. While this is taking place, the subject becomes conditioned to a new diet and, indeed, to captivity in general. Another important

GENERAL MANAGEMENT

aspect of primary acclimatization is quarantining which in many cases is a legal necessity. Basically, this means keeping the birds isolated and under close observation. Signs of stress or travel shock can appear at this time, and the birds' heavily taxed condition can manifest all manner of serious illnesses and defects. A course of a broad-spectrum antibiotic is considered routine by many importers but there are arguments against this, since the treatment can kill the beneficial bacteria as well as the harmful, and under some quarantine regulations all medicaments are prohibited.

Secondary acclimatization, in its mildest form, involves the subject's adaptation from one aviary to another, and, if tackled sensibly, there is no reason why it should be anything other than a routine event. There are, however, many tips to learn when mixing birds. A period of constant observation is always necessary as you must be prepared to intervene should all not prove well. Difficulties normally arise on introducing a newcomer to an established aviary and this always proves a worrying time. It is far safer and kinder not to make a habit of changing birds around; the hierarchy and balance of an aviary is very delicate and easily upset. However, such eventualities do inevitably arise from time to time, and each case must be treated on its merits, taking into account the disposition of all the birds involved and the design of the aviary. Again there is no substitute for sensitivity and experience but there are certain useful guidelines. It is best to introduce birds into an enclosure at midday, when they will already have fed yet still have the afternoon in which to find their way about and locate a roosting site (which will normally be the highest they can discover). If possible segregate the resident birds in the annex until all the newcomers have settled down. Provide an abundance of favored food in various places. Ensure that shelter and cover is adequate and varied. A certain amount of aggressive by-play is normal and even healthy but establish that this does not become a vendetta — "delicate" birds such as hummingbirds are among the worst offenders of all — while no chances should be taken with magpies, jay-thrushes and other robust territorial birds with carnivorous tendencies. Never endanger the equilibrium of an aviary during the breeding season — the best time to move birds is once it has passed its peak, when the days are still long, the weather reliable and young birds are due to be moved

41

GENERAL MANAGEMENT

anyway; also the ardor of birds is waning, and they are tired and preoccupied with building up their fat reserves for the molt and forthcoming winter.

All new birds acquired from outside sources should be kept under observation in a constant environment — which is even more important than warmth — draughts must be eliminated at all costs. New arrivals should be treated particularly considerately by working quietly, methodically and establishing a routine, the birds will quickly come to accept their new life. Diets are an important part of an acclimatization programme, and it is quite wrong to be too strict or theoretical. Far better at first to give the birds exactly what they want or will eat while gradually weaning them on to a balanced diet as time goes by. Millet sprays are especially enticing to apprehensive finches, and also, incidentally, for encouraging juveniles on to adult fare. Grapes, *soaked* sultanas, raisins and figs have a similar effect on softbills; and I know few parrots which can resist a peanut, banana, grape or orange.

If you are unlucky and a new (or established) bird ails, warmth, peace, subdued lighting and a course of antibiotics form a standard practice. The "oven treatment" (a short, sharp rise in temperature up to, say, 38° C (100° F) or even higher) has saved the lives of many birds: this seemingly drastic measure can bring a dying bird round and put it on the path to recovery. Obviously such treatment needs care, and never try it in a gas oven! A hospital-cage and an infra-red heat lamp must be on permanent stand-by. For further information on treating sick birds, see Chapter 8.

Catching a bird by net or hand is distressing to you but occasionally necessary. To the bird it is a traumatic experience which surprisingly often can have fatal consequences. Birds die from sheer fright (the most common cause), perhaps even a day or two later, or from injury sustained at the time of capture or by subsequent rough handling. Over-familiarity or in-experience can result in people overlooking the fact that cagebirds are small, delicate and sensitive creatures, easily damaged. Avoid repeated handling of birds at all costs. It (together with the preliminary catching) causes more fright, shock and distress than anything else, and no matter how carefully done it inevitably damages the plumage. Unfortunately there comes a time in the life of every captive bird when it has to be subjected to this undignified treatment. All the

GENERAL MANAGEMENT

Hospital cage. In homemade cages a domestic light bulb is sufficient as a heat source – located behind the bottom inspection panel.

same, there is a knack to it which only experience can perfect, but briefly the rudiments involve calmness, unflustered speed, smoothness and firmness. The very worst thing you can do is thrash about with a net, chasing the wretched birds all over the place until the victim surrenders from sheer exhaustion. In a large aviary it is always best to either drive the required bird from its co-inhabitants (which should not be needlessly frightened) into the annex or, better still, use a trap into which the bird can be baited or driven. Such traps are simple enough to design and make. I regard the best to be the baited variety, made out of wire-netting over a frame, which the birds enter by way of a short funnel; the hole of which they seem unable to find again. Another good trap is effected by a sprung door – triggered by the bird alighting on a sensitive perch inside the cage as it seeks the bait. Of the two, the former is simpler to make and has the advantages of not frightening the birds unduly and of having a capacity for more than one at a time.

Why will a bird lie peacefully in one person's hand but struggle violently in that of someone else? The answer rests in the person, not the bird. To conjure up a feeling of security, I believe, a bird must feel dominated; it must be held firmly, so that it realizes there is no chance of escape while at the same time feeling no pain or discomfort. The best way of holding a bird of magpie size or smaller is with its back against your palm and its head projecting from between your first and second fingers, which grip the neck. In this way the bird nestles snugly and escape is impossible; most

43

GENERAL MANAGEMENT

The correct way to hold most adult cage and aviary birds. Tasks such as ringing (banding) and trimming overgrown claws and beaks can be easily and safely undertaken with a bird held in this way.

birds submit peacefully if gripped firmly but not squeezed. It also leaves your fingers free to carry out ringing (banding) and other manipulatory tasks (see illustration).

It is very important, for many reasons, to maintain up-to-date records of your stock (see illustration). A card-index system takes some beating but whatever method you adopt it is essential that your birds are always easily recognizable. Banding with a colored plastic ring around the tarsus (see illustration) is the only sure method. (Parrots obviously have to be fitted with metal rings.) Nestlings can be close-ringed (see illustration) with coded metal bands, stamped with the owner's name, serial number and year. This is standard procedure by most breeders of exhibition birds. A

SPECIES			SEX ♂/♀		DATE OF HATCH	
RING NO.			PARENTS ♂		♀	
Mated to Ring no.	Date of 1st egg	Clutch	D.I.S.	Hatched	Reared	Remarks and Ring numbers of young

Records are invaluable. A simple breeding card like this can prevent all sorts of mistakes over the years.

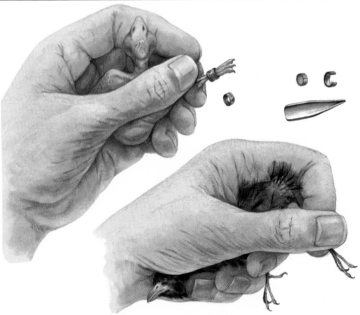

Ringing young birds. *Above:* How to place a *closed ring* on the leg of a nestling a few days old: the 3 front toes are bunched together and the hind toe is worked through the ring. *Below:* A juvenile bird can be rung with a split celluloid ring (in various sizes) shewn inset left and fitted with a special tool (*inset below*) or with a split metal ring (*inset right*) fitted with special pliers.

breeding register is kept by all experienced breeders, and the details of each ring should be entered therein. If, when the bird matures, its coded metal ring is duplicated by a colored plastic one, it can be positively identified with no disturbance. So that it does not need to be caught up twice, the best time to ring a newly acquired adult is on its transference from acclimatization cage to permanent home. British birds bred in captivity have, by law, to be close-rung soon after hatching if intended to be sold as proof that they were not wild-caught, otherwise nesting sites should not be disturbed. Leave the young alone until the nest has been vacated naturally or until they have to be removed from the breeding aviary, whereupon conventional split-rings should be used.

The need to keep cages, birdrooms and all appliances scrupulously clean cannot be over-stressed. Outside aviaries, too, although more natural, must be similarly maintained at a high degree of cleanliness — this does not necessarily mean tidy: an aviary including a "jungle" or wild element can be a great inducement

45

GENERAL MANAGEMENT

to breeding. An over-fussy approach can be as wrong as a slovenly one. A totally sterile aviary is not only an impossible ideal it is also a misguided one; do not forget that you want your birds to be as *hardy* as possible. However, this is not intended as a license for laziness, rather one for common-sense. Water must never become fouled or stagnant, nor should soil become sour; perches ought to be scrubbed regularly in a mild solution of disinfectant, as should other fittings. Feeding and drinking vessels should be cleaned in warm water daily, or whenever their contents are renewed, and rinsed thoroughly. Nesting equipment should be disinfected before and after each breeding season and stored out of season in a clean location. Although parrot nestboxes are left *in situ* all year, remember that they, too, need cleaning. In fact, to minimize the risk of disease and because of their destructive habits, parrot boxes are best *renewed* frequently. Many insect pests can plague birdroom and aviary, red mite *Dermanyssus gallinae* is one of the most notorious (see page 58), but there are various applications available to deal with all such eventualities. Maintain a constant vigil against these harmful influences. As a coating for all walls, emulsion cannot be bettered, nowadays the quality brands can be confidently used even outside. I have heard it said that limewash applied annually gives good protection against many pests, and is useful in birdrooms and on interior stone walls. White is always the best "color," as this provides the maximum of reflected light. Avoid gloss and lead-based paints.

Aerosols are ecologically harmful however useful, and an old-fashioned pressure spray for disinfecting walls and inaccessible corners is preferable. A small spray-gun, as used by gardeners, is a necessary tool in any birdroom. The plumage of birds kept inside may get too dry, and will benefit from periodic mist-spraying with tepid water. Many birds relish such bathing, others grow to, and some always hate it, but there is no doubting its material advantages.

One last word about aviaries and cleanliness. Most, hopefully all, keepers make their birds' reproduction the top priority. This being so, there comes a time most years when you will consider it prudent to leave an aviary or a corner of it well alone — neither entering into it nor disturbing it more than absolutely necessary. Do not worry about this, your birds will not suffer from a short period of aviary neglect, and it proves you have the right priorities. Wild birds are extremely intolerant of disturbance during the breeding season.

CHAPTER 7: BREEDING

It is the duty of anyone keeping more than a solitary pet Budgerigar or Canary to encourage the natural procreation of his or her birds. This is the crowning achievement; the accolade proving his birds to be healthy, "happy" and correctly, or at least sufficiently well, managed. With the growing awareness of the need for worldwide nature conservation nothing less will satisfy. Bird-keepers must become AVICUL-TURISTS in the true sense of the word. We can no longer afford *consumers* of nature. Even the proprietors of commercial collections are slowly realizing that it is what the majority of their patrons want. We must encourage our stock to engender its own replacements, this not only makes economical and ecological sense, it is also our moral and scientific duty.

It is a baffling truism that some birds will breed in captivity come what may, while others, possibly of the same species, resist even the most persistent encouragement. Without doubt the most productive birds are those with a long history of cage and aviary conditioning, while the highly specialized are the most barren. In between there are many degrees of what might be termed "breedability" but it is unfortunately true that if there were as many easy-to-breed as there are difficult birds, there would be less need for books such as this.

The breeding behavior of each species is sufficiently different to make generalization extremely difficult and often quite useless. However, the introductory passages and actual guide to the individual species in Part II contain specific information on such matters as nest sites, incubation periods, clutch sizes, hybridization and general breedability. Above all, the successful breeder of cagebirds needs flair. The conscientious keeper makes an exhaustive study of all available information on the species in question, both in the wild and captivity; his findings being transformed into tangible improvements in the management of his birds. It has been my experience that the smallest detail, the craziest notion or just sheer unceasing imagination can tip the scales and prompt a hitherto recalcitrant bird to get down to it. One thing is sure, a bird which is not

BREEDING

realizing its potential is wasted, and a cage or aviary in which young stock is not being produced needs serious reappraisal. Birds must never be shrugged off with an excuse like "Oh, they never breed!" It is up to the owner to diagnose the flaws in his system and correct them.

There are certain widespread factors which prevent birds from breeding in captivity. The commonest of all known ones is a supposed "pair" being in fact birds of the same sex. With species whose plumage is sexually alike, determining sex is a matter for an expert or, indeed, practically impossible. Buying a trio of birds instead of two can obviate the problem of acquiring a third later on. Even the possession of a known pair is by no means a guarantee of reproduction — quite often your problems are only just beginning! Birds may be as incompatible as people or be prevented from breeding by prevailing circumstances. Animals in captivity do not, of course, breed to please us or, wittingly, to make a gesture to conservation. They are simply fulfilling a natural function (the multiplication of their genes) and satisfying an instinct which was developed and formulated millions of years ago to suit that particular animal in its particular environment. To persuade an animal to breed in such an *un*natural habitat as a cage or aviary requires, I am afraid, luck followed by a deep knowledge of its biology, exemplary management, sensitivity and a carefully-designed living-space. Luck is so important that, good or bad, it can outweigh all other factors. Luck decrees the disposition of the birds you buy, and this more than anything else seems to determine their willingness to breed. If a bird or, more accurately; a pair of birds is conditioned into breeding: that is, a female into laying eggs and becoming broody, and a male into courting and nest-building etc it will take a lot of stopping.

Anyone who has endeavoured to discourage a domestic hen from staying broody will know just how strong the desire to reproduce can be. It is this drive that we have to try to instill into our cagebirds. Otherwise, most wild birds appear reluctant to breed in captivity. A caged life can lead to apathy, obesity and to a retrogressive outlook on life in general. If this condition is suspected, it requires much energy and resourcefulness on your part to counteract it. More often than not a fairly drastic measure is necessary — perhaps a change of aviary, mate, fitments, landscaping or fellow inhabitants. It is very tempting to leave an un-productive pair alone, year after year, in the forlorn hope that they will "settle down and come to their senses." Of course what usually happens is that things drag on, the birds getting older, until they eventually sicken and die, no nearer to breeding than they were years before. I believe that if after three years a pair or group of birds has not shown firm indications of breeding, serious and methodical reassessment is a necessity. Three years should be enough time for most birds to get accustomed to their living quarters, and it is surprising how many do suddenly begin to breed after such a period. Quite often birds begin to breed much more readily than this, while others never show any signs despite all your efforts. In such cases, infertility due to senility, infirmity, immaturity or an inadequate diet may prove to be the root cause.

Even accepting that the breeding behavior of each species is different and that individual assessment is essential, the following remarks apply in general to most situations. Assuming that we have a *pair* of birds in a reasonably suitable enclosure, with perches solidly fixed, an appropriate nesting device or area is the first requirement. This must be situated in the right place — away from rain and prevailing winds. Enough of the correct type of nesting material must be on hand, and this too needs more thought and research than might at first seem necessary. Avoid cotton, twine or any similar tough material which could prove lethal, and straw or indeed any dead vegetation which could harbour the fatal spores of *Aspergillus fumigatus*; there are many alternatives, including moss, coconut fibre, the packaging material known as "wood straw," cotton waste, wool, cow hair and woody twigs. Nests and their immediate vicinities should be as sterile and generally as clean as possible. One of the best ploys tempting birds to nest is to start the job for them. In a sense, this is the effect which a nestbox or basket has, but with passerines larger than finches you can even go to the extent of contriving a foundation of twigs: it is quite astonishing how often this pays dividends. Presumably a nest-building stimulus is triggered in the birds' awareness which starts the ball rolling.

The process of incubation is usually best left to the birds, artificial incubators being regarded as emergency failsafe devices or brooders. Removing eggs (and nestlings) to proven good parents is frequently done by

BREEDING

Nesting receptacles.
Upper left: Two styles of wicker nesting baskets suitable for small finches. *Lower left:* Finches and some softbills will also use open-fronted wooden boxes in preference to baskets. *Upper right:* Simple nest foundation as used by many large softbills. *Lower right:* Simulated nest placed high up will often trigger the breeding stimulus in some recalcitrant birds.

experienced breeders of finches and doves. Bengalese Finches and fantail pigeons are often used as foster parents, and it is wise to have some available in the same way as waterfowl and pheasant breeders use hens and bantams. You can help the natural incubation progress by making conditions as favorable as possible, but the best thing you can do for most birds is leave them well alone. Do not interfere or let your curiosity tempt you into "inspecting" the nest and eggs. I know to my cost of all the ways in which you can and will justify such interference; unless there are extenuating circumstances, defy it!

Unfortunately, even the possession of eggs is no guarantee of success. The axiom "Don't count your chickens ..." has never been more apt. Eggs can be infertile (clear) due to insecure perches or numerous other reasons, and fertile eggs become addled when the embryo dies and disintegrates early in its development. "Dead-in-shell" is so common in avicultural circles that the initials D.I.S. are ominously familiar to all breeders. The term is usually applied to an embryonic chick which dies on the point of hatching. Many unrelated reasons can result in D.I.S. An inexperienced mother can incubate inefficiently; a parent bird may carry a lethal gene which prohibits the fertilized egg from developing; an impoverished diet, one deficient in vitamins of the B group and E, can render an embryo incapable of survival; or one of several organisms such as *Coli septicaemia* or *Salmonella* can attack the developing chick. If D.I.S. is causing the failure of more eggs than would seem reasonable, it is of paramount importance to get some of the dead chicks autopsied in the hope of isolating the cause(s). It would be impossible to list all the possible reasons causing the failure of eggs to hatch but many can be traced back to a flaw in the management technique.

If all goes well and you, or your birds I should say, succeed in producing nestlings, you have a worrying and exhausting period to look forward to in which you endeavor to provide all that the parents need in order to help them rear their offspring. This is when an intimate knowledge of wild behavior and basic nutrition is invaluable. The importance of livefood (animal and vegetable) cannot be overemphasized for most seedeaters as will be seen in Part II. Variety is very important; always consider new ideas. Nothing is lost

BREEDING

by sensible inventiveness and much could be gained. Livefood of all sorts, greenfood, eggfood (see Chapter 9) — essentially *fresh* food — are the fundamental requirements of most young birds, and plenty of it. Growing birds demand high proportions of minerals and vitamins; growth is extraordinarily rapid and the high metabolic rate of birds burns up nutrients remarkably quickly.

Very few cagebirds are colonial breeders, most prefer seclusion and privacy although it must be said that the initial stimulus of a rival can goad a hesitant bird into breeding, thus constituting yet another weapon in the armory of the breeder. Until now most of this chapter has purposefully been devoted to what are best called wild birds — that is, birds transferred from their natural environments into artificial ones. The familiar cagebirds have a lengthy history of captive conditioning, therefore the problems they pose are considerably more sophisticated. These relate to channelling the birds' procreative urges along the best lines or at least those you desire. These are discussed more thoroughly in the relevant chapters of Part II. Basically, irrespective of color, variety and so on, only the best available cagebirds should be selected for breeding; as obvious as this might sound, it is surprising the number of owners who persevere with inferior stock either from misguided or sentimental reasons.

Breeding stock should be acquired in the autumn as young birds are then being dispersed. New arrivals will go into a birdroom or house, so the winter weather is not to be feared and they will be nicely settled in by the time spring arrives. The winter is a valuable time for reappraisal and stock-taking (both literally and mentally). It is then that the pressure is off and time can be taken to enjoy the company afforded by a contented birdroom. Nevertheless it is a busy time as preparations including repairing, cleaning and making equipment are underway for the approaching breeding season.

Pairs should be introduced to each other only when *both* are in full breeding condition, this can be at any time after late winter but varies with the year, locality and species. Preferably allow male and female a day or two to get acquainted: this is best accomplished in a breeding-cage divided by a wire partition. Once mating has been satisfactorily performed the nesting "furniture" may be put into place and nature allowed to take its course.

CHAPTER 8: TREATING SICK BIRDS

In life, sickness is to be expected. We anticipate it with insurance policies, prepare for it by early acknowledgment of its symptoms, and cope with it by a prompt visit to the doctor followed up by expert medical care. In severe cases, we place ourselves in hospital. We realize what is happening and face it resolutely. It is up to the owner to do as much for his pets because they are totally dependent on him. Although wild animals are hardier than us — they have to be to survive — sickness is always just around the corner, waiting to pounce on the unprepared, the foolhardy, the weak or the just plain unlucky. Such a blanket term as "sickness" has to cover not only the typical diseases (bacterial, viral and fungal) but also such conditions as damaged limbs, flesh wounds and plumage disorders.

Animals are sometimes good patients, but at other times they are not only uncooperative but downright antagonistic. One then has to fight not only the ailment but also the animal's instinctive fear of you, of being handled and, above all, its innate desire to hide its symptoms for as long as possible. It is this urge which must cause the death of many cagebirds each year. By the time a bird is seen to be ill, it can be too late. In the wild state, no animal wants to advertize the fact that it is functioning below par, which would make it easy meat for the nearest predator, and it has no call on the sympathy of others. If the animal is strong, nature may effect its own cure and give the animal another chance. In captivity, this safety mechanism works *against* the animal. Some experienced keepers and especially sensitive people can anticipate an animal's sickness or at least see through its disguise. I myself have often felt the curious sensation of walking past an aviary and being stopped in my tracks by, if you like, a sixth sense: a firm knowledge that things are not quite right despite all outward signs. I doubt if it is really a sixth sense, more likely some slight deviation from the norm arouses a developed sense. Close examination of the birds usually reveals some minuscule flaw in one which would certainly be overlooked by an insensitive or inexperienced keeper. So, most important of all, one's powers of observation must be developed to a high standard and keenly maintained there. It is not the slightest exaggeration to say that a *seemingly* healthy and robust bird can be but a tiny step away from death. I once watched as a bird which had aroused absolutely

SICK BIRDS

no suspicion in me, fell off its perch to hit the ground stone-dead (*Pasteurella pseudotuberculosis* was the cause). One must be forever vigilant and unceasingly on guard against complacency. Attention to detail in such matters as food and general hygiene will do much to cut down the incidence of disease. Stale and waste food, dirty water, grubby enclosures and slovenly cleaning are what germs are looking for; it is a constant battle. Botulism, for example, is a bacterial organism which causes the death of untold numbers of birds — in warm weather it multiplies rapidly in stagnant water.

Animals go to extreme lengths in order to conceal a weakness. I knew a Piranha fish, blind in one eye, which year in, year out, swam round its tank always in the same direction so as to keep its unprotected side hidden from the other fish which would certainly have made short work of it, had they known. Back to birds, at one collection I looked after, a splendid Black-shouldered Kite *Elanus caeruleus* gave me an uneasy feeling although I could not say why. Kept under intensive care and observation for some days, it seemed to be neither suffering nor benefiting. One day it suddenly deteriorated and looked wretched, gasping for air — each breath nearly choking it. Examination revealed a mass of spongy fungal tissue cramming the mouth and throat (*Candida albicans*, known to cagebird fanciers as "canker" or "thrush"). The kite must have been in considerable pain and discomfort for some time but had never shown it: only when it became chronic could it be hidden no longer and the bird then surrendered completely. That is the next thing you learn about amateur veterinary practice (maybe professional as well): as soon as an animal loses the will to fight, a stubborn death wish often takes its place. Conversely, as long as an animal has a spark of life, and as long as you can keep that spark alive, there is a good chance of recovery; animals are fundamentally very tough.

The listing of ailments which concludes this chapter concentrates mostly on those conditions which can be recognized and, in some cases, treated by the owner. But it should be remembered that professional advice is essential in the majority of serious cases. Even though most veterinarians have little experience of birds and, in my experience, are usually as baffled as the owner, they should be consulted on many counts, such as for laboratory diagnoses, access to a wide range of powerful pharmaceutical drugs and advice on their use. You can greatly help your veterinarian by carefully noting all the symptoms and explaining the whole situation to him accurately. General lethargy or a change in behavior perhaps as slight as a different posture, alert you to danger as much as the more obvious symptoms of discharges, diarrhoea, inflammation, constipation, bleeding and visible swellings. The first rule is isolation : this is better for the patient and reduces the risk of disease being transmitted to healthy stock. Tend sick birds *after* healthy ones, thoroughly washing and disinfecting your hands and utensils afterwards. Inexperienced birdkeepers should regard the hospital cage as an infirmary where the inmate receives professional medical care; certainly if after twenty-four hours an ailing bird has not responded to warmth, seek expert assistance immediately.

Bird Ailments

Abscesses are bacterial infections which are cleared up by simple and effective antibiotic treatment.

Aspergillosis is a dangerous and usually fatal disease caused by fungal infection of the lungs and air sacs through inhalation of the spores of *Aspergillus fumigatus*, which can be present in any decaying vegetation. No known cure but preventive measures include lacing drinking water with potassium iodide at the rate of 3.42 g per litre (30 gr per pint).

Broken and damaged limbs — consult professional veterinarian. Home doctoring can do more harm than good. Speed is essential and by the time you realize that you have made a mistake it is usually too late to rectify it. Dislocation and compound fractures are prone to infection and many other complications.

Cancer of various sorts attacks birds like many other animals. Symptoms are varied and not always apparent. Any bird which is consistently out of condition or in discomfort should be seen by a veterinarian. See next entry also.

Brown hypertrophy of the cere or when that of a male Budgerigar loses its blue color, usually indicates terminal cancer of the testicles.

Cere discoloration — see preceding entry.

Coccidiosis can be triggered off by environmental stress, often after the coccidia has lain dormant for many years; many healthy birds carry heavy infestations throughout life. Symptoms include listlessness, worsening of general condition, loose feathering,

SICK BIRDS

vomiting, diarrhoea and the ingestion of much grit. Professional diagnosis is essential and, if prompt, treatment with one of the modern sulpha drugs can be effective.

Colds and chills. Vague terms often used to describe any generally low condition. An infection of the upper respiratory tract, called Coryza, is the nearest avian equivalent to the common cold; symptoms include discharges from the eyes and nares. It is not usually serious but if left untreated, can spread to the lungs where it may become chronic. Isolate the affected bird in a hospital cage, and consult a veterinarian if condition does not soon improve.

Conjunctivitis. Any irritant of the eyes must be dealt with at once. Most infections respond to repeated antibiotic treatment, but a persistent disorder could well be symptomatic of a more serious condition and professional advice should be sought.

Constipation is revealed when a bird continually strains to pass droppings with little effect. There could be many causes (constipation is a symptom rather than an illness) but the commonest is incorrect feeding: the provision of more greenfood and vitamins of the B complex solve a mild bout, otherwise dose with olive oil. If things do not soon improve, seek professional advice.

Coryza — see Colds and chills.

Cysts, yellowish in color, quite frequently trouble Budgerigars, and require surgery.

Diarrhoea is symptomatic of many diseases but is not one in itself. The cause might be simply bad food, in which case it may well clear up when the source is removed, but meanwhile isolate the patient and obtain an expert diagnosis.

Egg-binding is reputedly common in cagebirds but in ten years of varied bird-keeping I have yet to encounter it. Perhaps I have been lucky, but a good balanced diet with cod-liver-oil added to seed in the breeding season, and sensible management (eg discouraging very young birds — under 8 months old — from breeding early in the year) greatly reduce its incidence. The hen will sit miserably straining, often on the floor of the cage, with feathers ruffled and a swollen anal area, she must be immediately brought into a temperature of about 28° C (85° F); if this and annointing the vent with an enema such as liquid paraffin or glycerine does not free the egg, seek expert advice without further delay. Egg-binding is most likely to occur with the first egg of the season and in cold weather.

Enteritis is inflammation of the intestines and is caused by infection or bad food. Many diseases can cause enteritis, which is accompanied by diarrhoea, greenish in color; coccidiosis is one, and the symptoms of this therefore also apply to enteritis. Veterinary advice must be sought if these symptoms appear.

Feather-plucking is the result of many avian disorders, although, like egg-binding, it need not be as common as it is. Parrot-like birds are especially vulnerable: the main causes are unbalanced diets (particularly a deficiency of vitamins A and D), environmental stress and unhygienic living quarters, which encourage ectoparasites. These can be killed by an insecticide (louse-powder), and diets can easily be improved, but nervous conditions induced by restricted cages, boredom or overcrowding are the commonest cause. A caged, lonely or frustrated bird has few opportunities to "express itself," feather-plucking is one which can quickly become a persistent habit; though difficult, it is not impossible to cure, however, it is better never to let the situation arise in the first place.

French Molt is puzzling, worrying and all too familiar to Budgerigar enthusiasts. Feather disorders, particularly of the wings and tail of juveniles, are usually attributable to this condition — the causes of which are still not known for sure. There are many theories but none is valid under all circumstances. Inherited factors resulting from overbreeding or inbreeding; oxygen deprivation in the chicks, possibly caused by the hen blocking the entrance hole to the nest; and the inhibition of "vital growth factors" to the eggs and "milk" secreted to the chicks caused by the provision of too much Vitamins A & D (present in cod-liver oil) which can, theoretically, result in a metabolic block are the currently popular ones. It is possible that a variety of such reasons contribute to the complexity of the problem. Some workers have found Biotin (Vitamin H, a growth factor and respiratory stimulant for the organism Rhizobium) and Vitamin K of use in treatment, but many young birds molt out perfectly normally with no treatment whatsoever, and are thereafter able to lead perfectly natural lives.

Goitre results from a malfunctioning thyroid gland. The most obvious symptom is wheezy breathing. Isolate, and consult a veterinarian. Treatment is effected by

SICK BIRDS

increasing the intake of iodine. Mineral blocks should always be available to hardbills.

Lice do not seem unduly to worry a healthy host in the wild, but of this we cannot be sure because very little is known about the causes of wild fatalities, and the evidence presented by birds in captivity indicates that lice (and mites) can seriously affect their host. Dusting with pyrethrum powder solves the problem. Birds heavily infested become very restless, but some skin disorders cause similar irritation.

Mites. Much of the preceding entry also applies. Some mites are blood-suckers, others feed on feathers and skin debris, and some are the so-called "itch-mites" (see Scaly Leg). *Dermanyssus gallinae* (red mite) is the most infamous of all: this is a sucking-mite which, except in severe cases, spends the day in the nest or birdroom crevices, venturing out at night to attack the birds. Treatment should be prompt and consists of dusting or spraying the victim with an insecticide, vacating the cage or room during the day and thoroughly sterilizing it.

Ornithosis (Psittacosis in parrots) is a serious virus disease which can be transmitted to human beings. If caught in the early stages it can be at least partially cured by antibiotics. Consult your veterinarian if ornithosis is suspected; it is most often found in newly imported birds which might *appear* to be suffering from a severe cold or even pneumonia, but many birds probably carry the disease and show no symptoms.

Overgrown beak and claws are also problems which can be greatly minimized by correct management, in this instance, housing. They should be rare in outside aviary stock, and are most frequently seen in caged birds living on slim machine-doweled perches. It is only a minor problem but one which requires attention (see illustration). The most important thing is to ensure that the cut is made beyond the vein, otherwise severe bleeding will occur. The vein becomes apparent if the claw is held up to the light but it is better to leave on the long side rather than endanger the blood vessel. A pair of sharp nail-clippers is preferable to scissors.

Pasteurellosis (*Pasteurella pseudotuberculosis*) is a common pathogen and particularly dangerous because of its sudden appearance and fatal consequences. It is difficult to combat, but follow the advice set out under Salmonellosis. Your best ally is probably a cold, dry winter.

Red mite — see Mites.

Respiratory disorders (see also Colds and chills) sometimes trouble birds, especially those housed in badly ventilated rooms. Symptoms such as gaping beak, asthmatic wheezing and evident discomfort should be viewed with alarm and professional advice sought. The causes are diverse and quite often extremely problematical.

Rickets is sometimes seen in young birds, especially softbills and Budgerigars. The cause is invariably an inbalance of the calcium/phosphorus ratio in the diet. A close watch should be maintained wherever possible for deformed legs, and immediate remedial action taken by increasing the intake of calcium. Calcium lactate tablets can be purchased at many chemists, and in emergencies, doses of Vitamin D_3 can be administered by a veterinarian.

Salmonellosis, caused by the *Salmonella* bacteria, is a common and often fatal disease which can be easily contracted by contact with rodents or, indeed, other birds. As always, scrupulous hygiene and good clean fresh food and water help to keep such bacteria at bay. Discourage wild birds from contaminating outside aviaries and encourage, by thoughtful design, the rapid drainage of rainwater. Do not be tempted to introduce such mammals as guinea pigs into planted aviaries. Symptoms are listlessness and diarrhoea coupled to excessive thirst and dysentery. Laboratory examination of droppings must be done at once. An extra word of warning: salmonellosis can be transmitted to humans.

Scaly Leg, together with **Scaly Face** and **Scaly Beak,** is caused by infestation of a small mite *Cnemidocoptes pilae*, and is readily betrayed by yellowish encrustations on the affected parts. It is not difficult to cure: the flaky crust should be removed and burnt, and a 10% solution of benzyl benzoate applied to the exposed area for a few days.

Worms can attack all birds but in particular, the parrot-like. If a bird loses weight and condition, and worms are suspected, laboratory examination of a faeces sample is needed so that the culprit can be identified and eliminated by drugs supplied by your veterinarian.

N.B. Birds which die from unknown causes should always be post-mortemed so that flaws in management, where they exist, can be rectified, and so that a possible epidemic can be forestalled.

Examples of overgrown beaks and claws.

CANARIES

CHAPTER 9: CANARIES

The myriad forms of Canaries developed by breeders over the last four centuries all owe their existence to *Serinus canaria*, a native of the Canary Islands, Madeira and the Azores. Of all finches, why the Canary? Undoubtedly its charm and beautiful song first attracted man, while its hardiness must have helped it become the archetypal cagebird. The achievements of Canary breeders, while less spectacular and useful than those of, say, the dog breeder, are of far more scientific interest.

Mutations occur naturally from time to time. In captivity, they can be judiciously preserved, and used to quite astonishing effect. By crossing with the Red Hooded Siskin, we now even have red Canaries (see *Red Factors*). Strictly speaking, these birds, together with the often sterile first-generation hybrids (mules) of other pairings, are not true Canaries, although they are adjudged so for the purposes of aviculture. The other two basic ground-colors on which all other shades are superimposed are yellow and white. This results in such types as Yellows (Buffs), Whites, Cinnamons, Blues (Greys) and Greens. Those unfamiliar with Canaries must not be misled into thinking that these colors are as intense as those found in Budgerigars; at a glance, most appear as subtle variations of the typical yellow. Apart from the wide range of color patterns, the plumage structure itself has been subjected to the same manipulation. It is a known fact of intensive bird-breeding that feather mutation occurs hard on the heels of color mutation. Stemming from such chance events, a bewildering variety of Canary designs now exists. The techniques of sex-linked color-breeding and genetic manipulation are often classed as an art whereas, in fact, they form a science. Many people devote their lives to the search for new types and the perfection of existing ones.

The actual *texture* of Canary plumage is of two sorts, confusingly called yellow (jonque) and buff (mealy, or frosted in Red Factors). The former has shorter, firmer and more colorful feathers, while those of buffs are rather the opposite. Canaries of white ground-color are harder to split, but the same rule, color apart, applies. It is important to recognize this difference because a breeding pair ought to include both, otherwise the so-called "double-yellowing" results in tight-feathered, over slim birds, while "double-buffing" has the reverse

Border and Fife Canaries
1 Self Cinnamon Border
2 Cinnamon and White Variegated Border
3 Clear Yellow Border
4 Eye-, Wing- and Tail-marked Buff Border
5 Clear Yellow Fife

CANARIES

effect. Correctly matched pairs produce an equal number of both viable sorts. Each type-breed differs to some extent in form, although this may be disguised by plumage eccentricities like those evinced by the Frilled Canary. On the other hand, the semi-circular Belgian Canary has one of the strangest silhouettes of the entire avian world.

Unlike all others, the Roller Canary was developed, in Germany, solely for its exquisite song with no account taken of its looks, which otherwise have to conform to strict standards of form and plumage. Because the Roller is a good songster and easily bred it makes an ideal pet, but highly competitive singing contests are also staged, and young pedigree Rollers of different strains are painstakingly trained by "school-masters" (prize-winning songsters), records and tapes to sing their "rolls" and "tours."

All the type-breeds evolved in different ways and places, many in Britain, at different times and for various reasons. Their names often reflect their origins, while others describe an aspect of the birds' appearance (the Lizard, Red Factor and Frilled); others like the Norwich Plainhead and Lancashire Coppy do both. The seven plates depict a wide cross-section of ideal Canaries, which serve in place of lengthy descriptions, so the following remarks are more in the order of potted biographies.

The Belgian Canary (page 69) is one of the oldest breeds but when exactly it originated in Belgium is not known. It was popular in Britain during the late 19th century, since when its popularity waned, the numbers decreasing until it seemed that it would die out. Belgians are not color-fed, and this accounts for their more insipid appearance when set alongside those breeds which are. Owing to the limited numbers once available, considerable in-breeding occurred which earnt them a reputation for being difficult to breed and delicate. This is no longer a problem.

The Border Canary (page 63) is the most popular breed of all. Ideal for beginners as it is a good reliable breeder, relatively cheap and readily obtainable. Like the Belgian, it must not be color-fed. Being so steady, it is eminently suitable as a foster. Borders are attractive, perky, neat little birds, available in a varied choice of colors. Answering the demand for a smaller Canary it originated in North England near the Scottish border, and was once known as the Cumberland Fancy.

Frilled, Gloster and Lancashire Canaries
1 Frilled
2 Wing-marked Yellow Gloster Corona
3 Variegated Gloster Corona
4 Buff Gloster Consort
5 Lancashire Plainhead
6 Lancashire Coppy

FRILLED, GLOSTER AND LANCASHIRE

63

CANARIES

Crested Canaries are known in various forms but the *Crest* or *Crested Norwich* (page 67) is the oldest breed. Unlike the Norwich Plainhead, it is not color-fed so appears in its natural paler color. The crest factor is dominant, and breeders avoid mating one Crest to another because this produces three kinds of progeny: the non-crested (Crestbred), the singular-character Crest, and the double-character Crest which, unfortunately, never survives. Therefore, singular-character Crests should be paired to Crestbreds, which results in fifty per cent of each viable type.

The Fife Canary (page 61) is one of the smallest breeds, and a recent innovation from Fifeshire, appearing in the 1940s. It owes its existence to the fact that a group of breeders in that part of Scotland considered the Border to be getting too large. The result of their work was a petite, richly-colored Canary with fine, firm feathers and a lively disposition. Its exact antecedency is not known. The Fife Fancy is currently gaining popularity, and as more breeders take it up, the variety of color strains is bound to increase. At present, the Yellow and Buff birds are still the most popular.

Frilled Canaries (page 63), are some of the most distinctive Canaries. There are Dutch, Italian and Parisian types, and it is essentially a European bird, for some reason never achieving the same popularity in America and Britain. It is a very old breed with origins probably in the now extinct Dutch Canary, which influenced many of today's type-breeds. It is an attractive bird with added advantages of being a reliable breeder and robust in nature.

The Gloster Canaries (page 63) consist of two types: the *Corona* has a short crest which fringes the eyes; the other is the *Consort*, which is a crest-bred bird (see *Crested Canaries*). This is another breed which is not color-fed and comes in many delicate hues. The current fashion in the Canary world is for small, neat, sprightly birds which have many practical advantages. And the Glosters are steady, reliable breeders, good for fostering, hardy, well-balanced and not expensive. All these features have helped their popularity spread rapidly around their world.

The Ino Canaries (page 71) are mutations which possess a diluted ground-color and red eyes. There are Rubinos of red ground-color, Lutinos of yellow, and Albinos of white. It is not albinism as we associate it

Lizard and London Canaries
1 Clear-capped Silver Lizard
2 Clear-capped Gold Lizard
3 Broken-capped Gold Lizard
4 Short-capped Silver
5 Over-capped Silver
6 Non-capped Silver Lizard
7 London

CANARIES

Norwich Canaries
1 Clear Buff Norwich
2 Clear Yellow Norwich
3 Heavily Variegated Norwich
4 Grizzle Crested Yellow Norwich
5 Variegated Crest-bred Norwich

with other animals but a genuine mutation. The character, being recessive, is seen only when carried by both parents. It was first recognized as such in 1964 when a Belgian fancier bred one from a pair of Cinnamon Red Factors. Since then they have been bred in many different hues.

The Lancashire Canary (page 63) is an old breed which probably first appeared, in Manchester, about 200 years ago. It is the largest of the "British" Canaries and includes both the crested (Coppy) and crestbred (Plainhead) varieties. It is not color-fed and is now usually seen as a Clear (unmarked) Yellow or Buff, but there is no reason why other color types should not be produced.

The Lizard Canary (page 65) is a popular, attractively marked breed of unknown origin: the only type-breed in which the plumage *markings* conform to a standard, which has remained unchanged for well over 120 years. Lizards are not birds for beginners because they require much experience and skill to maintain the correct spangling effect from one generation to another. There are three types: *Clear-capped, Broken-capped* and *Non-capped*. The yellow and buff variations in Lizards are called gold and silver. For exhibition purposes, they are known as "one-year birds:" young birds not attaining their characteristic markings until the first molt; subsequent molts see a marked depreciation in quality of color and feather. Color-feeding is commonly undertaken to increase the density of the natural colors.

The London Canary (page 65) became extinct in the 1930s but, unlike wild species, it is certainly within the bounds of possibility to revive it by experimental breeding. It was closely allied to the Lizard Canary, where must lie its resurgence.

Mule (page 73) is a term used to describe Canaries crossbred with other finches such as the Goldfinch and Linnet. As was fortuitously found with the Red Hooded Siskin, the progeny of such matings *can* be fertile, which disproved the converse belief which had long prevailed. The main value of hybridization in the domestic context is in the quest for new types and colors.

Color Canaries (page 71) is a self-explanatory term applied to most of the recent creations of scientifically-minded breeders. Color breeding is an exacting science and demands more space than is here

CANARIES

available. Needless to say, it is not for the in-experienced, and anyone whose interest leads them along this fascinating path will need to study the subject in depth.

The Norwich Plainhead (page 67) is perhaps the most superb of all Canaries. A truly beautiful testimony to man's understanding of selective-breeding, it probably appeared in East Anglia in the early 18th century, since when it has been subjected to constant improvement until today's splendid specimens appeared. Norwich Canaries are now available in many variations; they are color-fed which helps to account for their eye-catching brilliance. (See also *Crested Canaries*.)

The Red Factor Canary (page 71) is the most exciting recent development in the Canary world. Introduction of the red ground-color, along with black, had long been regarded as impossible, but since viable offspring were produced by crossing with the Red Hooded Siskin, it now seems that many new type-breeds are just waiting to be discovered. I see no reason why other members of the Fringillidae are not genetically close enough to produce fertile male hybrids when crossed with the Canary. Red Factors are still very much in the formative stage but already standards are being set down, and shades range from deep copper and rich orange red to delicate pastels. It is an exciting field.

Roller Canary. See *Song Canaries*.

The Scotch Fancy Canary (page 69). A most curious shape sets this bird apart from most others, and is its main claim to fame. It was once known as the Glasgow Don, and that city began its culture early in the 19th century. It is not as old as the Belgian Canary, which must have played a big part in its development. Apart from being a source of fascination, its placid disposition and good parental qualities make it the obvious choice for young ambitious newcomers.

Song Canaries. For reasons of space I have grouped these types together. The Roller Canary (page 73) is the best known and has already been mentioned on page 20-1. *The Malinois Canary* is closely related to the Roller but almost unknown in America and Britain, its main concentration being in Belgium. Another Canary bred mainly for its voice is the *Spanish Timbrado*, developed in Spain and now gaining popularity in America. Song Canaries are ideal for those requiring an aviary of colorful, active birds to liven up a garden.

Yorkshire, Scotch and Belgian Canaries
1 Clear Yellow Yorkshire
2 Self Green Yorkshire
3 Variegated Buff Yorkshire
4 Scotch Fancy
5 Belgian

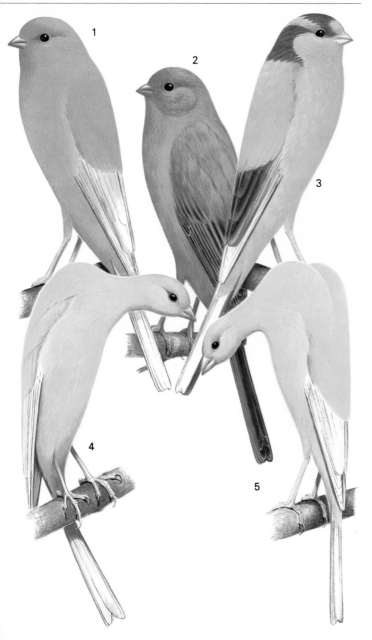

CANARIES

White-ground Canaries (page 73) are either the Dominant Whites, which originated in Germany over 300 years ago, or the Recessive Whites which emerged more recently from New Zealand. White-ground Canaries are now available in most of the type-breeds; the prototype being a Roller Canary. It is an exacting field, suited to the scientifically-minded.

The Yorkshire Canary (page 69) is a superior-looking breed of uncertain origin. It comes in many guises and is usually color-fed. The Yorkshire is currently very popular and provides the color-breeder with all the material he needs.

Whichever type of Canary is favored (and to maintain a healthy broad-based Fancy, each breed needs its band of disciples) the same general rules of management apply. Many of these are common-sense, but the less common ability to see the world through the birds' eyes is also valuable. The owner of the pet bird does not want to bother with science, and needs "only" to know about diets (Chapter 5) and the other basics of management(Chapters 4 & 6). It is important to remember that cages in living-rooms should be out of

New Color and Ino Canaries
1 Frosted Gold Agate Opal
2 Frosted Rose Brown Ino
3 Silver Isabel Ino
4 Apricot
5 Frosted Rose
6 Red Orange

draughts: sunshine, too, without facilities for shade is dangerous. The best cages are those which combine with a high stand to discourage cats etc. Most Canaries like to bathe, and by far the most convenient type of bath is the open-sided one which clips into the doorway.

Breeding procedures have been outlined in Chapter 7, and lack of space precludes an in-depth study of this involved subject, but there are a few points here to be made. One concerns softfood; it is as well to provide this throughout the year, increasing the supply during the breeding season. Homemade recipes are perfectly adequate but the commercially produced ones are perhaps safer and more convenient. Dried egg, biscuits and cod-liver oil are the main ingredients; bread and milk may be given as a change provided it is not allowed to turn sour. Since there need to be frequent small portions, softfood is usually given in "finger trays" which attach to the side of the cage. The natural color of some breeds (see above) is enhanced by color-food, which is similarly a softfood but one which contains a red coloring agent such as carotene.

Assuming that birds have been selected, paired off and settled into their breeding-cages, and that the

CANARIES

weather is seasonable, early spring sees intense activity in the birdroom. When cocks sing lustily, hens hunt for nesting material, and they feed one another through the wire partition, they are both in breeding condition, and the barrier can be removed. If mating is successful, the nesting receptacle (see illustrations) and a selection of moss and cow-hair can be introduced. The clutch of 4–5 eggs is laid on consecutive days. Once laid, each egg should be carefully removed and substituted with a pot egg. After the fourth has been laid the clutch can be reassembled in the nest — allowing at least four eggs to hatch concurrently after an incubation of 13–14 days. Towards the end of the incubation period it is important not to allow the eggs to dehydrate, which can occur if the hens do not have bathing facilities (some will not use them, and in such cases the eggs should be sprayed daily with a fine tepid mist spray). Young Canaries grow rapidly and are independent in about a month. After a short rest the hen will be ready for her second clutch and the cock may be allowed back in (some cocks will help with the rearing, others are a nuisance and have to be removed). By this time, the young should have progressed into a nursery-cage until they are ready to be transferred to a flight-cage for their first molt. Ensure that they are feeding themselves before they leave their parents.

Records must be maintained throughout. Details of the parents, clutch size, dates of "setting," and the progress of *each* egg, culminating in the juveniles' ring numbers etc comprise an accurate and comprehensive survey which will guide all future breeding policies. Human memory is such that these records should not be underestimated.

Ceramic nestpan and wooden box with ventilated base for canaries.

White-ground Song and Mule Canaries
1 Clear Recessive White
2 Clear Yellow Roller
3 Wing-marked American Singer
4 Goldfinch Mule
5 Greenfinch Mule

BUDGERIGARS

CHAPTER 10: BUDGERIGARS

If Canaries are confusing to the aspiring color-breeder, Budgerigars, despite their more recent appearance, present an even thornier problem. Intensive Budgerigar breeding is only about 100 years old, and it was not until Abbot Mendel's laws of inheritance were re-discovered early this century that the selective-breeding of domestic animals was better understood and put on a scientific footing. Until then, mutations were liable to be swamped by the typical form (as happens in the wild), and the early breeders stumbled along in the dark, gaining ground, which they could not hope to understand, by sheer chance. In 1925, The Budgerigar Club (later to become The Budgerigar Society) was formed from a meeting at the Crystal Palace Exhibition in London. This was the launch-pad which was much needed to direct the rapidly accumulating interest this humble little parakeet from the Australian outback was unwittingly creating. As with the Canary, its adoption by man was not really coincidental.

There are not that many wild animals which breed well enough in captivity to present themselves as viable propositions for domestication; and those which do, have to offer something else besides this compatibility. The Canary offered its song and charm; the Budgerigar too has an abundance of charm, but it also has much, much more. The Canary probably appeals most to either the scientifically-minded or those who simply enjoy the melodious company of a songbird. The Budgerigar similarly attracts the scientist, offering tremendous scope to the geneticist and color-breeder, but it has not the same diversity of form. As a pet, it surpasses the Canary. Being a member of the parrot family, its intelligence is superior, and it displays a considerable number of humanoid traits, which never fail to elicit our compassion. It climbs about using ladders etc; looks into mirrors; plays with bells and other childish toys; it has a much flatter, human-like face that has no obvious dagger beak to disquiet us (although its bite is far more effective!); it is not so keen on flying and therefore seldom alarms the faint-hearted by the sudden explosions of whirring feathers that seem to upset so many women; and it comes in a multitude of gaudy designs. But above all, it has one overwhelming asset which would negate all other arguments (as it does with the Mynah), it TALKS!

Normal or Green
Budgerigars
1 Light Green (Wild Type Normal)
2 Dark Green
3 Olive Green
4 Gray Green

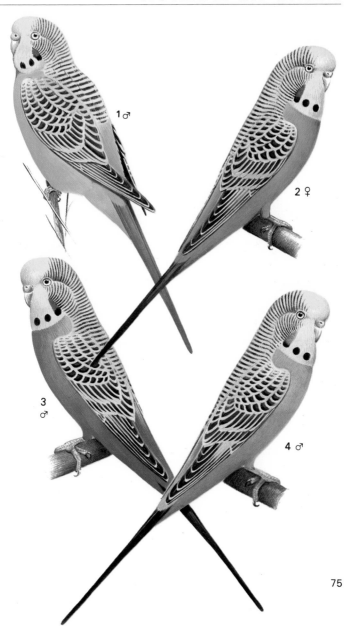

1 ♂

2 ♀

3 ♂

4 ♂

BUDGERIGARS

I firmly believe that man, who has treated the natural world so badly, likes to assume that because a friendly animal apparently talks to him, he is not totally corrupt! Of course, the talking Budgie is doing no such thing, he is merely mimicking *sounds*, but let's not destroy too many harmless illusions. If a Budgie does not talk to his owner, it will certainly chatter, and this to my mind, by virtue of its natural spontaneity, is even more attractive. And, of course, being a hardbill, it is as easy to maintain as the Canary, if not even easier. No-one need worry nowadays about catering for a Budgerigar, an industry exists for this very purpose. Senior citizens the world over cope perfectly well with their management, and neither is expense a problem, these same people gladly appropriate a tiny portion of their often meagre income to the needs of their beloved Budgies. The pleasure, company and indeed service these birds give their sometimes lonely or invalided owners provides one of the immediate arguments in favor of aviculture, because without it there would be no tame Budgerigars. And the few pompous naturalists who deride it would do well to realize that it is not the keeping and breeding of birds in captivity that is reprehensible but the outrageous fringes of the hobby, which cause inexcusable suffering.

As with Canaries, you need to know something of genetics in order to appreciate the value of mutations and color-breeding (see pages 88–92). There are then two very different schools of Budgerigar enthusiasts: the owner of the pet bird(s), who demands nothing more than a hardy, cheerful companion, and the serious breeder to whom Budgerigars become an obsession. In one sense, Budgies can give life; in another, they can take it or at least consume it. In quite another more sinister sense, the Budgerigar has been called the world's prettiest killer; this refers of course to the dreaded Psittacosis, which is no problem, let it be fully understood, with captive-bred pets and exhibition birds.

Despite the countless Budgerigar variations already alive and well, there are still many more waiting to be perfected and discovered. The search is still on for the true red Budgie (one up here to the Canary fraternity!) and the black Budgie too has so far delayed its entrance. As in the previous chapter, the facing plates provide a comprehensive selection of the color-varieties available, and do a far better job than could

Blue Series Budgerigars
1 Skyblue
2 Cobalt
3 Mauve
4 Violet Cobalt
5 Gray Blue

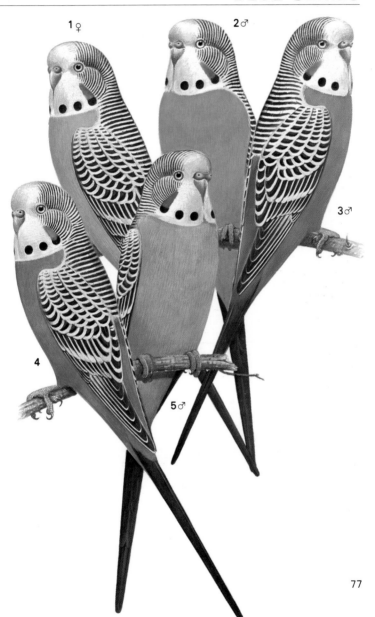

BUDGERIGARS

I with any written descriptions. The captions to each plate give the necessary generic information of the types opposite. The remainder of this chapter is therefore devoted to information which will hopefully assist not only the beginner and pet owner but also the more experienced fancier who can balance his own views against possibly different ones. Much of the value of an organized cagebird fancy is the free exchange of ideas and theories; there is not necessarily only one solution to every problem.

Management

Budgerigars are easy-going birds, happy in most styles of cage so long as they are roomy enough. Aviaries with a lengthy flight path are especially valuable for collections. For those requiring no more than a pet bird in their living-room, a large selection of excellent plain and fancy cages is to be found in most good pet shops. It is advisable thoroughly to wash and scrub a new cage in order to remove any dangerous particles which Budgerigars, in particular, are bound to find. Avoid cages which include ornate metalwork — it is not only difficult to clean but can easily trap a foot or, worse, a head. Most cages come ready fitted with seed-pots and drinking-fountains — which are superior to open-topped dishes for water, but you may need to provide an extra one for grit, although many owners rely on the "bird-sand" covering the floor to supply all necessary grits. I am convinced that you cannot supply too much variety of minerals and grit; cuttlefish bone (held in place by a special clip), oystershell, crushed eggshell, mortar, sea sand, chalk, granite chippings and, of course, the special mineralized nibbles are all beneficial. Indulge your birds in their desire to gnaw by supplying green twigs as well as the cuttlefish. Instead of loose sand, sheets of specially prepared sanded paper can be laid on the cage floor but are inferior, in my opinion, to proper bird sand although they do give the Budgies something to chew up! Around the base of the cage there should be either a glass or loose material shield to help prevent the floor in the vicinity of the cage from becoming littered with the debris of past meals. Glass shields which slide into slots on the cage exterior give a much neater and more pleasing appearance, although such cages are necessarily more expensive.

Providing bathing facilities for housebound birds is a rather messy problem; but in this respect, Budgerigars

Varieties
1 Slate Skyblue
2 Yellow-faced Skyblue
3 Fallow Light Green
4 Cinnamon Dark Green
5 Cinnamon Cobalt

BUDGERIGARS

are not so demanding as most, and I have found that an occasional spray with tepid water from a mist-gun is both enjoyed and quite sufficient. Cages should be positioned in a room as for Canaries. During warm weather, they may be put outside, but do not leave any bird in direct sunshine for too long, most detest it and the belief that they cannot have too much is a common fallacy of many people who keep "tropical" birds. Many owners allow their birds to fly around the room, some almost have free rein to come and go as they please. This is all very well, but ensure that windows are closed, house plants — which can be poisonous — are not accessible, there are no open fires and that valuable and/or fragile ornaments cannot be knocked over by a budgie making a forced landing on a shelf or mantlepiece. Budgerigars once used to a certain amount of liberty certainly enjoy it, and the exercise does their general constitution and mental state good. One stage on from this, but not necessarily a natural progression, is to have a flock of Budgerigars at complete liberty in one's garden (an illegal activity in North America). Not many gardens are suitable, however, as they need to be fairly large, have trees (nearby) and be free of disturbance. A flock intended for liberty has to be well used to its surroundings, preferably having been bred in the aviary which will later be used as the home base.

For those people who require more than one or two birds, I would strongly recommend a garden aviary in which a pleasant colony of multi-colored Budgerigars may be housed communally and allowed to get on with it. Such a policy is unsuitable for the breeder of show birds or color strains since no breeding control can be exercised over it. The conversion of a garden shed/greenhouse/summer-house/conservatory is always worth considering, although it is usually better, certainly easier and often no more expensive, to buy or build a purpose-designed aviary. The real enthusiast, however, will be content with nothing less than a fully equipped birdroom, complete with breeding-cages and outside flights. Such a complex is essential to the serious breeder as he will never have enough space available.

The design of aviaries, of which the main function is not decoration, should be as simple and uncluttered as possible. Budgerigars like to clamber about and gnaw, so perches of natural wood which can be easily

Red-eyed Budgerigars
1 Opaline Lacewing White
2 Albino or Red-eyed Clear White
3 Lacewing Yellow
4 Lutino or Red-eyed Clear Yellow

BUDGERIGARS

replaced are preferable to (expensive) dowelling. Coarse sand cannot, I think, be bettered as a floor covering for any outside area housing parrot-like birds. It is impossible to keep grass fresh and shrubs alive. Concrete or slab floors involve strenuous scrubbing and usually end up looking like a prison exercise yard. Sand or fine gravel floors need only raking over to maintain a fresh appearance, they facilitate speedy drainage and provide the birds with valuable trace-elements and a mental diversion. Wire-netting must be of good quality and frequently inspected for holes and weaknesses. A coat of bituminous or matt black paint on the outside is incredibly successful in concealing its presence and also makes it considerably easier to view the birds within. One can take more trouble with an ornamental aviary, planting various grasses and erecting interesting tree-limbs, a shallow pool and perhaps some rockwork; even so, the areas beneath perches should be sand. Other aspects of housing are dealt with in Part I.

Basic feeding requirements have been covered in Chapter 5. I would recommend the pet-bird owner and possibly even those who maintain a small stud, buying one of the tried and tested packeted mixtures, but for the more ambitious, it is cheaper to buy the various seeds separately, blending them himself. A good basic Budgerigar diet consists of 3 parts white millet, 3 parts canary seed and one part panicum millet; to this can be added small quantities of the supplementary seeds as mentioned on page 36. Do not forget the importance of fresh greenfood.

Unlike exponents of the colony system, those who like to exercise some control over their breeding stock give themselves a lot of necessary extra work. The idea is not very dissimilar to that described for Canaries insofar as pairing, housing and seasons go, although it obviously differs considerably in other ways. Male Budgerigars are in breeding condition when their ceres are a bright blue (those of the red-eyed and pied types are pinker) and when they move about energetically, quarrelling among themselves. Hens are also fractious, but their ceres are dark brown and they will hunt furiously for nesting sites.

Nestboxes are the subject of a surprising amount of discussion, but in the end, a certain amount of experimentation quickly shows which type of box is best suited to your particular birds. However, there are

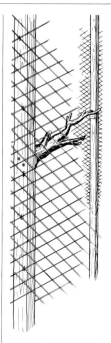

Probably the best kind of perch is a natural one fixed from one side of the aviary to the other. Such perches should be scrubbed and renewed regularly.

Opaline Budgerigars
1 Cinnamon Gray Opaline
2 Light Green Opaline
3 Dark Green Opaline
4 Skyblue Opaline
5 Cobalt White-flighted Opaline

BUDGERIGARS

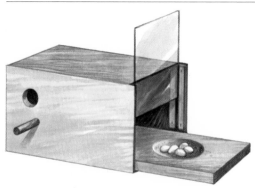

The ideal Budgerigar nestbox incorporates an inspection panel and removable base with concave nesting depression.

some important points to bear in mind when choosing or making them – looks or style being less important than functional ability. A feature of all good boxes is the removable concave base into which the hen will lay her eggs, and on which should be scattered a *small* amount of coarse sawdust. Another is an inspection door so that should anything need attention it can be seen at a glance. Nestboxes should always be thoroughly cleaned and disinfected before each breeding season. A growing tendency nowadays is to use disposable boxes made of sturdy cardboard, reusing only the loose wooden bases, and this trend has many points to commend it.

Some hens – either maliciously or accidentally – develop the annoying and expensive habit of breaking their eggs as they are laid. This problem can be solved if the concave base and nestbox are modified by drilling a hole therein, which allows the eggs as laid to drop through into a shallow translucent tray, in which is a layer of sawdust or other soft substance. The eggs can be collected and the complete clutch set under a reliable foster mother. Occasionally a neurotic or bad-tempered hen is encountered which can cause havoc in a breeding-aviary and must be removed.

Clutches of eggs vary between three and eight (four is an average for an older hen). Incubation, which lasts for about 18 days, seems to begin with the second egg. Therefore, on hatching, the ages of the young are staggered. Since eggs are laid on alternate days, there can be as much as a fortnight between the ages of the youngest and the oldest. This is not the problem it is with Canaries because they are all looked after equally

Clearwing and Graywing Varieties
1 Yellow-wing Light Green ♂
2 White-wing Skyblue
3 Opaline Yellow-wing Dark Green
4 Yellow-faced Opaline White-wing Cobalt (Rainbow)
5 Graywing Skyblue
6 Graywing Light Green

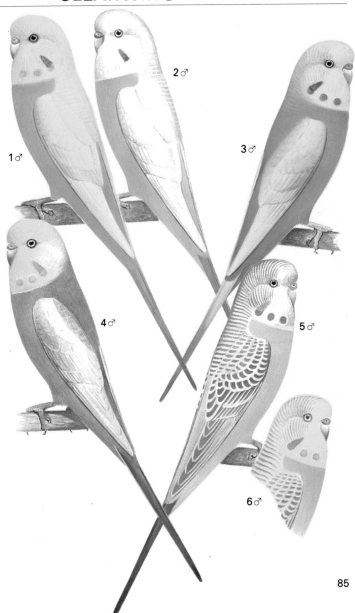

BUDGERIGARS

well. Young Budgerigars leave the nest after a month or so, by which time the hen, having begun her next clutch, will leave the weaning, which takes less than a fortnight, to the cock.

Nesting females spend most of their time in the box, and are fed there by their mates. For this reason it is wise not to introduce the nestbox until the newly matched pair have had a chance to become acquainted and mate, otherwise the eggs may well prove to be infertile. Other complications can also arise: some hens like to sit blocking the entrance hole, effectively cutting off the ventilation to the interior; it has been suggested that insufficient oxygen can cause French Molt in developing chicks (see page 57). It is therefore advisable to incorporate additional airholes elsewhere in the box. Needless to say, nestboxes in outside aviaries should be rainproof or situated under cover. Always supply an abundance so that jealousies are averted and the hens have a good selection to choose from.

Mention here of ventilation is appropriate because it is of vital importance in all cagebird environments but particularly for Budgerigars. All birdrooms should be light, dry and airy. Budgies are tough little birds so there is no need for stuffy conditions. The best type of birdroom is one incorporating a system of breeding-cages which can be extended or limited at will by the use of sliding partitions, which in turn are supported by pens for young stock or breeding pairs, and which open into lengthy outside flights. Single aviaries which combine an outside area (partially sheltered by opaque sheeting) and a shed which can be separated by sliding or hinged trapdoors is ideal for the small collection. Incidentally, food should be placed inside partly for reasons of convenience and hygiene but also to condition the birds into going inside. It is as well to make a habit of shutting Budgerigars in at night: this obviates the risk of sudden hard frosts which can cause frostbite to the toes of those birds which habitually choose to roost clinging to the wire-netting. This habit is doubly dangerous as it makes the birds vulnerable to marauding nocturnal predators which can cause direct physical injury or nightfright.

It is an indication of the birds' inherent hardiness that, left to it, they would happily breed, or at least attempt to, all the year round. They must be dissuaded from doing so for obvious reasons and in communal

Dominant Pied or Dutch Pied Budgerigars
1 Dominant Pied Graywing Cobalt
2 Dominant Pied Skyblue
3 Dominant Pied Light Green
4 Dominant Pied Opaline Dark Green
5 Australian Dominant Banded Pied Gray (Blue)

flights where males and females are left together nestboxes should be removed during the coldest months of the year. Even though some birds like to roost in them, they will not suffer if denied this "luxury." Three broods a year is quite sufficient: any more and you can easily overtax the hen, and, if I might mix my metaphors cook your golden goose!

Genetics

For those considering tackling color-breeding, which is probably the most fascinating aspect of pure aviculture, it may be of some help here briefly to explain the Mendelian laws of inheritance on which the modern science of genetics is based. Anyone sufficiently interested has to study the subject in depth, and while I would not agree with one learned author on Budgerigars, who states that the bird-breeder need only know certain elementary rules, it is true that he can disregard most of the finer points of the subject. What is elementary to the expert though, can be most baffling to the newcomer!

Life is passed on from one generation to the next by the fusion of male and female reproductive cells, called gametes. Each one contains a number of chromosomes — rod-like structures — which, in turn contain the genes which govern all inherited factors: not just color, which is our main concern. One might expect that because a young bird receives equal contributions from each of its parents, it would appear as an amalgam of them both, but this, as we shall see, is not so.

In birds (and butterflies), males possess an equal pair of sex-chromosomes, represented by the symbols "XX," whereas females' possess an unequal pair, a male "X" and a female "Y" which is shorter. (In all other animals, it is the male which possesses the unequal pair.) During mating, the chromosomes divide and should one of the male's X chromosomes fuse with the female's X, a male (XX) will result; should the male's X fuse with the female's Y, a female (XY) is born. The color factor of birds is carried by other chromosomes, but sometimes by the sex-chromosomes as well, and it is these colors which are called sex-linked. Theoretically, if a pure-bred wild type (Light Green) Budgerigar (which we shall call pure-type AA) mates with a pure-bred White Budgerigar (pure-type bb), the offspring, receiving one color factor from each parent, could be a combination of both (Ab), but while some will certainly carry the White factor (b), it will not show

Dominant and
Recessive Pieds and
Clear-flighted
Budgerigars
1 Australian Dominant Banded Pied Light Green
2 Yellow-flighted Light Green
3 Australian White-flighted Skyblue
4 Recessive Pied Cinnamon Violet (Cobalt)
5 Recessive Pied Cobalt
6 Recessive Pied Yellow-faced Skyblue
7 Recessive Pied Light Green

1♂

2♂

3♂

4

5

6

7

BUDGERIGARS

because Green is dominant over White; indeed, in Budgerigars, green is dominant over all other colors. Therefore the young of such a mating will be impure type Ab or, more accurately, A/b (the oblique stroke "/" represents splitting):

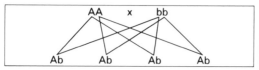

If son and daughter are mated together, the progeny so formed will comprise both pure-type AA and pure-type bb to the ratio 3:1, *but* fifty per cent of those young will carry the White factor b "hidden." That is to say that out of four young, one will be pure-type AA, one will be pure-type bb, and two will appear as AA but will in fact be impure Ab:

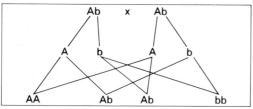

This Mendelian principle holds good for the inheritance of normal colors, but the sex-linked color factors carried by the male sex-chromosome are inherited in a different manner. Sex-linked colors are recessive, therefore to show in the plumage, a cock bird has to have gained contributions of the same gene from *both* its parents (if received from only one it will be carried in split form), whereas because of the peculiarities of the Y sex-chromosome, a hen cannot carry the sex-linked gene *X* without it showing in her plumage.

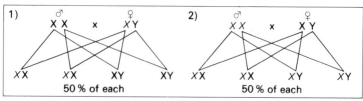

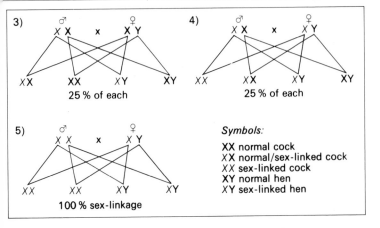

3) 25 % of each

4) 25 % of each

5) 100 % sex-linkage

Symbols:

XX normal cock
XX normal/sex-linked cock
XX sex-linked cock
XY normal hen
XY sex-linked hen

The other rules of inheritance, besides the Mendelian norm and the sex-linked phenomenon, relate to dominant inheritance, recessive inheritance and dark inheritance.

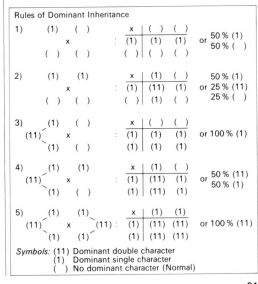

Rules of Dominant Inheritance

				x	( )	( )	
1)	(1)	( )					
		x		(1)	(1)	(1)	or 50 % (1)
	( )	( )		( )	( )	( )	50 % ( )

				x	(1)	( )	
2)	(1)	(1)					50 % (1)
		x		(1)	(11)	(1)	or 25 % (11)
	( )	( )		( )	(1)	( )	25 % ( )

				x	( )	( )	
3)	(1)	( )					
(11)		x		(1)	(1)	(1)	or 100 % (1)
	(1)	( )		(1)	(1)	(1)	

				x	(1)	( )	
4)	(1)	(1)					
(11)		x		(1)	(11)	(1)	or 50 % (11)
	(1)	( )		(1)	(11)	(1)	50 % (1)

				x	(1)	(1)	
5)	(1)	(1)					
(11)		x	(11) :	(1)	(11)	(11)	or 100 % (11)
	(1)	(1)		(1)	(11)	(11)	

Symbols: (11) Dominant double character
(1) Dominant single character
( ) No dominant character (Normal)

BUDGERIGARS

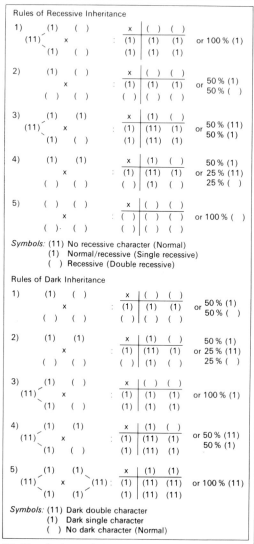

Rules of Recessive Inheritance

1)
$$\begin{array}{c} (1)\quad(\;) \\ (11)\diagup\qquad x \\ \diagdown(1)\quad(\;) \end{array} \quad x \quad \begin{array}{c|cc} x & (\;) & (\;) \\ \hline (1) & (1) & (1) \\ (1) & (1) & (1) \end{array} \quad \text{or } 100\% \ (1)$$

2)
$$\begin{array}{c} (1)\quad(\;) \\ x \\ (\;)\quad(\;) \end{array} \quad : \quad \begin{array}{c|cc} x & (\;) & (\;) \\ \hline (1) & (1) & (1) \\ (\;) & (\;) & (\;) \end{array} \quad \text{or } \begin{array}{l} 50\% \ (1) \\ 50\% \ (\;) \end{array}$$

3)
$$\begin{array}{c} (1)\quad(1) \\ (11)\diagup\qquad x \\ \diagdown(1)\quad(\;) \end{array} \quad : \quad \begin{array}{c|cc} x & (1) & (\;) \\ \hline (1) & (11) & (1) \\ (1) & (11) & (1) \end{array} \quad \text{or } \begin{array}{l} 50\% \ (11) \\ 50\% \ (1) \end{array}$$

4)
$$\begin{array}{c} (1)\quad(1) \\ x \\ (\;)\quad(\;) \end{array} \quad : \quad \begin{array}{c|cc} x & (1) & (\;) \\ \hline (1) & (11) & (1) \\ (\;) & (1) & (\;) \end{array} \quad \begin{array}{l} 50\% \ (1) \\ \text{or } 25\% \ (11) \\ 25\% \ (\;) \end{array}$$

5)
$$\begin{array}{c} (\;)\quad(\;) \\ x \\ (\;)\cdot\quad(\;) \end{array} \quad : \quad \begin{array}{c|cc} x & (\;) & (\;) \\ \hline (\;) & (\;) & (\;) \\ (\;) & (\;) & (\;) \end{array} \quad \text{or } 100\% \ (\;)$$

Symbols: (11) No recessive character (Normal)
(1) Normal/recessive (Single recessive)
( ) Recessive (Double recessive)

Rules of Dark Inheritance

1)
$$\begin{array}{c} (1)\quad(\;) \\ x \\ (\;)\quad(\;) \end{array} \quad : \quad \begin{array}{c|cc} x & (\;) & (\;) \\ \hline (1) & (1) & (1) \\ (\;) & (\;) & (\;) \end{array} \quad \text{or } \begin{array}{l} 50\% \ (1) \\ 50\% \ (\;) \end{array}$$

2)
$$\begin{array}{c} (1)\quad(1) \\ x \\ (\;)\quad(\;) \end{array} \quad : \quad \begin{array}{c|cc} x & (1) & (\;) \\ \hline (1) & (11) & (1) \\ (\;) & (1) & (\;) \end{array} \quad \begin{array}{l} 50\% \ (1) \\ \text{or } 25\% \ (11) \\ 25\% \ (\;) \end{array}$$

3)
$$\begin{array}{c} (1)\quad(\;) \\ (11)\diagup\qquad x \\ \diagdown(1)\quad(\;) \end{array} \quad : \quad \begin{array}{c|cc} x & (\;) & (\;) \\ \hline (1) & (1) & (1) \\ (1) & (1) & (1) \end{array} \quad \text{or } 100\% \ (1)$$

4)
$$\begin{array}{c} (1)\quad(1) \\ (11)\diagup\qquad x \\ \diagdown(1)\quad(\;) \end{array} \quad : \quad \begin{array}{c|cc} x & (1) & (\;) \\ \hline (1) & (11) & (1) \\ (1) & (11) & (1) \end{array} \quad \text{or } \begin{array}{l} 50\% \ (11) \\ 50\% \ (1) \end{array}$$

5)
$$\begin{array}{c} (1)\quad(1) \\ (11)\diagup\quad x \quad\diagdown(11) \\ \diagdown(1)\quad(1)\diagup \end{array} : \begin{array}{c|cc} x & (1) & (1) \\ \hline (1) & (11) & (11) \\ (1) & (11) & (11) \end{array} \quad \text{or } 100\% \ (11)$$

Symbols: (11) Dark double character
(1) Dark single character
( ) No dark character (Normal)

CRESTED BUDGERIGARS
1 Full-circular Crest (Skyblue)
2 Tufted Crest (Light Green)
3 Half-circular Crest (Cobalt)

NB. These rules apply irrespective of any colors which the birds might carry.

1♂

2♂

3♂

BUDGERIGARS

Talking Birds

It will be forever to the Budgerigar's advantage that many of their number can talk. Although it is by no means as talented as the Mynah bird in this respect, as a pet it wins every other round. Young males usually make the best pupils, and they should be taken from their kind soon after leaving the nest, when they can be sexed by the slight traces of blue on the cere and a more pronounced forehead. It is important to remove the selected bird as soon as possible from all contact with other birds even though this may mean hand-feeding him for a few days. The best tutors are women and children as they have a voice more identifiable to the bird, and it is best for only one person to undertake the task, as frequent changes of voice will tend to confuse him.

Serious training can begin only when the Budgie is finger-tame. If, whenever he is approached, his name is repeated, he will, if he is a good pupil, soon learn it; and one can then progress on to other words and even sentences. Once he has grasped the idea, he may well begin to pick up words on his own account, but take care not to frighten or confuse him.

It cannot be guaranteed that every Budgie will talk; some never do despite patient training. However, they will all chatter and play, and many will learn to do a few elementary tricks.

CHAPTER 11 : SEEDEATERS

This group sees our first real departure from fully domesticated cagebirds into the more complex world of wild birds, although it does still contain some genuine cagebirds. In some respects, its subjects constitute the most important part of the book for finches were the original cagebirds and today still have the widest appeal. The Canary, were it not so very important in its own right, belongs here — as it is, it demands a whole chapter to itself. The same could easily be claimed for the Bengalese and Zebra Finches but for reasons of space they have to be included here alongside their wild cousins.

The Bengalese is the oldest domesticated cagebird, it is indeed so old that its exact antecedents can only be guessed at. It is highly improbable that it has ever existed in the wild state. Most authorities believe it to be the result of cross-breeding, which took place either in ancient China or Japan, between at least three different wild species. It is surprising, given this ancient lineage, that there are not more varieties now available. The only commonly seen ones are the Chocolate-and-White, Fawn-and-White (page 140) with the charming Crest the only example of feather mutation. With today's increased understanding of genetics, it should be possible to breed new strains from the mutations which are continually being thrown up and by crossing with closely related wild species. Apart from scientific scope the Bengalese has much going for it. Its alternative name of Society Finch is indicative of its pleasant, easy-going nature. It generally makes an excellent foster parent, probably the best in the entire avicultural world, thinking nothing of taking on the half-grown young of completely different species or of helping to feed the young in other nests. If kept communally, more than one hen will often use the same nest, and it is amusing to see a string of hens emerging quite amicably from a nest which seems no larger than that suitable for just one conventional pair. Unfortunately this endearing habit does impair the hatching rate and has to be discouraged by serious breeders.

The Zebra Finch's history of domestication is not dissimilar to that of the Budgerigar, and follows not so very far behind in popularity. It originated in Australia, and probably came to Europe at about the same time as the Budgerigar. Its spread has been more explosive

SEEDEATERS

than that of the Bengalese, and it appears in many different variations, which is not surprising when one considers its free-breeding nature, which also makes it a useful foster-parent. In fact, its popularity spread so rapidly since 1950, that societies were founded all over the world, devoted exclusively to breeding, improving and exhibiting these cheerful little finches. I would strongly recommend anyone about to start a collection of cagebirds, especially a child, to begin with a pair of Zebra Finches. So popular is it, so easy to house, feed and breed, and so reasonably priced that, in avicultural terms, it is no longer regarded as a foreign bird and has achieved the status of a fully fledged cagebird alongside the Canary, Budgerigar and Bengalese. The wild Zebra Finch is known as Gray, from which have been developed some 15 mutations: Fawns, Whites, Pieds, Penguins and Silvers among them (page 134).

Diets vary remarkably little, the few basal seeds serving to provide the basic nutrition for all, although there is one interesting point which appears when comparing the *ingestion* methods of doves and finches: while doves consume each seed whole — hull and kernel — finches usually de-husk first. Therefore, when relating the food values of seeds, as set out in the table on page 36, to different species of hardbills, it should be borne in mind that the intake of doves and quail etc is very much higher in fibre (minerals) than that of finches and parrots, and lower, proportionately, in fats. The need for mineralized grit balances out: doves require it mostly for its abrasive qualities, and finches — which consume only the more oily kernel — require its minerals as well.

Pigeons, doves and quail are located in this chapter for the sake of convenience and because they are often to be found in mixed collections. Apart from food, they are unrelated in all other aspects: looks, behaviour, habits, anatomy and ecological function.

PIGEONS AND DOVES
Pigeons and doves are so familiar and cosmopolitan they need little introduction — except perhaps to emphasize that there is no real difference between them: the larger kinds are called pigeons, while the smaller ones are usually known as doves.

Several have long been kept in captivity and some have proved particularly suitable subjects for domestication. The incredible array of fanciful varieties has been produced from one common ancestor, and the keeping of these breeds has developed as a separate hobby, although a few ornamental varieties, such as fantails, are sometimes included with collections of cagebirds.

The more recently domesticated Barbary Dove is a typical ring-necked, creamy-buff dove from which a number of other varieties have been produced. Only one is common: a white variety with dark eyes that is misleadingly called the Java Dove, which conjurors sometimes use in their acts. The Barbary Dove was already well known as a cagebird in Europe in the first half of the 18th century when an early writer on birds, Eleazar Albin, said of it: "They are tame pretty birds and are kept in Cages by the Curious, in which they will breed and bring up their young." Another that is bred all around the world and is now generally considered to be domesticated is the diminutive Diamond Dove.

Most of the commoner pigeons and doves eat, as we have seen, seed and grain. There are others that eat different types of food and a number that feed almost exclusively on fruit, but it is the former that concerns us here. A wide choice of such species is usually available. Few are brilliantly colored but they are attractively clad in subdued shades that merge into each other. Frequently the plumage of the sexes is alike, though the females are sometimes duller. The seed-eating species have a lot to commend them, for they are relatively easy to look after and many are willing to nest. A few of the smaller types do well in large box cages that offer them some seclusion, otherwise they are better off in aviaries. No species can be regarded as delicate and, as a rule, none is aggressive towards other species, even very small ones, but often they will not tolerate the presence of other pigeons and doves, and it is seldom possible to keep more than one pair of the same species together.

Several small doves are regularly available in addition to the Diamond. There are the long-tailed Cape or Namaqua Dove, the wood doves from Africa, and the Ruddy Ground Dove or Talpacoti Dove and other gray-brown species from Central and South America. Pairs of these tiny doves (sometimes called miniatures), are suitable for cages and planted aviaries along with waxbills etc; they are not generally quarrelsome and thrive on the same kind of treatment. On a larger scale is the Red Collared Dove, followed by

SEEDEATERS

an assortment of medium-sized doves, of which the best example is the ubiquitous Barbary Dove. As well as the common species that are illustrated, a number of others are seen from time to time, most are ring-necked or collared species from Africa and Asia, but there are also the Central and South American relatives of the Mourning Dove *Zenaida macroura*. In aviaries they are suitable companions for most large finches — particularly buntings and cardinals, Budgerigars and lovebirds, starling-sized softbills and even pheasants. Although they seldom interfere with small birds such as waxbills, the latter are intimidated by their sheer size and they should not be mixed. In common with the miniatures, the bigger doves spend a lot of the day on the ground, but also like to perch high up and their avaries need to be at least 198 cm ($6\frac{1}{2}$ ft) high and have a few stout branches for them to perch on. The aviaries should be sited in a position which affords a good all-round view, so that they are not startled by sudden movements. If this happens, pigeons and doves are liable to panic and fly wildly about, injuring themselves.

Doves appear quite unaffected by direct sunshine, and even during the hottest time of the day will spread their feathers to sunbathe. They adopt a similar posture to rain-bathe — which they thoroughly enjoy. What they do not like is wet, windy weather, but provided there is a shelter and they are acclimatized, most seed-eating species are not worried by the cold, and can remain outdoors all year-round in mild temperate climates. The tiny ones, however, should not be expected to withstand hard weather and may need to be brought indoors or at least shut inside a frost-proof shelter each night during the winter.

The Diamond Dove and other small types which do so well with waxbills require a similar diet to them, consisting mainly of small yellow and white millet and canary seed. From the Red Collared Dove upwards, they eat mostly white millet but also some of the larger grains. Many species like some greenstuff and a few will eat mealworms, maggots and a little insectile mixture or fruit.

As males and females frequently look so alike, the potential breeder is faced with a problem when trying to select true pairs. Often the only satisfactory way is to see the males displaying. Display often entails the male pursuing the female, inflating his neck or chest to show off distinctive markings, and fanning the tail to reveal bold patterns. Once a true pair is established, nesting is often assured. A few will even nest in quite small cages, but they are exceptions, for most are more likely to nest successfully in an aviary.

The nests doves make are little more than a flimsy platform of twigs. Even when there are bushes and trees growing in an aviary, they seldom manage to build an adequate nest without some assistance in the form of a support. This can be merely a piece of wire-netting (with sharp edges removed) fixed in a suitable place, although a wire, wicker or wooden tray is better. A suitable tray for doves would measure 235 sq cm (36 sq in) × 2½ cm (1 in) high, and for pigeons 524 sq cm (81 sq in) × 5 cm (2 in) high. Trays should be sited in a sheltered spot (high up for the larger species) and, if necessary, screened with evergreen foliage. A variety of twigs and grasses can also be provided.

The majority of doves lay two white eggs that are incubated by both parents for a period of 12–18 days. During the first few days, the sole food fed to the squabs – as the young are called – is a nutritious curd-like substance known as pigeons' milk, which both sexes produce in the crop. Little or no special food is needed while they are rearing young, just a good varied diet perhaps with the addition, if they will take it, of a little canary-type rearing food or chick starter crumbs. The young develop rapidly and those of some small doves can fly before they are two weeks old. A few species will breed almost all the year round, but despite the temptation, they should not be allowed to raise more than three broods a season.

QUAIL

Quail are small, plump, fowl-like birds belonging to the Pheasant family. There are two main groups – one in the New World, and one in the Old. The Old World quail are stumpy-tailed birds; most males have striking head and throat markings; otherwise both sexes are cryptically colored so that they blend well with the grasslands and undergrowth. They walk and run along the ground, only rarely taking to the wing, although they can fly well. The Japanese or Coturnix Quail has been domesticated by the Japanese mainly to capitalize on the hens' prolific egg production – up to 200 a year. It has been introduced, with varying degrees of

SEEDEATERS

success, into parts of the United States and Hawaii as a gamebird, and is also a popular ornamental bird, as are the Harlequin and tiny Painted Quails. Although China forms only a small part of its range, the latter is commonly known as the Chinese Painted Quail and, particularly in America, incorrectly as the Button Quail.

The true buttonquail or hemipodes are superficially like ordinary quail, but their alternative name of bustardquail suits them much better as they are anatomically closer to the bustards than to the true quail. Most works on buttonquail state that it is the hen which plays the dominant role in family life; this statement can easily confuse the reader because while it is true that the hen is larger, more colorful and noisy, and dominates the male, in most but not all species it is the cock around which the family revolves. It is he who generally chooses and prepares the nest-site, incubates the eggs and rears the young. The hen can be a nuisance at rearing time but she should be given a chance all the same.

Quail in general are a great asset to aviculture because the ground area in aviaries is often under utilized. So quail, which are simple to feed — eating ordinary finch fare, fairly hardy, and friendly, sociable birds, are especially valuable in mixed collections where they provide color, activity and interest to otherwise wasted ground-space. Their prolific egg-laying can be turned to both your financial and scientific advantage, not to mention the quails' own numerical one, if you can overcome one or two problems which seem inherent with quail. They are nervous, excitable birds whose actual chick production often falls short of their great fecundity. The Painted Quail, which is probably the best known of all, regularly lays many more eggs than necessary in a random, haphazard manner. Some of these eggs, if not infertile, can be incubated artificially with any young produced set under a reliable foster, but I have never found this practice anything but frustrating. Avoid frightening your birds so that they do not erupt vertically to crash into the wire-netting, injuring or even killing them-selves. Additionally, you must provide them with ample cover and a few well-chosen nesting shelters. Quail like to be dry and out of the wind, and to my mind, the best aviaries for them have a surrounding wall of a few courses of bricks; this also helps to discourage them from patrolling the cage perimeter — which can develop

100

FINCHES AND ALLIES

into stereotyped behavior, serving no useful purpose and irritating you. Hen quail should be brought into a warmer environment in the winter, otherwise egg-binding can easily occur with often fatal consequences, as outside they will hide from view. I believe this causes the deaths of many hens each year, and certainly contributes to their reputation of delicacy; it also helps to explain why, come summer, hens are always in short supply. When rearing young, the normal diet should be supplemented with eggfood, live insects and chick crumbs.

FINCHES AND ALLIES

By and large, finches are suitable for either cage or aviary, and are, together with the Budgerigar, most people's idea of the typical cagebirds. This hardly does credit to the many other suitable types but it does accurately sum up their many advantages.

For our convenience we can divide finches into the following categories: the Emberizidae (buntings, American sparrows etc), Fringillidae (seedeaters, goldfinches and allies), Estrildidae (waxbills etc) and Ploceidae (whydahs, weavers etc).

The Emberizidae. Some confusion exists with this family for it includes the finch-type birds which are our immediate concern but also tanagers and honey-creepers, which, aviculturally, are classed quite differently — as softbills. It has been suggested that the latter two be accorded familial rank of their own, with the buntings and cardinals assigned to the Fringillidae; if this theory is adopted, the Emberizidae automatically ceases to exist. Fortunately, we can ignore such taxonomic arguments here; for our purposes, a finch is a finch is a finch!

Considering that there are some 319 hardbill members of this family, surprisingly few — about 5 per cent — are well known as cagebirds. To the fore are the distinctive cardinals from the New World, which are splendid aviary birds, being large, showy, tough and highly melodious. Curiously enough, the definitive one is not strictly speaking a true cardinal but a cardinal-grosbeak (from a different sub-family); the Virginian Cardinal, so called on account of its scarlet plumage, is a marvellous bird, a good mixer and a delightful songster, at its best in a large planted aviary. As with most of the true cardinals, it is quite willing to breed in captivity. The Red-crested Cardinal is typical of the

SEEDEATERS

remainder but is probably not as suitable as the Green Cardinal for those with limited resources. Cardinals are best mixed with species larger than waxbills, such as weavers and whydahs. They are omnivorous in their food requirements, eating many insects and much fruit and greenstuff.

The buntings are not quite as tough as they look, and must be acclimatized carefully. They require a varied diet too, if they are to be bred and keep their fine colors. Many of those seen in collections are of South American origin, and these days, with tightened export restrictions, they are becoming increasingly difficult to obtain.

The Fringillidae. This family contains 122 species, including all the canaries, siskins, goldfinches and many more interesting avicultural subjects. All are true seedeaters, enjoying (depending on their size) seeds ranging from sunflower and hemp (bullfinches and greenfinches) down to niger (relished by most). As with all small seedeaters, the millets and canary seed form the basis of most diets. Outstanding in this category as cagebirds are the following species: Green Singing Finch (a type of canary), Red Hooded Siskin, Linnet, Redpoll, Scarlet Grosbeak (Indian Rosefinch), Bullfinch and Hawfinch.

The Estrildidae. The single most important avicultural family. Within its 124 species are all the waxbills, parrot-finches and mannikins, which, of course, includes the Zebra Finch and Bengalese. Very few are little known, and of all the many bird families, it is the one which gives the biggest impression of having been created for the aviculturist. They are essentially Old World birds, and the smallest seedeaters.

Easy to manage, willing to breed, suitable for cage and aviary, reasonably priced, dainty, colorful, ideal for the novice, perhaps the only thing they lack is a melodious voice. Regarding management, much of what was said in Chapter 6 applies to waxbills. They need a varied diet, livefood at rearing time, protection from frosty nights within a dry, draught-proof shed, an abundance of nesting sites in mixed collections; in other words, good, basic management.

The Bengalese and Zebra Finches' requirements are much the same regarding housing, feeding and breeding, and they are two birds which are perfectly happy living in cages. The standard Zebra Finch cage should measure at least 76 cm (30 in) long ×

FINCHES AND ALLIES

31 cm (12 in) deep × 38 cm (15 in) high; and the most suitable nestbox is the common finch type with a half-open front. They also make good aviary birds, but obviously if color-breeding is the main object, it requires as much method and control as that outlined for Canaries and Budgerigars, and cages or special breeding pens must be used. More breeding information will be found in Chapter 7 and throughout the species text; but anyone considering specializing in one of the breed fancies should endeavour to join the appropriate local club or society because the subject calls for serious application.

The Ploceidae. This important family of 150 species, including the weavers and whydahs, is the third assemblage of Old World seedeaters (in this case, almost exclusively African), and presents a range of birds which although well-suited to an aviary life individually, are not ideal in all respects. They are no trouble to feed or house, and although well able to look after themselves are not a danger to smaller birds except when breeding. However, as soon as reproduction is considered, more serious problems arise. Most weavers are highly gregarious and will diligently build elaborate nests, but their record of reproduction is poor, probably attributable to this well-developed social life. They need much space, and males are sometimes polygamous. Otherwise they are hardy (if well acclimatized) seedeaters with the usual need for animal food at rearing time.

The *Viduinae* whydahs can for the most part be treated as weavers, but due regard must be taken of their parasitic habits – which seriously prejudice breeding prospects. Indeed, they are best housed with weavers for ease of management and visual appeal. On no account should they be mixed with smaller finches from which it is hoped to breed, since whydahs, apart from being large, ponderous birds, will certainly interfere with breeding waxbills. If, on the other hand, whydah reproduction is the prime objective, then the reverse applies, and the *correct* species of waxbill or mannikin must be "sacrificed" so that they may act as hosts for the whydahs.

The Ploceidae is certainly a subject in need of a concerted captive-breeding programme, and one which demands an experienced, specialist approach.

SEEDEATERS

Barbary Dove *Streptopelia "risoria"*. Domestic Collared or Ringed Turtle Dove; Blonde Ringdove.
Domesticated (there is a feral population in Los Angeles, Calif., USA) and ideal for the beginner. It is usually very tame, and thrives on the recommended seed and grain. It will live outdoors or in an indoor cage, nesting readily. A white variety with dark eyes is commonly called the Java Dove (see page 14). The Collared Dove *S. decaocto* that has lately spread to western Europe from Asia looks very similar.

Necklace Dove *Streptopelia chinensis*. Spotted Dove.
The Necklace Dove is a fairly free-breeding aviary bird that requires similar management to the Barbary Dove. There are a number of races that vary in size and color. Freshly imported birds need to be acclimatized before they can be expected to live outdoors without heat during a hard winter.

Laughing Dove *Streptopelia senegalensis*. Palm or Senegal Dove.
This species can also be a free breeder, and requires similar food and care to the Necklace Dove. It is generally quiet and a good mixer. All doves are graceful and elegant: assets to most communal aviaries. They should not be disturbed when nesting.

Zebra Dove *Geopelia striata*. Barred or Peaceful Dove; Barred Ground Dove.
The Zebra Dove should be treated in the same way as the small doves on the next plate. It can be a free breeder in an aviary, and, as one of its alternative names suggests, is an eminently suitable bird for mixed collections. If anything, it can be almost too quiet, and will often sit for long periods out of sight.

Emerald Dove *Chalcophaps indica*. Green-winged Dove.
As well as seed and grain, this handsome dove will consume some fruit and live insects, such as maggots. Once well acclimatized it can live outside with equanimity all the year round, provided there is a comfortable shelter. Given suitable conditions, it will breed freely and be a dutiful parent. It can be used for fostering more "difficult" kinds.

1 *Streptopelia "risoria"* 12 in/305 mm Domesticated
2 *S. chinensis* 12–13 in/ 305–330 mm Several races over much of SE Asia from India to Taiwan, and south to Indonesia Introduced many places
3 *S. (Turtur, Stigmatopelia) senegalensis* 9½–10 in/ 240–255 mm Common over much of Africa and W Asia Introduced W Australia
4 *Geopelia striata* 8½–9 in/215–230 mm Malay Peninsular and Indonesia to Australia
5 *Chalcophaps indica* 10–10½ in/ 255–265 mm India to Taiwan, and south through Indonesia to Australia

SEEDEATERS

Diamond Dove *Geopelia cuneata*.
Common and inexpensive, the Diamond Dove is ideal for novices. Pairs will breed in large cages or aviaries and do well in mixed collections, where they eat the same food as finches and require similar care. Among the captive-bred mutations is the so-called Silver, which is actually gray. As with so many doves, to maximize their breeding potential it is imperative to provide some kind of firm base on which they can build their flimsy nests.

Cape Dove *Oena capensis*. Namaqua, Masked or Long-tailed Dove.
This species is regularly available and inexpensive and has the added advantage of pronounced sexual dimorphism. It does best in warm, dry conditions; it is neither as hardy nor such a free-breeder as is implied in many books.

Blue-spotted Wood Dove *Turtur afer*.
Of the wood doves, this is the most often available, followed by the darker-billed Emerald-spotted *T. chalcospilos* and, more rarely, the Tambourine Dove *T. tympanistria*. The latter is the only one that is easy to sex, for the female lacks the male's clear white breast.

Ruddy Ground Dove *Columbina talpacoti*. Talpacoti Dove or Ground Dove.
This is just one of the small American doves that are occasionally available; others include the smaller Pigmy Dove *C. minuta* and the Croaking Ground Dove *C. cruziana*, which has a distinctive yellow base to its bill. Like the preceding doves, given similar care to the waxbills with which they mix so well, pairs will breed in small planted aviaries. The Ruddy builds a more substantial nest than most doves.

Red Collared Dove *Streptopelia tranquebarica*. Red or Dwarf Turtle Dove.
This easily sexed dove is not steady enough to keep in a cage. Housed in an aviary, however, it can be a free-breeder, and once acclimatized is hardy. It requires the same treatment as the preceding species.

Painted Quail *Coturnix chinensis*. Chinese Painted, Blue-breasted, King, Button or Blue Quail.
The smallest of all quail; extremely well suited for the floors of well-sheltered, planted aviaries housing finches etc. It nests readily if a secluded corner is

1 *Geopelia cuneata* 7–7¾ in/180–195 mm Australia. ♀ paler red orbital skin and slightly duller plumage tinged brown
2 *Oena capensis* 8½–10 in/ 215–255 mm Africa south of the Sahara, SW Arabia and Madagascar ♀ has purplish-black bill and no black mask
3 *Turtur afer* 8 in/ 205 mm Africa south of the Sahara excluding the Cape
4 *Columbina talpacoti* 7 in/180 mm N South America, Mexico, Trinidad and Tobago ♀ has lighter colored eyes, olive-brown above and paler buff below
5 *Streptopelia tranquebarica* 9 in/ 230 mm India and Andamans to China, Taiwan and N Philippines

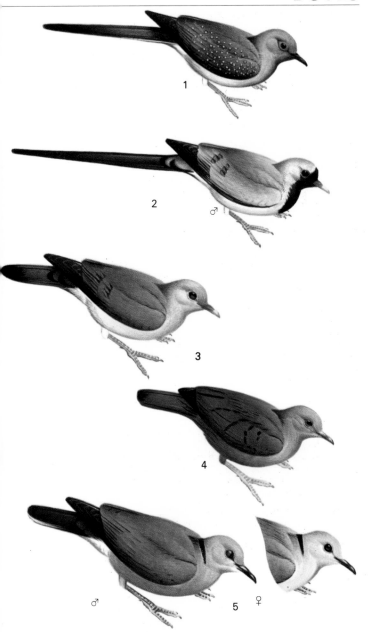

SEEDEATERS

provided; the male guards tenaciously while the female undertakes the incubation and rearing. A clutch may consist of ten or more eggs — about 6–8 young being generally produced, which are taught to feed by crumbs or live insects being dropped in front of them. Chicks are independent at about 4 weeks. There are Silver, Pied and White mutations.

Harlequin Quail *Coturnix delegorguei.*
Slightly larger but needing exactly the same treatment as the Painted Quail. All quail have nidifugous young which are able to run about as soon as they hatch, squeeze through tiny holes, and easily escape or become trapped. Chicks hatched artificially must have access to a heat lamp during rearing; the temperature gradually being reduced.

Japanese Quail *Coturnix japonica.*
This quail, of which there are a number of forms, may be a subspecies of the Common Quail *C. coturnix*

1 *Coturnix (Excalfactoria) chinensis* 4½–6 in/ 115–150 mm India to China and Taiwan, and south to Indonesia and Australia. *(Text begins preceding page.)*

2 *C. delegorguei* 6–6½ in/150–165 mm Africa south of the Sahara, excluding western forests

3 *C. japonica* 7½ in/ 190 mm Assam and China to Taiwan and south to Thailand and Philippines

108

4 *Colinus virginianus*
8½–9 in/215–230 mm
E and C USA to S
Mexico
5 *Lophortyx
californicus* 9–10 in/
230–255 mm W USA
(Oregon to S
California)

(Gruson, 1976), but its appearance differs sufficiently for this to be uncertain. However, both are hardy, albeit prone to nervousness — which must be guarded against. No matter how hardy quail are, they hate damp weather and must always have a dry sandy area.

Bobwhite Quail *Colinus virginianus*. Virginian Colin; Bobwhite.
Hardy and a free-breeder, the Bobwhite is a showy inexpensive bird suited to most roomy aviaries and is a typical New World quail, as is the next species.

California Quail *Lophortyx californicus*.
The largest of the commonly kept quail. It, like the Bobwhite, is very hardy and thrives on a variety of seeds and greenstuff. Most quail, given the correct conditions, are reliable parents and the young, if warm, dry and well fed, easy to rear. If problems are encountered, eggs of various quail species have been hatched under Barbary Doves, Budgerigars etc.

SEEDEATERS

Most buntings live near the ground and are usually good mixers but their increased size alone can be a disturbing influence to small waxbills. Most can be encouraged to breed, and lay 4–5 eggs which hatch in about 12 days. The young are often reared exclusively on live insects. Out of the breeding season, the males of some species resemble the respective females.

Cinnamon-breasted Bunting *Emberiza tahapisi.* Cinnamon-breasted Rock Bunting.
A splendid occupant of a roomy aviary where it has a chance to display its undulating flight. Always active, peaceful and a good mixer except when breeding, which can be encouraged in this instance by the provision of nest-baskets high up.

Golden-breasted Bunting *Emberiza flaviventris.*
This handsome and common species often proves very

1 *Emberiza schoeniclus* 6 in/ 150 mm Much of W and C Palearctic ♀ has brown head and distinct moustachial streaks; white throat and outer tail-feathers; buff eyestripe
2 *E. (Fringillaria) tahapisi* 5–5½ in/ 125–140 mm Much of Africa south of the Sahara ♀ has tawny crown streaked with black; throat duller black
3 *E. flaviventris* 6–6½/ 150–165 mm Much of

Africa south of the
Sahara excluding
western forests
♀ overall duller
4 *E. citrinella* 6½ in/
165 mm Much of W
and C Palearctic
♀ duller, much less
yellow
5 *E. bruniceps*
6–7 in/150–180 mm
C and E Palearctic
6 *E. melanocephala*
6½–7 in/165–180 mm
SE Europe and W and
C Asia (Italy to China)
♀ similar to ♀ *bruniceps*
but with pale yellow
underparts

tricky to acclimatize, but thereafter is hardy providing it
has a frostproof shelter. If kept one pair to an aviary and
given plenty of livefood it should breed well.

Reed Bunting *Emberiza schoeniclus*.
Yellowhammer *Emberiza citrinella*. Yellow or Common
Bunting; Scribbling Lark.
Common birds throughout much of the Old World. The
Yellowhammer's distinctive song has made it even
more famous. The Reed Bunting is an avid bather.

Red-headed Bunting *Emberiza bruniceps*.
Black-headed Bunting *Emberiza melanocephala*.
Considered by some to be races of the same species,
they need the same captive management; both are
peaceful, gentle and have beautiful songs. Males are
often available when females are not.

6 ♂

5

♀

♂

4 ♂

SEEDEATERS

In the New World, small bunting-type birds are called sparrows or finches. As with all South American species, captive-breeding is now of vital importance. Most thrive on a good seed mixture supplemented by greenstuff, fruit, livefood and budding twigs etc.

Saffron Finch *Sicalis flaveola.*
A popular, hardy, frequently imported and inexpensive bird suited to beginners since it is easy-going, free-breeding and the male has a pretty song. Two or three broods a year is usual, and all they ask is an ordinary finch nestbox or Canary nestpan. The young require the usual variety of food.

Cuban Finch *Tiaris canora.* Melodious Grassquit or Finch.
A robust, delightful, larger-than-life finch which is rarely exported nowadays. It is well able to look after itself and can be troublesome in a collection of small finches. It is best on its own in a cage or mixed with weavers etc, whose nests it will take over and convert.

Olive Finch *Tiaris olivacea.* Yellow-faced Grassquit; Cuban Olive Finch.
Much better suited to a collection of mixed finches than the Cuban Finch, since it is less quarrelsome, and easily looked after — breeding well. Live insects are less important than is the case for many other bunting-like birds.

Black-crested Finch *Lophospingus pusillus.* Pygmy Cardinal.
A distinctive little "crested-finch" which is rather pugnacious when breeding. Livefood is essential when rearing young — in which the male gets very involved. The young have to be removed after about three weeks if the parents wish to go down again.

Lined Finch/Seedeater *Sporophila lineola.*
The seedeaters are sociable songsters and good mixers. They are reliable breeders and require a good mixture of seeds and a little live/soft-food.

Crimson Finch *Rhodospingus cruentus.* Rhodospingus or Purple-crowned Finch.
A popular and attractive little "softbill" finch. To indulge in its amazingly rapid breeding cycle (11 days incubation, 8 for fledging) it needs a roomy, planted aviary with a warm shelter. It will become territorial but not troublesome.

1 *Sicalis flaveola*
5–6 in/125–150 mm
Tropical South and Central America; introduced Jamaica
♀ slightly duller
2 *Tiaris canora*
3½–4½ in/90–115 mm
Cuba and introduced New Providence
♀ altogether duller with black face replaced by chestnut
3 *T. olivacea*
(nominate race)
3½–4½ in/90–115 mm
Mexico to NW South America; Greater Antilles ♀ considerably paler
4 *Lophospingus pusillus* 4¾–5 in/120–125 mm C South America ♀ has gray crest and lacks black throat
5 *Sporophila lineola* 4–4¼ in/100–110 mm NE South America
6 *Rhodospingus cruentus* 4–4½ in/100–115 mm Ecuador and Peru

FINCHES

1 ♂

2 ♂

3 ♂

4 ♂

5

♂

♀

♂

♀

6

113

SEEDEATERS

These birds are all members of the Emberizidae, but the Virginian Cardinal belongs to the Cardinalinae subfamily (see next plate). They are superb aviary birds, and require much the same care as the buntings, but are stronger and can be aggressive when nesting, which they will do in a surprising assortment of places. The young need a great variety of livefood, which is best dusted with a multi-vitamin preparation if the all-too-common leg deformities are to be avoided. Two or three broods of 2–3 eggs are laid each year, which hatch in about 13 days.

Green Cardinal *Gubernatrix cristata.* Yellow Cardinal.
Not as colorful as many but a superb exhibition bird, as it is a strong songster and steady. I have never found it quarrelsome when mixed with softbills, doves or quail but others have found it argumentative. It breeds readily.

Pope Cardinal *Paroaria dominicana.* Red-colored or Dominican Cardinal.
Very popular as a cagebird in its native Brazil. It is difficult to breed owing to the fact that the sexes are alike; however, if a true pair is obtained, it should breed reliably and peacefully.

Yellow-billed Cardinal *Paroaria capitata.*
Slightly smaller than its cousins and proportionately less hardy and not at all quarrelsome. It is in fact, probably the best of all for a mixed aviary as it is also a free-breeding species.

Red-crested Cardinal *Paroaria coronata/cucullata*
Fearless songsters which are best housed on their own in a small planted aviary where they will build an untidy but substantial nest quite low down. It requires similar treatment to other large cardinals. It is apt to lose its bright coloring in captivity.

Virginian Cardinal *Cardinalis cardinalis.* Virginian Nightingale; Scarlet, Red or just Cardinal.
Although not closely related to the true cardinals this "cardinal-grosbeak" (see next plate) is a superb aviary songster which requires similar care. It is prolific and best housed and seen in a spacious, well-planted enclosure.

1 *Gubernatrix cristata* 7–7½ in/180–190 mm Brazil south to N Patagonia ♀ paler, yellow on face replaced by white
2 *Paroaria dominicana* 6¾–8 in/170–205 mm E tropical South America
3 *P. capitata* 6½ in/ 165 mm E Brazil ♀ duller, grayish back
4 *P. coronata/ cucullata* 7–7½ in/ 180–190 mm E South America south of Bolivia and S Brazil
5 *Cardinalis (Richmondena) cardinalis* 8–9 in/ 205–230 mm SW USA and N Mexico, introduced elsewhere

1 ♂

2

3 ♂

4

5

♀

♂

115

SEEDEATERS

This group of small, colorful buntings all belong to the same subfamily as the Virginian Cardinal. They are similar to other buntings in their habits and requirements but are perhaps even less hardy, requiring good, warm winter accommodation. Females are unfortunately valued little by trappers (except as food), so it is the brighter colored males which proliferate frustratedly in our aviaries.

Versicolor Bunting *Passerina versicolor*. Varied or (misleadingly) Painted Bunting.
Infrequently exported, the female can be identified even when the male has freshly molted out, when it appears much duller and browner. It requires a certain amount of live insects, especially during the touch-and-go acclimatizing period.

Painted Bunting *Passerina ciris*. Nonpareil Bunting.
One of the most beautiful of all North American birds, the Painted Bunting is a surprisingly free-breeder, if a true pair can be obtained; young males resemble females, so one has to be careful when choosing birds in the autumn. Adult males are liable to have their bright red colors fade to yellow if they are not housed in planted aviaries or color-fed. It is less insectivorous than the preceding species and altogether more robust.

Rainbow Bunting *Passerina leclancheri*. Orange-breasted or Leclancher's Bunting.
This secretive species needs special care and wary acclimatization. It has a poor record of reproduction, which could be due to incorrect feeding since it needs a mainly softbill diet.

Lazuli Bunting *Passerina amoena*.
The Lazuli Bunting is similar in its requirements to the Rainbow Bunting, and is likewise bred only rarely. By all accounts, it is always peaceful and a good mixer. There are not many hardbills which live exclusively on seeds, and a diet deficient in animal food can result in a loss of color and condition.

Indigo Bunting *Passerina cyanea*.
This species is in great demand due to its strange color and haunting song, but it, too, requires careful acclimatization and sensitive after-care. It is fairly pugnacious in itself. The brilliant blue of the male is largely replaced by a rich brown when not breeding.

1 *Passerina versicolor* 5–5½ in/125–140 mm SW USA through Mexico to Guatemala
2 *P. ciris* 5–5½ in/ 125–140 mm S USA to N Mexico; winters to Panama
3 *P. leclancherii* 4¾–5½ in/ 120–140 mm SW Mexico
4 *P. amoena* 4¾–5 in/ 120–130 mm From Canade down W USA to Baja California, east to Oklahoma
5 *P. cyanea* 5–6 in/ 125–150 mm From Canada down E USA to N South America, west to Arizona This and the preceeding species are known to hybridize where their ranges overlap.

BUNTINGS

117

SEEDEATERS

The birds on this and the following 14 plates are all finches of one sort or another, and as such require much the same basic management. Canary seed takes over from the buntings' millet as the staple diet, added to which are all the other items which go to make it varied. Softfood and/or live insects are an invaluable aid when rearing young.

Chaffinch *Fringilla coelebs.*
Two species of chaffinches and the Brambling *F. montifringilla* comprise the Fringillinae subfamily. The Chaffinch has not such a free-breeding nature as, say, the Linnet or Goldfinch; but when it does breed it builds a delightful nest and becomes very insectivorous; it also enjoys tree-seeds, chickweed etc.

Black-headed Canary *Serinus alario*. Alario Finch.
This relative of the ordinary Canary is just one of 35 *Serinus* species, all of which can be intimidatory when nesting; they should not be mixed with smaller finches. It has a pretty song, breeds well and is easy to maintain, enjoying seeding-grasses, weeds etc.

Green Singing Finch *Serinus mozambicus*. Yellow-fronted, Yellow-eye or Icterine Canary.
Renowned for its longevity, pleasant song, gentle ways, free-breeding and lively nature, this little finch is much sought after for both cage and communal aviary. It becomes insectivorous when rearing young and will also take much greenfood and ordinary Canary rearing-food.

Gray Singing Finch *Serinus leucopygius*. White-rumped Seedeater.
Drabber than the Green species but possessing an infinitely better song. It similarly becomes territorial when nesting but no problems are encountered if overcrowding is avoided.
    The Yellow-rumped Serin or Seedeater (synonyms: Black-throated Canary; Angolan Singing Finch) *Serinus atrogularis* is similar but has a necklace like that of a female *mozambicus*. The lemon-colored rump is usually seen only in flight.

Serin *Serinus serinus.*
The smallest of European finches, the Serin is in all ways an attractive bird if a trifle delicate under acclimatization. Ultimately very long-lived, but young birds need to be watched carefully when molting.

1 *Fringilla coelebs*
6 in/150 mm Common over much of the Palearctic (several races)
2 *Serinus alario* (nominate race)
4½–6 in/115–150 mm S Africa The other race *leucolaema* mainly from SW Africa differs in ♂ having white throat and facial-markings; ♀ also has paler throat
3 *S. leucopygius*
4–5 in/100–125 mm Senegal to Sudan
4 *S. mozambicus*
4–5 in/100–125 mm Much of Africa south of the Sahara ♀ is duller and has necklace of black spots
5 *S. serinus* 4½ in/ 115 mm S Europe, N Africa and W Asia

SEEDEATERS

A cosmopolitan group of 24 "goldfinches" popular as cage and aviary birds on account of their intrinsic beauty and sweetness of song. Their captive conditioning over many generations has made them adaptable and free-breeding. Insects are not so important but greenfood and a varied seed mixture (especially chickweed) are necessary when rearing young; an aviary left to rank plant growth is your best ally.

Goldfinch *Carduelis carduelis.*
Its exceptional beauty is further enhanced by a charming song and the fact that this species makes an ideal living-room cagebird. In mixed aviaries it is often too friendly and a male can soon be responsible for numerous unwanted hybrids. To make their exquisite nests, they need a wide variety of fine pliable material — rootlets, feathers and cobwebs.

Siskin *Carduelis spinus.*
Conveniently called the Eurasian Siskin, this remarkably homogeneous species is, to quote Restall (1975) "the cagebird *par excellence*," which really says enough. It needs good basic management, and likes nothing better than a bundle of alder or birch branches hung up in its aviary.

Red Hooded Siskin *Carduelis cucullatus.*
Red or (mistakenly) Hooded Siskin, which is quite another species (*C. magellanicus*).
Imported and valued chiefly for its unique red factor, which is transmitted in some degree to Canaries by mating a cock to a Canary hen. However, nowadays, it deserves to be recognized in its own right – otherwise it could vanish altogether. It possesses a lively personality and a fine voice (both sexes), but needs careful acclimatization and frostproof quarters.

Black-headed Siskin *Carduelis notatus/ictericus.*
Cocks are imported much more frequently than hens because they are used extensively in hybridization work. It needs the same care as the Red Hooded.

Greenfinch *Carduelis chloris.*
A vigorous and popular, free-breeding bird which is thoroughly conditioned to captivity and much used in color-breeding, but many youngsters die inexplicably at molt time. It is also kept as a household pet solely on account of its voice.

1 *Carduelis carduelis* 4¾ in/120 mm Much of the Palearctic; introduced Australia, Uruguay and Argentina
2 *C. spinus* 4¾ in/120 mm Much of the Palearctic, Philippines ♀ resembles ♀ *Serinus serinus* on previous plate except that it has a less stout bill and yellow at the sides of the tail
3 *C. (Spinus) cucullatus* 4¼ in/110 mm Venezuela, Trinidad, NE Colombia; introduced (?) Cuba and Puerto Rico
4 *C. (Spinus) notatus ictericus* 4¼–4¾ in/110–120 mm S Brazil south to N Patagonia ♀ duller, lacks black head
5 *C. (Chloris) chloris* 5½ in/140 mm Much of the Palearctic; introduced Australia, Uruguay ♀ duller

FINCHES

1 ♂

2 ♂

♂   3   ♀

4 ♂   5 ♂

SEEDEATERS

Linnet *Acanthis cannabina*.
Many people consider the Linnet to have the sweetest song of all finches, and for this reason it has been kept as a cagebird for a very long time. It has also an enviable reputation as a gentle, free-breeding aviary occupant, but its quiet charm is lost when it is mixed with more showy kinds.

Redpoll *Acanthis flammea*.
Similar in most ways to the Linnet but less common; there are 7 distinct races. *Acanthis* finches need few insects when breeding, and feed their young mostly on regurgitated seeds.

Scarlet Grosbeak *Carpodacus erythrinus*. Common or Indian Rosefinch.
A hardy, eye-catching bird more suited to aviary than cage. The male requires a certain amount of color-food if it is to retain anything like its natural coloring. Otherwise, it needs the usual diet for large finches, which includes budding fruit twigs, fruit and some livefood when rearing young.

Bullfinch *Pyrrhula pyrrhula*.
One of my favorite finches: a magnificent and free-breeding bird which requires similar treatment to the preceding species. There are several races — the nominate Siberian or Northern is larger than the British (*pileata*), and is commonly seen. A well planted aviary and one of the canthaxanthin color-foods is the best way to maintain its color.

Black-tailed Hawfinch *Coccothraustes migratoria*.
Black-headed, Chinese or (mistakenly) Japanese Hawfinch.
This handsomely massive bird requires similar treatment to other large finches. Despite its large beak it has a peaceful, retiring demeanor. A thickly-planted aviary will assist breeding attempts but it will also need much livefood.

Red Crossbill *Loxia curvirostra*. Common or Spruce Crossbill.
An attractive, although destructive subject, which does not mix too well but has an enchanting aloof manner. It should be fed on the larger seeds, and loves fircones. If housed in single pairs it may breed willingly once established.

1 *Acanthis (Carduelis) cannabina* 5¼–5½ in/ 135–140 mm Common over much of the Palearctic ♂ resembles ♀ when not breeding but with less streaking below

2 *A. (Carduelis) flammea* (nominate race) 4¾–5½ in/ 120–140 mm Much of the Palearctic, Canada; introduced New Zealand ♀ lacks red on breast

3 *Carpodacus erythrinus* 6–6½ in/ 150–165 mm Much of Eurasia, India, Burma, China and Thailand

4 *Pyrrhula pyrrhula* (nominate race) 6–7 in/150–180 mm Much of the Palearctic Other races have less or no red at all

5 *Coccothraustes (Eophona) migratoria* 7–8 in/180–205 mm C Asia to Japan Bill yellow in winter; ♀ duller, head brownish

6 *Loxia curvirostra* 6⅓–6½ in/ 160–165 mm Holarctic, Himalayas, China, Philippines

SEEDEATERS

This plate begins a sequence of 12, each of which is devoted to the remarkable waxbill group – the most typical of all small cagebirds. Waxbills are ground-feeders, and will nest given the correct conditions and a good varied diet with the emphasis on the smaller seeds.

Melba Finch *Pytilia melba.* Green-winged Pytilia or Crimson-faced Waxbill.
This is a species more suited to the experienced owner than novice since it is tricky to acclimatize and maintain, and virtually impossible to breed successfully other than in a planted aviary abundantly supplied with small live insects. Moreover, it can be very pugnacious when nesting and has therefore to be housed with care.

Aurora Finch *Pytilia phoenicoptera.* Red- (Crimson-) winged Pytilia or Waxbill.
This waxbill should be treated almost exactly like the Melba Finch, although it is possibly not so terrestrial. It thrives only if given plenty of warmth, fresh-air, insects and sunshine.

Green Twinspot *Mandingoa nitidula.*
Another waxbill needing rather special care and attention; similar to the two preceding species although it naturally prefers forests. It is so active that it should be housed only in the most spacious of enclosures.

Peter's Twinspot *Hypargos niveoguttatus.*
This attractive species again needs similar management to the above but is less troublesome and demanding. It will readily nest in thick shrubbery at ground level, and is a delight to watch when so engaged. It needs only a little livefood.

Red-headed Bluebill *Spermophaga ruficapilla.*
Less frequently seen but similar in most ways to the twinspots. It enjoys small sprouting seeds but will also accept those up to the size of oats and sunflowers. Breeding is difficult, but successes are beginning to be announced and a densely-planted aviary with abundant livefood would certainly be advantageous.

Quail-finch *Ortygospiza atricollis.* West African Quail-finch.
Very aptly named birds, the *Ortygospiza* finches

1 *Pytilia melba*
$4\frac{3}{4}$–5 in/120–130 mm Much of Africa south of the Sahara excluding the western forests and the SW tip
2 *P. phoenicoptera* (nominate race)
$4\frac{1}{2}$–$4\frac{3}{4}$ in/ 115–120 mm Senegal east to Ethiopia and Uganda One of the three races has a red bill ♀ duller
3 *Mandingoa nitidula* (nominate race)
4–$4\frac{1}{2}$ in/100–115 mm Much of Africa south of the Sahara A few distinct races exist ♀ paler with little or no red on face
4 *Hypargos niveoguttatus*
$4\frac{1}{2}$–5 in/115–130 mm East Africa and to the south
5 *Spermophaga ruficapilla* $5\frac{1}{2}$–6 in/ 140–150 mm C and E Africa

SEEDEATERS

are quite unlike all others, and have developed along the lines of true ground-birds which they also resemble in their captive management. On no account should they be kept in cages since they require lushly turfed and planted aviaries, which are well sheltered and provisioned with low-growing cover in which they will construct their intricate nests and roost. Quail-finches are prone to panic in exactly the same way as quail, and this must be guarded against.

Quail-finches are reputed to rear their young solely on grass-seeds but it is more likely that in well-planted aviaries they find all the insects they need themselves. They need warmth in the winter; and a corner of clean sand together with bathing facilities will help to keep their feet in good order.

Red-billed Firefinch *Lagonosticta senegala.* Common, Senegal or, just, Firefinch.
A delightful subject for aviaries of mixed finches which, although hardy once acclimatized, is not very prolific or long-lived. It is peaceful and will build a

1 *Ortygospiza atricollis* (nominate race) 3½–4 in/90–100 mm West Africa in a belt from Senegal southeast to S Sudan and Uganda ♂ has upper mandible black when not breeding; ♀ has black replaced by earth brown and is altogether paler *(Text begins previous page.)*
2 *Lagonosticta senegala* 3½–4 in/ 90–100 mm Much of Africa south of the Sahara

3 *L. rubricata*
4¼–4½ in/
105–115 mm Much of
Africa south of the
Sahara Jameson's
Firefinch *L. jamesoni* is
very similar but is paler
red and has an
unnotched 2nd
primary

4 *L. (Estrilda)
caerulescens* 4–4¾ in/
100–120 mm W Africa
from Senegal to W
Central African
Republic

loose nest in a variety of sites. Firefinches are parasitized by the viduines.

Blue-billed Firefinch *Lagonosticta rubricata*. African or Dark Firefinch; Ruddy Waxbill.
Less frequently encountered than the foregoing species but needing the same treatment. Breeding firefinches are charming birds, troubling none of their aviary companions. They produce 3–4 eggs which hatch within 12 days; the young are reared almost exclusively on eggfood and live insects.

Lavender Finch *Lagonosticta caerulescens*. Lavender, Gray or Bluish Waxbill.
Unusually colored and popular but needing increased attention until thoroughly established. It is insectivorous when breeding, but the Black-tailed Lavender Finch *E. perreini*, which is less frequently imported, is even more so. It is a darker bird with black bill, legs and undertail-coverts. They will both build their own nests.

SEEDEATERS

Purple Grenadier *Uraeginthus ianthinogaster.* Grenadier Waxbill.

More secretive than the typical cordon-bleus, but not really shy or timid, the Purple Grenadier is a stunning bird well suited to the progressive waxbill enthusiast, but hardly a subject for the beginner. Like all waxbills, it enjoys hopping about on the ground picking up seeds which have been scattered there, and it needs copious amounts of insect life when rearing young.

Violet-eared Waxbill *Uraeginthus granatina.* Violet-eared Cordon-bleu.

Like the foregoing species, with which it sometimes shares the same synonym, this is another rare and expensive bird, much desired for its beautiful plumage. It is trustworthy once established (which can be difficult) but somewhat delicate in cold weather. It is lively and willing to breed, but does require substantial amounts of livefood.

Red-cheeked Cordon-bleu *Uraeginthus bengalus.*

A popular inhabitant of many collections. The fact that it is commoner does not mean that it is any the less in need of sensitive handling than the Violet-eared. Five eggs per clutch is usual, incubation and fledging each takes about 14 days; incubation is shared by both parents, and the young assume adult guise in about 3 months. Like all waxbills, they have the best chance of rearing young in outside planted aviaries, provided they are not overcrowded; however, it is still necessary to provide extra insects for the best results.

Blue-capped Cordon-bleu *Uraeginthus cyanocephalus.* Blue-headed Cordon-bleu or Waxbill.

Not quite as common as the Red-cheeked, but possibly the easiest on this page to maintain and breed. Do not underestimate the importance of livefood for most waxbills in the breeding season, a rich eggfood is also an invaluable supplement. The first few days in the life of a chick are crucial, and it is then that an effort must be made to provide the tiny insect-life the parents will be seeking. The Blue-breasted species *U. angolensis* is also frequently kept and resembles a female *bengalus.*

1 *Uraeginthus ianthinogaster* $5\frac{1}{2}$ in/ 140 mm E Africa
2 *U. granatina* $5-5\frac{1}{2}$ in/ 125–140 mm S Africa
3 *U. bengalus* $4\frac{1}{2}-5$ in/ 115–130 mm Much of Africa south of the Sahara except southernmost tip
4 *U. cyanocephalus* $4\frac{1}{2}-5$ in/115–130 mm E Africa ♀ rather paler but positive identification can be gained by the lack of the notch on the 2nd primary possessed by both *bengalus* and *angolensis*

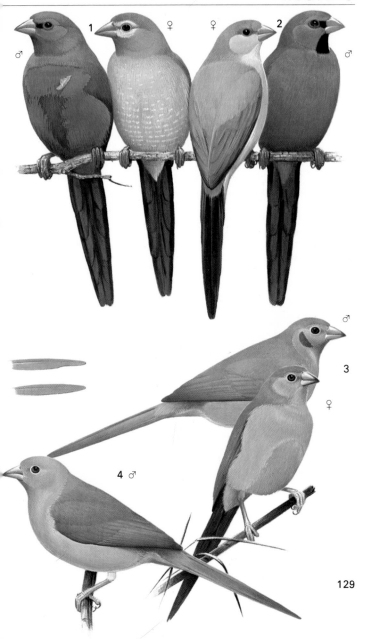

SEEDEATERS

Red-eared Waxbill *Estrilda troglodytes*. Red- (Pink-) cheeked, Gray, Senegal or, wrongly, Common Waxbill.

The definitive waxbill; this and the following two waxbills are suitable for beginners. Housed in a cage or an aviary, they will thrive on a good seed mixture, and be good mixers. None is especially delicate but unless the climate is particularly good, it is wise to give them indoor accommodation during cold and wet weather.

St. Helena Waxbill *Estrilda astrild*.

More properly called "Common Waxbill" than the preceding species. It is a better breeder than the Red-eared, although much of that species' reputed "difficulty" can doubtless be attributed to bad management and incorrectly sexed pairs: males can be easily distinguished when they indulge in their charming courtship dance around the females.

Crimson-rumped Waxbill *Estrilda rhodopyga*. Rosy-rumped, Ruddy or Sundevall's Waxbill.

Available only from time to time in small numbers, it needs much the same care as the previous two. It has bred on several occasions: these waxbills usually lay 3—5 eggs which hatch in 11—12 days. They will use the standard nestboxes.

Black-cheeked Waxbill *Estrilda erythronotos*.

Available only occasionally, when it is usually rather expensive. It is delicate when newly imported, and needs warm, dry conditions, and a good, varied diet that includes much livefood. Restall wisely advises against their purchase unless a "well-planted outdoor flight with plenty of sunshine and a well-lit, warm and dry shelter" is available.

Black-crowned Waxbill *Estrilda nonnula*.

Rare, expensive and usually tricky, the Black-crowned Waxbill is best left to experts, who should treat it with the same circumspection as the Black-cheeked. Almost identical, the Black-headed Waxbill *E. atricapilla*, can be quickly identified by its black undertail-coverts and vent.

1 *Estrilda troglodytes* $3\frac{1}{2}$—4 in/90—100 mm C Africa from Senegal to Ethiopia and Uganda ♀ can be paler 2 *E. astrild* 4—$4\frac{3}{4}$ in/ 100—120 mm C Africa south and east to Mozambique; St Helena; introduced Portugal and Brazil ♀ usually has less red and black on underparts 3 *E. rhodopyga* 4—$4\frac{1}{2}$ in/100—115 mm E Africa ♀ can have red paler 4 *E. erythronotos* 4—5 in/100—130 mm CE Africa south to Rhodesia 5 *E. nonnula* 4—$4\frac{1}{2}$ in/ 100—115 mm Fernando Po, Cameroun and Gabon to Kenya and Tanzania ♀ can be duller on underparts

1 ♂

2 ♂

3 ♂

4

5 ♂

SEEDEATERS

Orange-cheeked Waxbill *Estrilda melpoda.*
An ideal bird for the beginner since it is regularly imported, inexpensive, relatively hardy, amusing and of heartening longevity. What was said for the first three species on the preceding spread also pertains here, especially in connexion with courtship and breeding. It has more breeding potential than records suggest, but like the Red-eared Waxbill, must have peace and quiet, and be undisturbed after it has begun nesting.

Yellow-bellied Waxbill *Estrilda melanotis quartina.*
Dufresne's Waxbill *Estrilda melanotis melanotis.*
Considerable confusion exists about the correct identification of the Yellow-bellied Waxbill group. Most aviculturists call the black-headed form the Dufresne's. The species is both quietly colored and mannered, and well-suited to a cage or life with a collection of other small waxbills. It is said to be delicate but is probably no more so than other birds of similar genre – all of which should be given extra warmth and dryness in the winter, and livefood at all times.

The Dufresne's is less frequently available than the Yellow-bellied. Both require the same treatment.

Golden-breasted Waxbill *Estrilda subflava.* Zebra or Orange-breasted Waxbill.
A diminutive but tough little bird which has the best chance of breeding successfully in a well-planted aviary (with a wire-mesh gauge of no more than 10 mm ($\frac{7}{8}$ in)). It needs a lot of tiny insects – the skins of maggots and mealworms are too tough.

Green Avadavat *Amandava formosa.*
Not such a good bet for the beginner as the next species since it is harder to acclimatize, more expensive and not so brightly colored. For successful management, it should be regarded more as a cordon-bleu.

Red Avadavat *Amandava amandava.* Tiger Finch; Red Munia or Waxbill.
A superb cage and aviary bird, the male of which becomes much browner and more female-like when not breeding. It is one of the best birds for the novice on account of its hardy nature, lovely coloring, pretty song and free-breeding inclination – it deserves much more attention from serious breeders as well. There are several races including the Strawberry and Yellow-bellied Finches.

1 *Estrilda melpoda* 4 in/100 mm Tropical W Africa, east to Lake Tanganyika
2 *E. (Coccopygia) melanotis quartina* 3½–3¾ in/90–95 mm Ethiopia and Sudan
3 *E. (Coccopygia) m. melanotis* 3¾–4 in/95–100 mm E South Africa ♀ lacks black on face and is duller
4 *E. subflava* 3½–3¾ in/90–95 mm Much of Africa south of the Sahara, excluding equatorial forests and SW Africa ♀ paler and lacks eye-stripe
5 *Amandava formosa* 4–4¼ in/100–110 mm C India
6 *A. amandava* 4 in/100 mm W Pakistan through India, Sri Lanka and Burma to SW China and Indonesia; introduced in places

1

2

3 ♂

4 ♂

5

♀

6

♂

SEEDEATERS

Zebra Finch *Poephila guttata.*
The different forms of Zebra Finch which dominate this plate all owe their existence to a wild grassfinch from Australia, which is now firmly domesticated and forms a complete branch of aviculture on its own. The prototype – the Normal Gray – has been, and still is, subjected to intensive selective-breeding which has resulted in numerous types, including the Chestnut-flanked White, Silver, Cream, Penguin and Pied, for each of which a "standard" has been settled upon.

The Zebra Finch, quite apart from its importance to the specialist, is an ideal bird for the beginner. It is difficult to imagine a bird more suited to captivity, or easier to feed and look after, or a better mixer. It will breed freely in either environment and will, given the chance, build a delightful bottle-shaped nest. The young are easy to rear on the usual rearing-food; live insects are *not* needed. The adult diet is panicum millet, a small amount of large millet, small canary seed and, occasionally, a little niger and maw. A suitable grit must be available at all times.

Diamond Sparrow *Emblema guttata.* Diamond Firetail or Spot-sided Finch.
Only captive bred birds are now available outside Australia, and no great difficulty should be experienced in increasing the stock of this chubby, sparrow-like finch which is, indeed, so prone to fatness that it is far healthier and happier in an aviary than a cage. Breeding and rearing should not be much of a problem, provided a *true* pair is obtained; but some males can be aggressive.

Cherry Finch *Aidemosyne modesta.* Plum-headed, Modest, Plain-colored or Diadem Finch.
Care and attention is much the same as for the above but it is rather more nervous and needs sympathetic handling. All Australian finches are surprisingly hardy once they are used to a new home, whether it is cage, pen or aviary, and the Cherry Finch is no exception. The biggest problem is matching up a compatible pair, and for this reason they are best obtained in a mixed flock; fortunately they are all good mixers.

1 *Poephila (Taeniopygia) guttata* (Normal Gray) 4–4½ in/100–115 mm
1a Chestnut-flanked White, ♀ as ♂ but minus throat-markings, chestbar, lobe and flank-markings, paler beak, and the head may carry some light flecks of gray on top
1b Pied (have about 50% dark and pale on flanks and upperparts), ♀ like Normal ♀ but in pied form, beak paler
1c Penguin, ♀ as ♂ but minus flank-markings and with the cheek-lobes white; the back is a little paler Australia and some islands; domesticated
2 *Emblema (Steganopleura) guttata* 4½ in/115 mm ♀ has narrower breast-band SE Australia
3 *Aidemosyne modesta* 4–4½ in/ 100–115 mm ♀ lacks chin-markings E Australia

♂ 1 ♀

1 a ♂

1 b ♂

1 c ♂

2

3 ♂

SEEDEATERS

Australian grassfinches are only available abroad today as captive-bred stock. It is a superb, varied group of birds of interest to all fanciers: easy to manage, hardy once established and free-breeding – they do not need live insects in the same quantities as many waxbills. If breeding difficulties are encountered, Bengalese or Zebra Finches are adequate fosters. They prefer to build their own nests but will often use an open nestbox as a base. The sexes are usually very similar, but males are sometimes more boldly marked and brighter colored.

Parson Finch *Poephila cincta*. Black-throated Finch. Not so aggressive as the Long-tailed, and it is wise to house in a small flock so that pairing is optimized. Avoid cross-breeding with other *Poephilae*.

Long-tailed Grassfinch *Poephila acuticauda*. The cheapest of the wild grassfinches, but still more expensive than many African waxbills. Breeding presents few problems, although its belligerent behavior can necessitate separate accommodation or the company of comparably sized birds. Heck's Grassfinch is no longer recognized as a valid race.

Bicheno's Finch *Poephila bichenovii*. Banded, Double-bar, Owl(-faced) Finch.

1 *Poephila c. cincta* 4–4½ in/100–115 mm E and NE Australia *P. c. uropygialis* from S Cape York has black upper tail-coverts
2 *P. acuticauda* 6½–7 in/165–180 mm (including 2½ in/65 mm tail) N and NW Australia, excluding Cape York
3 *P. (Stizoptera) bichenovii* 4–4¼ in/ 100–105 mm N and E Australia: white-rumped race (*bichenovii*) to the east; black-rumped race (*annulosa*) to the west

FINCHES

4 *P. (Neochmia)*
ruficauda 4½–5 in/
115–125 mm Coastal
belt from NW to NE
Australia ♀ has smaller
mask.
5 *P. personata*
(nominate race) 5 in/
125 mm N Australia;
nominate race abuts
leucotis from Cape
York which has some
white below the eye

Because of its active temperament, this attractive grassfinch should be housed in a roomy, planted aviary — where, after a lengthy settling-in period, a true pair will be good nesters (unfortunately, true pairs are hard to find). A rare subspecies, the Black-ringed Finch *P.b. annulosa*, is very similar in looks, habits and requirements, but can be distinguished by its black rump.

Star Finch *Poephila ruficauda.* Ruficauda; Rufous-(Red-)tailed Finch.
Rather meek perhaps but ideal aviary birds in every other respect. In common with other grassfinches, two or three broods per year can be expected of about 4 eggs each; hatching takes 13 days, and fledging about 20. Livefood appears to be useful but not essential.

Masked Grassfinch *Poephila personata.*
Fine, noisy birds which breed best if kept in a flock in a large planted aviary. According to Rutgers (1964), it has a strange fixation for lumps of charcoal, which are always found in its wild nests.

137

SEEDEATERS

Parrot-finches require similar care to their grassfinch relatives, but possibly have an increased dependence on live insects; certainly in the wild all Erythrurae are efficient hawkers of termites. Incidentally, grit, in particular crushed eggshell, is said to be of special importance to parrot-finches.

Gouldian Finch *Chloebia gouldiae*. Purple-breasted or Lady Gould's Finch.
The Gouldian Finch is without doubt the most spectacular of all finches. It can now be regarded as domesticated, but the habit of using Bengalese as fosters to optimize the birds' breeding potential is generally *harmful* to ensuing Gouldian populations. The establishment of Gouldians is worrying. Their love of hot weather must not be ignored and, at all times, they need dry, draughtproof quarters. They also need a rich staple diet with increased amounts of insects. Although their instincts have been sadly dulled by domesticity, Gouldians still only *thrive* in a tropical-house environment which imitates their rainy-season wild breeding-time.

Pin-tailed Parrot-finch *Erythrura prasina*.
Blue-faced Parrot-finch *Erythrura trichroa*.
Red-headed Parrot-finch *Erythrura psittacea*.
To help conserve space, these three examples of the desirable parrot-finches are discussed collectively, since their management differs little. The first named is also called the Pin-tailed Nonpareil and Long-tailed Munia, and is exported in huge numbers from SE Asia. The Blue-faced is also called the Tri-colored.

For a long time, they, like the Gouldians, had a "delicate" reputation; now this has been dispelled, with the help of modern antibiotics, they are being kept and bred with more confidence — however, they are still on the expensive side. They are active birds at their best in aviaries, where they mix well. They need a grassfinch diet, and if the sometimes difficult acclimatization can be successfully achieved (buy captive-bred whenever possible), they can be expected to live long and productively; and, hopefully, the massive exploitation of birds such as the Pin-tailed will be a thing of the past. Their breeding particulars are basically the same as those of the grassfinches, and they should be given some live insects when rearing young.

1 *Chloebia (Erythura, Poephila) gouldiae* 4¾–5½ in/ 120–140 mm N Australia possibly excluding the extreme NE Color forms (l to r): Black-headed ♂♀, Red-headed ♂ and Orange-headed ♂
2 *Erythrura prasina* 5½–6 in/140–155 mm (including 1 in/25 mm central tail feathers) Malaysia and the Greater Sundas ♀ also has shorter tail Perhaps up to 5% of birds have red replaced by gold
3 *E. trichroa* 4½–5½ in/ 115–140 mm S Pacific islands from Celebes through the Moluccas, New Guinea to Micronesia in the north and Loyalty Is's in the south; NE Australia ♀ likely to have less blue and duller
4 *E. psittacea* 4–4¾ in/ 100–120 mm New Caledonia

SEEDEATERS

The Lonchura *branch of the Estrildidae is of immense importance to aviculture. It consists of about 35 Old World species, which in many ways can be regarded as typical finches. Certainly, from an avicultural viewpoint, they provide few surprises – so the cheapest become ideal birds for children and novices.*

Indian Silverbill *Lonchura malabarica*. White-throated Munia.
Considerably rarer than the African, otherwise it requires the same treatment, and has the same virtues.

African Silverbill *Lonchura cantans.*
For some inexplicable reason this bird has come to be regarded as a race of the last species. The African Silverbill is a bird of quiet ways and colors but none the poorer for that. It is exceptionally free breeding in cage or aviary, and builds a lovely little nest. Its feeding and breeding particulars are much the same as for other prolific waxbills (no livefood is needed). Difficulty may be found in sexing the birds, and it is as well to buy a few, whereupon the gentle song of the male will be heard; the colony can be left together, if desired.

Pearl-headed Silverbill *Lonchura caniceps*. Gray-headed Silverbill or Mannikin.
Not as prolific as the above two but a useful subject for anyone wishing to progress on to a lesser known type. General management is as for other mannikins, but it should always be given livefood when young are in the nest.

Bengalese *Lonchura striata,* **dom.** Society Finch. (Domesticated.)
The wholly admirable Bengalese performs a service to aviculture which is hard to overemphasize: it is friendly, peaceful and evidently considers reproduction as the most important thing in life. Its value as a versatile foster parent alone earns it a prominent position in even the most sophisticated collection. While its cheerful, hardy constitution in various forms make it a source of delight to children, amateurs and experienced keepers the world over. Their general management is simple, and similar to that of the Zebra Finch.

1 *Lonchura (Euodice) malabarica* 4¼–5 in/ 105–125 mm
Afghanistan through India to Sri Lanka
2 *L. (Euodice) cantans* 4–4½ in/100–115 mm
A belt from Senegal to Sudan
3 *L. caniceps* 4–4¾ in/ 100–120 mm
S Ethiopia, Uganda, Kenya and Tanzania
4 *L. (Munia) striata,* dom. (*domestica*) 4–5 in/100–130 mm
Domesticated
4a Chocolate and white
4b Fawn and white

SEEDEATERS

Striated Mannikin/Munia *Lonchura striata.* Striated Finch; White-rumped (-backed) Mannikin or Munia.
A subspecies of this mannikin (*L.s. acuticauda*) played a part in the original appearance of the Bengalese — and this adequately reflects its prolific and easy-going nature. The young are easy to rear on the usual fare and do not require live insects.

Nutmeg Finch/Mannikin *Lonchura punctulata.* Spotted Munia; Mascot or Spice Finch; Spicebird; Ricebird.
One of the most popular mannikins, having all the usual attributes but not breeding so well as many, and it is wise to offer livefood. It requires sensitive handling but will settle down eventually in cage or mixed aviary. There are various similar races which become available from time to time.

Chestnut-breasted Mannikin/Finch *Lonchura castaneothorax.*
Similar in habits to the Nutmeg Finch, except that it is more likely to build its nest in a low shrub rather than higher up — it will incorporate an entrance passage which accurately suggests a preference for peace and quiet. Pairs vary considerably in their individuality, so be prepared to experiment with conditions, diets and rearing techniques.

White-headed Mannikin/Munia *Lonchura maja.* Pale-headed Mannikin; Maja Finch; White-headed Nun.
Hardy and long-lived,if properly established, it has all the advantages of other mannikins, but can be strangely reluctant to breed and needs a fair amount of encouragement; the fact that it likes to build its own nest is probably partially to blame. The Javan White-headed Munia *L. ferruginosa* is similar but has black under the throat.

Tri-colored Mannikin *Lonchura malacca.* Tri-colored Nun or Munia; Three-colored Mannikin; and (misleadingly) Black-headed Munia.
Much of the above also applies here. It may well be that dense vegetation consisting of much reed or bamboo will help improve the present indifferent breeding results. It is certainly as much in need of a dedicated and specialist approach as the closely allied Black-headed Mannikin (see next plate).

1 *Lonchura (Munia) striata* 4$\frac{1}{2}$ in/115 mm
The Andamans and India through to S China and Taiwan, and south to Sumatra
2 *L. (Munia) punctulata* 4–5 in/ 100–125 mm India through to Taiwan, and south to Indonesia; introduced elsewhere including E Australia
3 *L. (Munia) castaneothorax* 4–4$\frac{1}{2}$ in/100–115 mm Coastal N and E Australia; New Guinea
4 *L. (Munia) maja* 4–4$\frac{3}{4}$ in/100–120 mm Malay Peninsular, Sumatra and Java
5 *L. (Munia) malacca (ferruginosa)* 4$\frac{1}{4}$–4$\frac{1}{2}$ in/ 105–115 mm S and C India, SW China, Taiwan, and south to Indonesia; introduced elsewhere

SEEDEATERS

Black-headed Mannikin *Lonchura atricapilla*. Black-headed Munia or Nun; Chestnut(-bellied) Munia.
For some reason it is often made con-specific with the Tri-colored Mannikin, which is also, therefore, confusingly called the Black-headed Munia. It is equally suitable as a pet or mixed aviary inhabitant, and is the most commonly kept "wild" mannikin. Funnily enough, it is not a reliable breeder, and requires a thickly-planted area; otherwise, it is easy to feed, eating just seeds etc, and maintain, and is hardy and sociable even with tiny waxbills. It is eminently suitable for the emerging serious breeder.

Magpie Mannikin *Lonchura fringilloides*.
The African species, such as this, used to be accorded their own genus — *Spermestes*. This type also has a poor breeding reputation, but it is more likely that this is a reaction to badly-mated "pairs" or incorrect housing: it is probably not suitable for mixed aviaries, and would do best in a thickly-planted, *sparsely* inhabited flight.

Bronze-winged Mannikin *Lonchura cucullata*. Bronze Mannikin.
People who find this species hard to breed often have the advice meted out of housing separately in small cages, but this cannot correct badly-matched "pairs." There is no good reason why it should not breed given the *right* conditions. The thin song of the cock is the only way of telling the sexes apart, so it is best to buy (from) a group and provide special accommodation. It can become aggressive when nesting. If young are produced some livefood should be added to the adult's diet.

Black-and-white Mannikin *Lonchura bicolor poensis*.
Rufous-backed Mannikin *Lonchura bicolor nigriceps*.
Both these races are free-breeding. Regularly available, and require similar management to other *Lonchura* species. The Rufous-backed Mannikin is probably even more peaceful than the Black-and-White and it breeds freely amongst small waxbills, creating few problems providing aviaries are not over-crowded, and that seed is provided in separate dishes so that there are as few reasons as possible for squabbling. *L.b. poensis* is frequently known as the Fernando Po or Black-breasted Mannikin; *L.b. bicolor* (the Blue-billed Mannikin) lacks the wing and rump markings.

1 *Lonchura (Munia) atricapilla* 4½ in/ 115 mm Mostly S India and Burma
2 *L. (Spermestes, Amauresthes) fringilloides* 4½–5 in/ 115–130 mm Senegal across tropical Africa to Uganda and the eastern seaboard
3 *L. (Spermestes) cucullata* 3½–4 in/ 90–100 mm Much of Africa south of the Sahara, excluding equatorial forests and SW Africa
4 *L. (Spermestes) bicolor poensis* 3½–4 in/90–100 mm Tropical W Africa, east to Kenya
5 *L. (Spermestes) b. nigriceps* 3½–4 in/ 90–100 mm Kenya down coast to Mozambique and Natal; S Arabia

SEEDEATERS

Java Sparrow *Padda oryzivora*. Rice Bird or Munia; Paddy or Temple Bird.

One of the most popular, frequently imported and beautifully marked and feathered of all cagebirds. The trade in Java Sparrows is, however, banned in the US due to the fear that the already feral flocks will become as great a menace to grain crops as they are in their native Indonesia: its scientific name means "Eater of rice in paddy fields!" The wild Java Sparrow is not the best of breeders but some of the domesticated mutations are, for example the White and Pied varieties.

The Java Sparrow is not quarrelsome and mixes well in most collections of finches, where it eats the usual fare and is predictably fond of whole/paddy rice. It displays a desire for some insects and softfood at rearing time. Establishment needs to be extensive and careful before it will go to nest, for which purpose it seeks a hollow log or Budgerigar nestbox (it mixes very well with Budgerigars). If a pet is the primary objective, the purchaser ought to go for one of the domesticated strains, as they are inherently well conditioned for captivity. They are at home in cage or aviary, and can winter without heat if properly acclimatized.

Cut-throat *Amadina fasciata*. Ribbon Finch.

Probably the best known of all small African finches, this and the next species require similar care to the Java Sparrow, but noise and disturbance must be avoided when breeding. The East African race, *A.f. alexanderi*, differs in being browner, with a broader red throat-band, and heavier scale-like markings. Both races will breed well given the correct conditions and livefood. Males can be dangerous to small waxbills when nesting, but females tend to be much more fragile and need extra careful acclimatization.

Red-headed Finch *Amadina erythrocephala*.

Rather less prolific and much rarer than its cogener but otherwise very similar in habits etc. It demands individual attention if it is to be bred regularly, and will not tolerate any degree of over-crowding or disturbance.

1 *Padda oryzivora*
5–6¼ in/125–150 mm
Java and Bali; widely introduced elsewhere including Indonesia
1a Normal
1b White variety
2 *Amadina fasciata*
4¼–5 in/110–130 mm
Semi-arid belt from Senegal to Sudan and Uganda
3 *A. erythrocephala*
5–5½ in/125–140 mm
SW Africa

SEEDEATERS

For background information on these unusual birds see page 103. Although immensely decorative and undemanding with regard to their maintenance, when breeding is considered, the situation becomes much more complicated.

Paradise Whydah *Vidua paradisaea*. Widow Bird.
Although it can be confused with the Broad-tailed Paradise Whydah *V. orientalis* (whose range includes West Africa), males of the latter have the long tail feathers broad along their entire length instead of tapering to a point. Both are common, trouble-free birds (eating the usual seeds), suitable for the beginner. They parasitize the Melba Finch in the wild, and will also use it as a host in captivity.

Pintailed Whydah *Vidua macroura.*
As males have a reputation for being spiteful, this robust bird is best housed with large companions or in a thickly-planted aviary. Over its wide range, it parasitizes several small birds, including the St. Helena, Red-eared and Orange-cheeked Waxbills.

Queen Whydah *Vidua regia*. Shaft-tailed Whydah or Widow Bird.
Rarely available nowadays. In the wild, this whydah parasitizes the Violet-eared Cordon-bleu and, perhaps, the Red-cheeked too; and using these hosts has bred in captivity.

Fischer's Whydah *Vidua fischeri*. Straw-tailed Whydah.
It is available occasionally, but does not so far seem to have bred; presumably because its natural host is the rare and expensive Purple Grenadier.

Senegal Combassou *Vidua chalybeata*. Indigo Bird; Steel Finch.
The hardy and delightful Combassou is commonly kept, and if mixed with firefinches, which it parasitizes, there is every chance of its breeding; however, occasionally, it will also build its own nest and raise its young. There are several races, as well as other species, that are all remarkably alike. Another similar bird is the Steel Blue Whydah *V. hypocherina*, only in this case, breeding males have long Pintailed-like tail-feathers.

1 *Vidua (Steganura) paradisea* 5–6 in/ 125–150 mm (tail of ♂ in breeding plumage can be 12 in/305 mm long) Eritrea and Sudan south to Natal, and including Angola in the west
2 *V. macroura* 4½–5 in/ 115–130 mm (tail of ♂ in breeding plumage can be 10 in/255 mm long) Much of Africa south of the Sahara; some nearby islands
3 *V. regia* 4½–5 in/ 115–130 mm (tail of ♂ in breeding plumage 7–8 in/180–205 mm long) S and C Africa
4 *V. fischeri* 4½–5 in/115–130 mm (tail of ♂ in breeding plumage 5½–8½ in/ 140–215 mm long) E Africa
5 *V. (Hypochera) chalybeata* 4–4½ in/ 100–115 mm Senegal, Gambia and Mali

1

2

3

4

5

SEEDEATERS

Yellow Sparrow *Passer luteus.* (Sudan) Golden Sparrow.

A nicely-colored species, which is hardy, lively and will breed on the colony system, building a typical sparrow nest — large and untidy — in a suitable aviary. It needs a considerable amount of livefood when rearing, and a varied diet at all times. The Arabian Golden Sparrow *P. euchlorus,* which is more yellow, is occasionally imported and needs the same insectivorous treatment.

Yellow-throated Petronia *Petronia xanthocollis.* Yellow-throated Sparrow.

The petronias are rock-sparrows with similar habits to other sparrow-weavers. This species is one of the prettiest and friendliest, especially so when bribed with mealworms. It will nest readily in holes, crevices and correctly sited nestboxes.

Speckle-fronted Weaver *Sporopipes frontalis.*
Scaly-crowned Weaver *Sporopipes squamifrons.*

Both these species are confusingly sometimes called "Scaly-fronted Weaver." *S. squamifrons* has the less enviable reputation of the two, but in truth, they are both pretty amenable birds which mix well. It is possible that *frontalis* is rather retiring, but both should breed well given suitable sites — nestboxes, old weaver nests etc, in which they will also roost. The males have pleasant, quiet songs. Specimens housed in cages can become very lethargic and eventually ill, so they are far better off in aviaries.

Red-billed Quelea/Weaver *Quelea quelea.*
Red-headed Quelea/Weaver *Quelea erythrops.*

The first named is the commonest at home and abroad, and is a serious pest of crops in its native Africa. Both require similar treatment in captivity, which varies little from the standard weaver management, as outlined elsewhere in the book. They are possibly the most industrious nest-builders in the entire bird kingdom, but breeding records are dismal considering the huge numbers imported. To encourage nest-building in aviaries, they should be housed in flocks, and an abundant supply of stout grass-blades provided, together with a varied diet including, preferably, some partially germinated seeds, insectile food and live insects should young be produced.

1 *Passer (Auripasser) luteus* 4$\frac{3}{4}$–5 in/ 120–125 mm A belt from W Algeria to the Red Sea
2 *Petronia xanthocollis* 5$\frac{1}{2}$ in/140 mm Persia to India ♀ has duller chestnut shoulder and smaller throat-spot
3 *Sporopipes frontalis* 4$\frac{1}{2}$–5 in/115–125 mm Senegal to Eritrea and Ethiopia
4 *S. squamifrons* 4 in/ 100 mm S Africa
5 *Quelea quelea* 4$\frac{3}{4}$–5 in/120–125 mm Very common over much of Africa south of the Sahara
6 *Q. erythrops* 4$\frac{1}{2}$–5 in/ 115–125 mm Distribution as for *quelea* but less common

SEEDEATERS

The true weavers have many attributes and few adverse features: they are hardy, inexpensive, gregarious and easy to keep. But unfortunately they rarely follow up their energetic and clever courtship and nest-building by actually breeding successfully. It is a large group with many similarly garbed members; ideally they have to be housed in spacious, planted flights. The males of most species have an "out-of-color" phase when they resemble the brown-streaked females.

Baya Weaver *Ploceus philippinus.*
Very aggressive when busy in its wonderful nest, the Baya Weaver is safest housed on its own unless much space and cover or large companions are available; however it requires standard weaver care. The cock has a strange display in which he flutters around the hen, continually uttering his hoarse little song, and, kept in a flock, these birds provide much entertainment.

Half-masked Weaver *Ploceus vitellinus.* Vitelline (Masked) Weaver.
Considered by some to be a race of the Southern Masked Weaver *P. velatus*, the Half-masked is a small, enchanting yet hardy bird, better off in an outside aviary, where it might well breed, building a beautiful pouch nest. It will lay about 4 eggs which hatch in about 12 days.

Masked Weaver *Ploceus intermedius.*
Another lively, desirable weaver which builds a round nest with a short, hanging entrance tunnel; it is semi-gregarious, occurring in the wild in flocks of about 10 pairs — which build their nests close to water.

Black-headed Weaver *Ploceus cucullatus.* Spotted-backed, Village, Rufous-necked, V-marked Weaver.
It is common in Africa, and shows a fondness for human settlements. For safety's sake, it should be housed on its own (preferably in a female-rich flock) or with other large birds, because of its strength.

Napoleon Weaver *Euplectes afra.* Yellow (-crowned) or Golden Bishop. Includes the Taha race *E.a. taha*.
Hardy, providing it has an adequate shelter, this striking bird needs a varied diet if the male is to retain his vivid coloring. If enough trouble is taken, breeding can be induced, but the polygamous male likes to build many nests, from which the females choose. His display is energetic and aggressive to all finches.

1 *Ploceus philippinus*
5½–6 in/140–150 mm
W Pakistan to SW China and Vietnam; Java and Sumatra

2 *P. vitellinus* 4¾–5 in/ 120–125 mm Senegal to W Sudan ♀ when breeding is darker: more green above and more buff below

3 *P. intermedius* 5–5½ in/125–140 mm Nominate illustrated race in S Sudan and Ethiopia to Kenya and Somalia Another race *cabanisii* occurs in S Africa

4 *P. cucullatus* 6–7 in/ 150–180 mm Nominate illustrated race from Senegal to Central African Republic Other races occur over much of Africa south of the Sahara excluding the extreme S and SW

5 *Euplectes afra* 4½–5½ in/ 115–140 mm Nominate illustrated race: W Africa, Senegal, Fernando Po and the Congo east to Sudan; other races to the E and S

SEEDEATERS

Long-tailed Whydah/Widow Bird *Euplectes progne.*
This and the shorter-tailed Jackson's Whydah *E. jacksoni*, which is further differentiated by the males' yellowish shoulders, are birds which demand an especially large aviary. Unfortunately, they also have other factors working against their consistent captive propagation. In need of a specialist approach.

Yellow-mantled Whydah/Widow Bird *Euplectes macrourus.* Yellow- (Gold-) backed Whydah/Widow Bird. Probably also polygamous, which complicates breeding attempts, this species is another in need of seclusion and a well-planted aviary. *Both* sexes in eclipse plumage show yellow wing feathers.

Red-collared Whydah/Widow Bird *Euplectes ardens.*
Red-naped Whydah/Widow Bird *Euplectes laticauda.*
Sometimes considered to be con-specific. The former is the best known, and an aggressive customer, especially to birds with red in their plumage, and for this reason must never be mixed with *E. hordeacea.* Breeding is a complex matter, best left to the expert.

Crimson-crowned Bishop/Weaver *Euplectes hordeacea.* Black-winged Red Bishop.
A typical weaver in most respects, and as hardy as the Napoleon Weaver overleaf, the Crimson-crowned Bishop will build (as will other weavers) against wire-netting on any suitable protruberance, so this should be borne in mind when planting aviaries. This species bears an uncanny resemblance to the Red-collared Whydah (below) in matters of color, display and voice.

Red Bishop *Euplectes orix.*
This nominate race is also called: Grenadier Weaver; Red, Scarlet or Crimson Grenadier. There are four other races, including the most commonly imported Orange Bishop/Weaver *E. o. franciscana.* Astonishingly colored birds which need a varied diet, rich in semi-germinated grain and insectivorous food if they are to retain their vivid colors through successive molts. They, and also the Zanzibar Red Bishop *E. nigroventris*, can be tough and quarrelsome with definite polygamous tendencies. Again, they need thickly planted aviaries, preferably with some reeds (a pheasant aviary is often perfect) if breeding is to be a serious proposition.

1 *Euplectes (Coliuspasser) progne* 6–9¼ in/150–235 mm (♀ smallest, ♂ in breeding plumage has a tail 13–18 in/330–455 mm longer) S and E Africa
2 *E. (Coliuspasser) macrourus* 6–7 in/150–180 mm (♂ in breeding plumage has a tail some 2½ in/65 mm longer) Trans C Africa from Senegal to Indian Ocean coast, avoiding equatorial jungles
3 *E. (Coliuspasser) ardens* 5–6½ in/125–165 mm (♀ smallest, ♂ in breeding plumage has a tail up to 9 in/230 mm longer) Much of Africa south of the Sahara except equatorial jungles and SW Africa
4 *E. (Coliuspasser) laticauda* 6 in/150 mm (♂ in breeding plumage has a tail 3–4 in/75–100 mm longer) E Africa
5 *E. hordeacea* 6–6½ in/150–165 mm Much of Africa south of the Sahara except equatorial jungles and south of Zambia.
6 *E. orix* (nominate race) 4¾–6 in/120–150 mm Trans C Africa from Senega to S Red Sea; in E Africa south to Malawi
All males are shown in breeding plumage

PARROTS

CHAPTER 12: PARROTS

Speaking both aviculturally and ornithologically, the parrots are unique. No other large group of birds is so well defined or so distinctive. Unlike virtually all others, a member of this family, even if never seen before, is immediately recognizable as such despite the fact that it is extremely varied and large (about 328 species). Parrots can be as small as the tiny *Micropsitta* (pygmy) parrots from the Papuan region— only about 9 cm ($3\frac{1}{2}$ in) long — or as large as the macaws from South America, which can measure 102 cm (40 in), but they all have certain features in common such as a relatively large head, no visible neck and strong grasping feet; the most diagnostic feature of all, however, is the stout, strong, highly accentuated downward-curving beak.

In the wild, parrots are pan-tropical in distribution, whereas, in captivity, they are found virtually everywhere. Budgerigars apart, parrots are still immensely popular as cage and aviary birds; their suitability is due to certain factors which combine fortuitously to excellent effect. These factors repay consideration because they will help to influence those whose minds are undecided about the branch of aviculture in which to specialize. To my mind, parrots offer more scope to the serious and casual aviculturist than any other group of easily kept and housed birds.

Very much in their favor is the true parrots' disinclination to fly — thus, they do not so easily offend even those who have the common and over-sentimental view of captivity. And their position finds a closer parallel with that of a dog than it does to that of a softbill or even a finch. Parrots are mostly quite happy to clamber about an aviary or sit for hours on end preening, chattering, playing or feeding. It is quite common, even usual, for an "escaped" parrot to sit on the top of its cage trying hard to get back in. If one does fly away, it normally heads for another collection and makes that its home-base. Other points in their favor are their comparatively high intelligence; adaptable, friendly, mischievous and playful natures; simple diets; inherent hardiness and amazing longevity. They inevitably have their disadvantages too: amongst the most serious are the harsh, loud, generally unpleasing voices of many, which can all too easily upset neighbors, and their somewhat anti-social behavior towards each other. Breeding parrots often have to be housed on their own (although there are communal nesting species such as the Budgerigar, lovebirds and certain conures), otherwise very serious fights can occur. Here it should perhaps be emphasized that the difference between those psittacines called parrots and those called parakeets is that the latter are the smaller, long-tailed varieties which *are* strong in flight. It is rather confusing that the smallest species are again called parrots (or parrotlets) and lovebirds, and that the largest — the macaws — are long-tailed species; so it is not wholly to do with size.

Size is of no great account when choosing parrots either, providing the correct accommodation is available. Many macaws live happily on stands in living-rooms with little recourse to exercise, although such facilities should be regularly provided. Popular as cage parrots are the colorful and amusing Amazons, whereas the parakeets are more suited to aviaries, as are the marvellous cockatoos, because they are much better flyers and are only then seen at their best. In fact, anyone who has seen free-flying cockatoos would never happily confine them in anything but the roomiest of flights. Macaws too are splendid in flight, and many zoos and bird gardens now keep free-flying specimens, and they present an unforgettable spec-tacle. Unfortunately, liberty parrots, especially the bigger ones, do present problems since they are very destructive in their habits and especially fond, in my experience, of such things as plastic guttering and telephone wires! It is not difficult to imagine them becoming pests in fruit-growing areas etc and for this reason it is illegal to keep liberty parrots (including Budgerigars) in parts of America and elsewhere (consult local government or police for precise information). This is not as yet a problem in northern Europe; but over and over again parrots have proved themselves to be highly adaptable and resourceful birds. A happy medium between complete liberty and captivity can be achieved by allowing a small number of birds their freedom but at the same time ensuring their return for the winter or whenever deemed desirable by always providing their food inside an aviary — allowing their retention at any time.

Of the more commonly kept parrots, the somewhat strange and easily defined lovebird genus of Africa is one of the most remarkably attuned to captivity. It is only a comparatively small group of nine species, and yet each, bar one, is a familiar cagebird. They are so

PARROTS

easily bred that most nowadays come from domesticated strains. And mutations bred according to the Mendelian principle are now a common aspect of their culture, as they are with the Cockatiel — another splendid cage and aviary subject. This is an Australian parakeet with much in common with the Budgerigar; it is the best choice for someone interested in expanding their Budgie experience, and is difficult to fault as an aviary occupant. It is gentle, friendly, sociable at all times with its own kind and all smaller birds, a free breeder, excellent parent (also suited to fostering more difficult types), hardy and of quiet and pleasing voice. As a pet or cagebird, it is also desirable — learning a few words, whistling tunes and becoming very tame — although, being a strong flyer, it is better off housed in a larger, flighted area. For all its tameness it is, however, a rather nervous bird, and care must be taken not to scare it, especially when it is nesting.

I have not yet mentioned the best known of all parrots, namely the African Gray — a monotypic species which owes its popularity largely to its impressive powers of mimicry, which, as we have seen with mynah birds, can overrule all contrary features. In the case of the African Gray, any unsuitability stems not from problems of management, because it is easy to keep, but more from the fact that it is usually kept singly. In this way its interest in mimicry is sustained to the detriment of all breeding ambitions — which, by definition, should be the preoccupation of an aviculturist. No more than with any other animal can you have both a devoted pet and a normal wilding with natural instincts — one aim inevitably prospers at the expense of the other. It is to be hoped that more and more captive stock is allowed to live as naturally as possible and encouraged to breed, and that fewer and fewer are regarded as animated toys. I fervently hope that people who feel the desire for the companionship of an animal — a healthy and normal emotion given the stress of modern living — will choose from the wide selection of domesticated forms already available, which are included in this book, leaving the development of more to the breeder, and to avoid brainwashing a wild animal, like the African Gray, into a false and sterile existence.

The following subsections divide the parrot family up using avicultural and not necessarily ornithological criteria. They concern, in turn, cockatoos, Australian

158

parakeets, lovebirds, the brush-tongued parrots, Asian parakeets, macaws, neotropical parakeets, and the true parrots from that region, which includes the evergreen Amazons.

COCKATOOS

There are 17 species of unmistakable and spectacular Australasian cockatoos, all of which possess mobile crests — used to display anger, fright, pleasure and sexual arousement. Most cockatoos are white, many having suffusions of pale pastel coloration, and a few are either gray or black.

Cockatoos need a little more care taken over their diets than most other parrots, and require more variety, especially fruit and greenstuff. They have a wide range of vocal abilities, sometimes being disagreeably noisy but also chattering, whistling and "talking." The smaller varieties can live indoors as pets, but being fairly free breeders, are better housed in pairs or groups in lengthy aviaries where they have a chance to indulge their superb, swift and direct flight. A healthy cockatoo is always active and lively. An allied species the Cockatiel is dealt with below.

AUSTRALIAN PSITTACINES

Australia is altogether richer in parrots than many people would imagine. It is the home of a fantastic assortment of spectacular, vividly-colored birds, even discounting those discussed in the preceding two sections. Aviculturally, they can be split into three groups: the grass parakeets (*Neophema* spp.), rosellas (*Platycercus* and *Barnardius* spp.) and a mixed bag which contains the remaining species including the important *Polytelis* and *Psephotus* genera.

Located under this heading are parrots to suit most tastes and requirements. There are many notable free-breeders, which is just as well in view of the Australian Government's ban on bird exportation. The grass parakeets are a group of smallish, attractively colored and easily managed birds all of which are now virtually domesticated. The striking rosellas (alternatively "broad-tails") have domesticated representatives, are equally willing to breed, and present no great problems to successful management (see also Chapter 4).

Other interesting Australian psittacines include the well-known Cockatiel and Budgerigar and quite a few lesser knowns as well which are more the preserve of

PARROTS

the experienced breeder. The Red-rumped Parakeet is one which is suitable for the less experienced, being a good breeder. Like most parakeets, breeding pairs should be housed separately from other parakeets, although many do not object to the presence of smaller birds such as finches.

LOVEBIRDS
Of the nine species of African lovebirds six are illustrated and discussed individually. It is a well defined genus, consisting of attractively colored, small-bodied *true* parrots, noted for their friendly disposition towards each other, even whilst breeding. Splendid birds for both the inexperienced and the specialist color breeder, the neotropical parrotlets are often regarded as counterparts to the lovebirds.

LORIES & LORIKEETS (Brush-tongued parrots)
This group of over 50 idiosyncratic parrots have nectar or, more accurately, softbilled diets as their main distinguishing feature. They are totally Australasian in the wild and among the most visually striking of all parrots – a lory or lorikeet would nicely fit the bill as a typical tropical bird. Despite their rather specialized diet, they make good avicultural subjects – more suited to outdoor aviaries than internal cages on account of their liquid and messy droppings, which are expelled with considerable force! No parrot-lover should be discouraged from keeping these friendly, playful and amusing birds providing that a suitable well-sheltered aviary is available.

The diets for nectar-feeding parrots, given they are *different*, are amongst the easiest to provide and afford scope for infinite variation and experimentation. There are few hard and fast rules as they seem to thrive on just about any combination of fruit, honey and the concentrated, powdered invalid or baby foods which can be bought at any chemist, grocer or supermarket. A liquidiser is very useful as it enables you to mix up all sorts of highly nutritious and tasty meals with the minimum of fuss. You need not worry too much about the strength of the prepared liquid mixture, since the stronger it is the less the birds will take, and it requires only a little experimentation to discover the correct proportions to last the birds from one meal to the next. It is probably best to mix two a day – morning and evening – especially during the long, hot summer

LORIES AND LORIKEETS

Nesting receptacles suitable for most medium to large parrots.

days. In the winter, a warm meal in the evening is beneficial, so lukewarm water may be used for mixing. Fresh fruit can be supplied separately and/or liquidized into the meal. As a rough guide, a pair of lories' daily diet might be: 2 dessertspoons of a complete powdered invalid food, 1 of baby food, 2 of honey, $\frac{1}{4}$ orange and $\frac{1}{4}$ apple to about $\frac{1}{2}$ l ($\frac{3}{4}$ pt) of water. I have tried literally hundreds of variations without noticeable effect. Some books give the dangerous direction to feed only fruit and seeds to these brush-tongued parrots; this is bad advice, although lorikeets do enjoy a certain amount of sunflower seed and millet etc.

Deep nesting-boxes must be provided all-year-round, as they should with most parrots; they will be used for roosting if not breeding, and go a long way to counteracting even the coldest of nights. I have never found *Trichoglossus* or *Lorius* susceptible to cold weather, providing they have the facilities outlined here, and have even known them breed in the depths of winter. But some do unfortunately foul the boxes, necessitating periodic cleaning and renewing of the sawdust and shavings in the base.

161

PARROTS

Outstanding as aviary birds are the Chattering Lory and the varied races of the Rainbow Lorikeet.

OLD-WORLD PARAKEETS

Contained within this category are both familiar and unfamiliar avicultural birds — all of the genus *Psittacula*. They are ring-necked, long-tailed parakeets mainly from the dense forests of the Indian subcontinent. The Indian Ringnecked is the most frequently kept of all parakeets, and one of the most popular of all parrots; it is a subspecies of the African Ringnecked or Rose-ringed Parakeet — another familiar aviary bird but one which lacks the variety of color mutations displayed in the Indian race. The *Psittacula* parakeets do not mature for three years, and this discourages some breeders; they are quarrelsome early in the breeding season and should be housed in separate pairs. Possibly the Indian Ringnecked and Malabar parakeets are the most compatible. They all require similar management.

NEW-WORLD PARROTS

Macaws. The largest of all parrots and very popular incumbents of most zoos and bird gardens, the macaws are long-tailed, vividly colored birds, whose center of distribution is the Amazon Basin. Although they are kept in private homes their harsh, ear-piercing screams do not make them very suitable as house birds, and their very hugeness demands much space in which to move about. It must be acknowledged, however, that a great many are kept singly as pets on T-stands, and by all outward appearances very successfully. There can be no denying, though, that macaws are seen at their best in flight, and are thus to be seen in an increasing number of zoos. Failing these facilities, macaws may be kept full-winged in spacious aviaries or, if you are brave and experienced, feather-clipped, at semi-liberty on a dead tree or something similar — where they will clamber about, performing various amusing acrobatics. Feather-clipping Macaws demands two people: even if tame, macaws resent being manhandled, and can easily bite through the strongest gauntlets. So it is not a task to be undertaken lightly or by anyone who has not actually seen it performed.

Macaws are very tame (if they have been brought up correctly) and may enjoy being handled gently by their owners. They are not susceptible to cold once acclimatized but do not enjoy it when accompanied by wind and rain, and so must be provided with sturdy, adequate shelters in which their food of seeds, fruit and nuts can be placed. Macaws take a long time to mature, and even then their breeding is still very much a matter of random selection. It is not surprising that most captive macaws live unreproductive lives, but a surprising number of hybrids have been produced. Great trouble ought to be taken to provide the correct environment: if possible, a group of macaws should be housed together so that compatibility of the sexes is optimized. Unfortunately, their initial high cost prohibits such management to most people, and if this is so, it is best to go, albeit reluctantly for some of the smaller and cheaper psittacines (see below).

Neo-tropical parakeets and parrotlets. South American parakeets are often called conures and the two terms are synonymous. The parrotlets are the smallest neo-tropical psittacines, and consist of two (sometimes three) genera, of which *Forpus* is well-known. The seven species of *Brotogeris* parakeets, equally well-known, come scientifically within the parrotlet group, and are dimensionally on a par with them. Unlike *Forpus*, those of the *Touit* genus are virtually unknown to aviculture. *Brotogeris* parakeets are very popular in North America as pets, and also present a challenge to breeders, since past records leave much to be desired.

Conures fall into two main genera: *Aratinga* and *Pyrrhura*. They have loud, harsh voices but their intelligent and pleasing dispositions help to compensate for this disadvantage. Ideal as outside aviary birds: they are hardy, less expensive than macaws, very sociable with members of their own genus, and should breed well on the colony system. Some, especially the *Aratingas*, are conservative in taste but they all eat much fruit and should be offered an extremely varied diet.

Of the remaining parakeets, those of the *Bolborhynchus* genus are mostly little known to aviculture. They are only slightly larger than the parrotlets, and the Sierra and Lineolated species are the only two at all familiar. The monotypic Quaker Parakeet which is unusual in the parrot family in that it builds a large nest, also comes within this section.

Amazons and other small neotropical parrots. Included here, for convenience, with the large

PARROTS

Amazona genus are various other small true parrots, such as the two species of popular and charming caiques — the Black-headed and White-bellied — which are, according to the authority Rosemary Low, among the most sociable of all parrots. There are additional races of these two species (such as the Pallid, which is the best known) but, unfortunately, none is a reliable breeder. The Red-capped Parrot *Pionopsitta pileata* is the only member of that genus encountered in captivity on the eastern side of the Atlantic, and its appearance seems highly irregular even so. Similarly, with parrots of the *Pionus* genus, only one, the Blue-headed Parrot, is frequently kept and bred in Europe, which is a pity because by all accounts they are ideal as pets, and also offer much scope in aviaries. Rosemary Low affirms them to be the most neglected of all neo-tropical parrots.

And so on to the famous Amazon parrots, which, with the exception of the African Gray, are the best known of all short-tailed true parrots. Argument about the number of species in this genus will doubtless continue for a long time: some believe there to be only about 20, while Gruson (1976) lists 27. However many are eventually decided upon, the fact remains that within their number is a wide variety of essentially different birds. Some are suitable as pets while others are not, and for many reasons, the ownership of an Amazon is not to be undertaken lightly. I can do no better here than quote directly from Rosemary Low's valuable book *The Parrots of South America*: (Amazon parrots are) "[a]ffectionate, unreliable, intelligent, demanding, mischievous, strong-willed, noisy, even dangerous." And that comes from a self-confessed parrot addict! She is quite right, of course, and "noisy" in itself does not fully convey the considerable anti-social effect their regular screaming can have both on your own nerves and those of any close and not so close neighbors! The "unreliable" and "dangerous" tags owe their existence mostly to the very protective behavior many Amazons display when one enters their aviaries at breeding time. They are also prone to bite viciously when handled and can indeed be downright dangerous to a child. A beginner would be well advised to seek experience with one or more of the smaller species such as the *Brotogeris* and *Pionus* (see above). But it would be very inaccurate to imply that they are totally unsuited to captivity — were that true, their

Parrots and other exotic birds were originally brought to Europe by sailors returning from voyages to exotic lands. They quickly became popular at home, and until recently many parrots arrived by similar means, although quarantine restrictions now often make such casual importations illegal.

popularity would not be nearly so evident. As it is, there are a great many highly contented Amazons in foreign lands and probably nearly as many highly contented owners. Without much doubt, the Yellow-fronted Amazon is by far the most suitable species on most counts. This species was the first to be bred in England, as recently as 1967. Today as more emphasis is placed on breeding, there is no reason why Amazons should not be bred in ever-increasing numbers. But beware of their fearless aggression at such times.

PARROTS

Great White Cockatoo *Cacatua alba*. White-crested or Umbrella Cockatoo.

One of the biggest cockatoos; the female can be identified by her brown irides. Because it makes such a splendid pet, moving slowly and deliberately, and talking well, it has rarely had the chance to capitalize on its enormous breeding potential. All cockatoos are extremely destructive to woodwork, so nestboxes have to be very sturdy and/or renewed regularly.

Moluccan Cockatoo *Cacatua moluccensis*. Salmon-crested or Rose-crested Cockatoo.

Very similar in most respects to the Great White: an equally good pet but some specimens indulge in habitual screaming which cannot be tolerated indoors. The proper place for all captive cockatoos is mated in large aviaries or even at partial liberty.

Roseate Cockatoo *Eolophus roseicapillus*. Galah; Rose-breasted Cockatoo.

Rather smaller, the Galah is especialy suited to aviary life as it is a proven breeder. It does not make such a good pet as the Moluccan unless obtained when very young. The female can be recognized by her paler eye color.

Leadbeater's Cockatoo *Cacatua leadbeateri*. Major Mitchell's or Pink Cockatoo.

Active, with good breeding potential, this attractive species is similar to the Roseate in most ways. It is bred occasionally when 3 or 4 eggs are laid, incubation is shared and the young, as is common with parrots, take a very long time to mature.

Greater Sulphur-crested Cockatoo *Cacatua galerita*.

Its management needs to be the same as the Great White's, but this species has a much better breeding record, and so should be regarded as aviary breeding stock and not as a pet. Incidentally, teased pets forget their imposed domesticity and become spiteful. The Lesser Sulphur-crested Cockatoo *C. sulphurea*, a slightly smaller bird, is another commonly kept species – popular with children and adults alike.

Palm Cockatoo *Probosciger aterrimus*. Great Black Cockatoo.

A marvellous and spectacular bird – the largest of all cockatoos. Unfortunately rare and expensive, and so should never be kept as a pet despite the fact that it

1 *Cacatua (Kakatoe) alba* 18–18½ in/ 455–470 mm N and C Moluccas
2 *C. (Kakatoe) moluccensis* 20–21 in/ 510–535 mm S Moluccas
3 *Eolophus roseicapillus* 13½–14 in/ 345–355 mm Interior of Australia
4 *C. (Kakatoe) leadbeateri* 13½–16¼ in/ 345–415 mm ♀ has paler eyes Interior of Australia except NE, E and extreme SW regions
5 *C. (Kakatoe) galerita* 18–20 in/ 455–510 mm ♀ has paler eyes N and E Australia; New Guinea and adjacent islands
6 *Probosciger aterrimus* 23–24 in/ 585–610 mm ♀ has smaller upper mandible New Guinea and some adjacent islands; Cape York peninsular in N Australia

PARROTS

makes a good one – not being nearly as ferocious as it looks. Rarely, if ever, bred in captivity; however, all cockatoos should be supplied with deep nesting receptacles with layered rotten wood and peat etc.

Eclectus Parrot *Eclectus roratus.* Temple Parrot.
Possibly the most awe-inspiring of all true parrots, and unusual in that the female is even more striking than the male. The Eclectus is expensive and rightly the province of the dedicated breeder; but it is not difficult to keep and breed once mature and established. Treatment is very similar to that outlined for the cockatoos.

Australian King Parakeet *Alisterus scapularis.* King or Red Lory.
Despite its old-fashioned alternative names, this bird is *not* a nectar-feeder but a conventional seed-nut-and-fruit-eating parrot – all of which should be supplied daily, together with maize and greenstuff. It is expensive but long-lived, hardy but a slow-breeder; and needs housing in a spacious quiet flight with a choice of large, deep nesting boxes.

Crimson-winged Parakeet *Aprosmictus erythropterus.* Red-winged Parrot.
Rarely available and expensive outside Australia, this parakeet needs a large flight to itself with plenty of "furniture," an *extremely* varied diet which includes fresh twigs, fruit and greenstuff. The males can be very aggressive but breeding results are occasionally announced.

Adelaide Rosella/Parakeet *Platycercus adelaide.*
This first-mentioned of the rosella-broadtails is considered by some to be a race of the next species. Either theory could be correct, or it could even prove to be a natural hybrid of the Pennant's and Yellow Rosellas. However, it remains an extremely desirable bird which needs the same care as those discussed on the following page.

Pennant's Rosella/Parakeet *Platycercus elegans.* Crimson Rosella.
A reasonably free-breeding species which remains expensive to foreign aviculturists. It is a delightful aviary bird and fairly sociable, for a parakeet. Treatment as for other rosella-broadtails.

1 *Eclectus roratus*
13–13¾ in/
330–350 mm Different races occur throughout the Moluccas, New Guinea (except central highlands), surrounding islands, Bismarck Archipelago and the Solomon Islands; one race (*cornelia*) from Sumba in the Lesser Sundas, another (*macgillivrayi*) from extreme NE Australia
2 *Alisterus scapularis*
15¼–17¾ in/
400–450 mm ♀ mainly green, only lower belly red; some blue on rump and blackish bill Coastal regions of E Australia from N Queensland to S Victoria
3 *Aprosmictus erythropterus*
11¾–12¾ in/
300–325 mm On ♀ green replaces black, red on shoulders and blue on rump reduced N and NE Australia and S New Guinea
4 *Platycercus adelaide*
14¼–15 in/
360–380 mm Plumage variable ♀ can sometimes be told by smaller head Around Adelaide, South Australia and to the north
5 *P. elegans*
14¼–15 in/
360–380 mm ♀ can sometimes be told by smaller head SE Australia

PARROTS

Stanley Rosella/Parakeet *Platycercus icterotis*. Western or Yellow-cheeked Rosella.

Housing and management for this slightly smaller species is just the same as for other rosellas but it is less plentiful despite being freely bred. Large numbers of these double-brooded parakeets can be produced providing they are housed on their own and interference is kept to a minimum. Some rosellas mix well with other birds if not breeding.

Eastern Rosella *Platycercus eximius*. Common, Red or, just, Rosella; Rose Hill Parrot.

The most accessible of all rosellas, and a firm favorite of many collections. It needs the usual varied diet, and once it has started to breed, does so quite reliably (if not frightened). The young can be reared on seed, soaked bread, hard-boiled egg, greenstuff, fruit and fresh fruit- and privet-twigs; they are liable to be extremely nervous on leaving the nest but soon settle down. The Golden-mantled Rosella *P.e. ceciliae* probably does not exist in its wild form in captivity outside Australia because it has been so inter-bred with the Eastern. It is almost certainly a true subspecies and not a variety of the Eastern, and its absence now in aviaries elsewhere illustrates the dangers of hybridizing and mixing blood.

Yellow Rosella *Platycercus flaveolus*. Yellow-rumped Parakeet.

Less frequently seen, the Yellow Rosella is probably an equally good breeder, and requires the same management as its relatives.

Mealy Rosella *Platycercus adscitus palliceps*. Blue Rosella: a subspecies of the Pale-headed Rosella.

Another entirely hardy, free-breeding bird which requires the usual treatment. It is often difficult to split the sexes when buying a pair of these rosellas, and this should be borne in mind by both the purchaser and vendor, and if possible an agreement of exchange agreed upon should the sexes prove to be the same.

1 *Platycercus icterotis*
9¾–11 in/
250–280 mm
SW Australia. ♀ duller, some green on crown and underparts.
2 *P. eximius* (*ceciliae* illustrated) 11–11¾ in/
280–300 mm ♀ duller
SE Australia,
Tasmania; introduced
New Zealand
3 *P. flaveolus*
13–14¼ in/330–360 mm
Riversides of SE
Australia
4 *P. adscitus palliceps*
11¾ in/300 mm
E Queensland and NE
New South Wales

2 ♂

1 ♂

3

4

PARROTS

Rock Pebbler Parakeet *Polytelis anthopeplus*. Regent Parrot; Rock Peplar or Black-tailed Parakeet.
A firmly established aviary breeding species which has the attributes of being hardy, a good mixer and parent. It eats the usual seeds (including hemp), fruit and greenstuff; and nests in a deep nestbox which should have a layer of rotten wood in the base. Five or six eggs are laid in each annual clutch which hatch in about 3 weeks; the young fly in another 5.

Princess of Wales Parakeet *Polytelis alexandrae*. Princess Alexandra, Princess or Queen Alexandra Parakeet.
Very similar in most respects to the Rock Pebbler with regard to its captive management and breeding particulars. In-breeding is a real problem with much Australian stock abroad, and care must be taken to avoid it; in this instance, it has resulted in a quite unwarranted reputation of delicacy.

Barraband Parakeet *Polytelis swainsonii*. Superb Parrot.
Certainly superb in its coloring, the Barraband is also a good, hardy aviary breeding bird which should be left outside all year round provided with adequate shelter to enable it to nest in northern winters.

Red-rumped Parakeet *Psephotus haematonotus*. Redrump; Red-backed or Blood-rumped Parakeet.
A free-breeding, virtually domesticated bird which mixes well with most other birds except, as is usual, those of its own kind. An attractive dilute Yellow mutation — in fact a pastel form of the normal Redrump — is now well established. It usually proves to be an industrious nester and exemplary parent, which will lay several clutches of 4 eggs each year if a nestbox correctly primed with rotten wood is available; breeding should be discouraged in the winter. As with most parrots, the young must be removed after a few weeks if they are not to be molested by their fathers.

Mulga Parakeet *Psephotus varius*. Many-colored or Varied Parakeet.
Not so frequently seen as the next species, the Mulga Parakeet nevertheless requires the same diet of small seeds (eg. canary, millet), greenstuff and fruit etc. It is more nervous than the Redrump until established, whereupon it becomes quite hardy but obviously needs a frost- and draught-proof, dry, shelter.

1 *Polytelis anthopeplus*
15–15¾ in/380–400 mm
♀ dull green with bright yellow shoulders Two populations: E of Adelaide and SE Australia

2 *P. alexandrae*
15–17⅜ in/380–450 mm ♀ has blue parts duller Interior of W and C Australia

3 *P. swainsonii*
13¾–15¾ in/350–400 mm Riversides of SE Australia

4 *P. haematonotus*
9¾–10⅜ in/250–270 mm ♀ lacks red rump SE Australia

5 *Psephotus varius*
10⅝–11¾ in/270–300 mm Southern half of Australia's interior

1♂

2♂

3♂

♀

4

♂

♂

5

♀

PARROTS

Cockatiel *Nymphicus hollandicus.*
The monotypic Cockatiel with its wonderful temperament, gentle nature, quiet ways and hardiness is the
best choice of all for the young parakeet breeder. It can
be bred, like the Budgerigar, on the colony system and
mixes well with other species. It is easy to feed on the
usual mixed seeds and greenstuff; most psittacines are
immensely fond of privet sprays, and the Cockatiel is no
exception. There are numerous mutations available.

*Grass Parakeets are popular, dainty and colorful birds,
many of which are at least double-brooded and quite
prolific, laying on average 5 eggs (incubation takes less
than 3 weeks). They are good aviary birds which in
some cases have been virtually domesticated. They
need a quality diet of small seeds, fruit and fresh green
twigs. They are quite hardy but need dry shelters in the
winter. Many are noticeably crepuscular in their habits.
The Elegant Grass Parakeet Neophema elegans (not
illustrated) is unusually colored in yellowish olive-
green with pure yellow underparts; the frontal band
and leading edge of the wings are a mixture of deep and
light blues; the tail is yellow excepting the two
elongated central feathers which are blue-green.*

Bourke's Parakeet/Parrot *Neophema bourkii.* Blue-
vented or Pink-bellied Parakeet.
Probably the most familiar and widely bred of the
grass parakeets, and the most suitable for those with
restricted space.

Splendid Grass Parakeet *Neophema splendida.* Scarlet-chested (-breasted) Parakeet.
Astonishingly beautiful, this species is also a free-
breeder and a reliable parent, but highly priced.

Turquoisine Grass Parakeet *Neophema pulchella.*
Chestnut-shouldered or Beautiful Parakeet.
Another delightful species which is a consistently
reliable breeder but, as with the rosella-broadtails, great
care must be taken to avoid in-breeding.

Blue-winged Grass Parakeet *Neophema chrysostoma.*
Blue-banded Grass Parakeet.
A free-breeding species which mixes well with birds
of many sorts and tolerates its own kind better than
many. It is a model parent and often tends its young
long after they have left the nest.

1 *Nymphicus
hollandicus*
$9\frac{3}{4}$–$12\frac{1}{2}$ in/
250–320 mm
Throughout most of
Australia's interior
2 *Neophema bourkii*
$7\frac{1}{2}$–9 in/190–230 mm
♀ slightly duller, blue
on forehead is often
reduced Central
Australia
3 *N. splendida*
$7\frac{1}{2}$–$8\frac{3}{4}$ in/
190–220 mm ♀ has
blue lores, green
breast; blue duller on
face, may be missing
on wing Interior of SW
and C Australia, east to
NSW border
4 *N. pulchella* $7\frac{3}{4}$–8 in/
195–205 mm E NSW,
SE Queensland, N
Victoria
5 *N. chrysostoma*
$7\frac{3}{4}$–$8\frac{1}{2}$ in/
195–215 mm ♀ duller,
smaller frontal band,
underparts greener SE
Australia, Tasmania
and some Bass Strait
islands

PARROTS

Lovebirds, short-tailed true parrots from the Ethiopian region, are excellent cage and aviary birds, of which several mutations exist. They are free-breeding, hardy and cheerful, apart from being visually and behaviorally most appealing. Conventional parrot care is sufficient, and the smaller species can breed well housed as a colony if the correct sex-ratio is maintained. They carry fresh strips of willow, privet etc into their nests, reputedly to keep them moist, but there have been successful breedings in very dry conditions too.

Masked Lovebird *Agapornis personata*.
Possibly the best known and most widely bred of all lovebirds. Two-chamber nestboxes (which become crammed with slivers of wood) allow the hen to begin her second clutch while the young from the first are still being reared.

Fischer's Lovebird *Agapornis fischeri*.
Like the previous species, the Fischer's is a typical lovebird — suitable for beginners, and, therefore, very popular. Young lovebirds need a rich seed-mixture, plenty of fruit and greenstuff and perhaps a little softfood.

Peach-faced Lovebird *Agapornis roseicollis*. Rosy-faced Lovebird.
Another free-breeding bird, but it is larger and more pugnacious, for which reason it ought to be housed in separate pairs. To collect nesting material, these lovebirds insert it into their feathers and clamber awkwardly to their nestbox; so aviaries should be well supplied with branches — flight is not so important. A blue mutation occurs which is most attractive.

Abyssinian Lovebird *Agapornis taranta*. Black-winged Lovebird.
Quieter than many and so a good choice· for a household situation. It needs standard care, and should breed when established. As always with lovebirds, provide a surplus of nesting-boxes.

Red-faced Lovebird *Agapornis pullaria*.
All lovebirds can remain outside in the winter but a good shed is needed so that the nestboxes can be removed to discourage out-of-season breeding. However, in this case, simulated termite hills made of compacted peat or loam, and not nestboxes, should be available to encourage captive-breeding.

1 *Agapornis personata* 5¾ in/145 mm NE Tanzania, possibly (introduced?) S Kenya
2 *A. fischeri* 5½–6 in/ 140–150 mm N Tanzania, possibly (introduced?) S Kenya
3 *A. roseicollis* 6 in/ 150 mm SW Africa, east to Victoria Falls
4 *A. taranta* 6½ in/ 165 mm Highlands of Ethiopia
5 *A. pullaria* 6 in/ 150 mm ♀ has a more orange face, underwing coverts green instead of black
A belt from the coast of W Africa between parallels 0° and 10° east to S Sudan and Lake Turkana (formerly Rudolf)

1

2

3

♀

4

♂

5 ♂

177

PARROTS

Madagascar Lovebird *Agapornis cana*. Gray-headed Lovebird.

Immediately identified by its pale head, this species looks dissimilar to the mainland African lovebirds on the preceding plate, and is seen less frequently than most. However, it needs the same form of management.

Celestial Parrotlet *Forpus coelestis*. Pacific or Lesson's Parrotlet.

Parrotlets are good aviary birds, but small cages — wherein they often become very quarrelsome — should be avoided. They are perfectly hardy if given a good shelter. and breed reliably but some, especially this species, display cannibalistic tendencies towards their young; so it helps if disturbance is kept to a minimum.

Turquoise-rumped Parrotlet *Forpus cyanopygius*. Blue-rumped or Mexican Parrotlet.

A lively bird which needs company and plenty of exercise if it is not to become lethargic. All parrotlets should be offered a varied seed, fruit and greenstuff

1 *Agapornis cana*
5–6 in/125–150 mm
Madagascar and surrounding islands
2 *Forpus coelestis*
5 in/125 mm Pacific coast from Ecuador south to N Peru
3 *F. cyanopygius*
5–5½ in/125–140 mm
♀ has blue replaced by yellowish-green NW Mexico; Tres Marías Islands

4 *Loriculus galgulus*
4¾ in/120 mm ♀
duller, lacks red throat
and yellow on lower
back, blue crown and
yellow mantle barely
visible Malay
Peninsular; Sumatra
and adjacent small
islands (not Java);
Borneo

5 *L. vernalis* 5 in/
125 mm ♀ slightly
duller Coastal belt
from SW India round
to Burma and then
across Thailand to E
Vietnam; Andaman
Islands

diet, although difficulty is often encountered in getting them to accept strange items. And they are prone to nervousness until established.

Blue-crowned Hanging Parrot *Loriculus galgulus*.

This, and the next species, are members of a small group of diminutive parrots which spend much of their time hanging upside down. They are tricky to house because of their extremely messy droppings (due to a nectivorous and frugivorous diet), which tends to make them unsuitable for indoor sites. Ideally, they need well-planted outside aviaries (which, if roomy enough, can be shared with small birds of all sorts) but provision must be made for extra warmth in cold weather, since they lack the toughness of the lories and lorikeets.

Vernal Hanging Parrot *Loriculus vernalis*.

An active, lively and delightful aviary bird which should breed well on the lovebird principle. Similarly, hanging parrots are true parrots, to which climbing is more important than flying.

3 ♂

4 ♂

5 ♂

179

PARROTS

Chattering Lory *Lorius garrulus*.
The most familiar lory to most aviculturists, the Chattering is a marvellous aviary inhabitant. Most lories, it seems to me, develop quite their own personalities. I once kept a male Chattering Lory who was deeply attached to a female Jobi Lory *L. lory jobiensis* (a subspecies of the Black-capped Lory); she laid many eggs, and they reared one youngster but the other chicks vanished mysteriously when a few weeks old, and this spotlights a common psittacine breeding problem, that of proven or suspected cannibalism.

Purple-naped Lory *Lorius domicellus*.
In some ways it is unfortunate that the liquid nature of these bird's droppings and their piercing voices make them totally unsuitable as cagebirds, but in other ways it is to their advantage since the best alternative is to keep them paired in outside aviaries where they will likely breed. This species, like the others, is hardy once acclimatized, surprisingly easy to keep, and visually and behaviorally most attractive. They get up to many antics — enjoy "dancing" on springy twigs and even swinging on ropes like monkeys.

Lorikeets.
It is invidious really to have to select one or two of these astonishing birds, but it is necessary for reasons of space and the fact that lorikeets still have a mistaken reputation for being delicate and difficult (two over-used expressions which often serve to hide aviculturists' own short-comings). As with the lories, they should be regarded as aviary birds — where they will have full rein to indulge their acrobatic talents and display their amusing and friendly personalities.

Ornate (Ornamented) Lorikeet *Trichoglossus ornatus*. Rainbow Lorikeet *Trichoglossus haematodus.* Swainson's, Blue Mountain, Blue-bellied Lorikeet etc.
There are many similarly patterned races of the Rainbow Lorikeet — all of which require the same treatment. In cold or wet weather they, and other acclimatized brush-tongued parrots, need to have access to a dry shed or "nestbox;" but it is not wise to let them nest during the winter months, which many will, given the chance, in the northern hemisphere. The Ornate Lorikeet has been bred several times in captivity. All Lorikeets will breed given a fair chance.

1 *Lorius garrulus* (*flavopalliatus* illustrated) 11½–12 in/ 290–305 mm N Moluccas
2 *L. domicellus* 11 in/ 280 mm S Moluccas – Ceram and Amboina; introduced Buru
3 *Trichoglossus ornatus* 9½–10 in/ 240–255 mm Celebes and major offshore islands
4 *T. haematodus* (*moluccanus* illustrated) 10–10½ in/ 255–265 mm Bali east through Indonesia and New Guinea to New Caledonia and Loyalty Islands; coastal regions of Australia from N Western Australia east round to Eyre Peninsula; Tasmania
5 *T. h. capistratus* (Edwards's Lorikeet)

PARROTS

*These principally Asian parakeets are good, hardy
aviary birds which can occasionally be mixed with
finches. They take 3 years to mature and breed but will
then do so quite freely; they make good parents and
can rear up to six young per clutch after an incubation
of over 3 weeks.*

Alexandrine Parakeet *Psittacula eupatria.* Alexandrine
Ringneck; Large Indian Parakeet.
A large parakeet which is best housed on its own in a
lengthy spacious flight although I have not always
found it as intolerant of other birds as its reputation
implies. It is found in different mutations as well as the
several bona-fide subspecies.

Plum-headed Parakeet *Psittacula cyanocephala.* Includes the smaller Blossom-headed Parakeet *P.c.
rosa* which can be further identified by its paler head.
All these parakeets should receive the same type of
mixed seeds, supplemented by green food, fruit and
germinated grain. Nestboxes should be of the conventional sort and interference kept to a strict minimum. A rearing food of brown bread soaked in milk
and mixed with honey is highly successful.

Moustached Parakeet *Psittacula alexandri.* Banded or
Red-breasted Parakeet.
A slightly larger species which needs the same
treatment as other parakeets and makes one of the best
pets since it is always fairly quiet. But at breeding time it
becomes more wary and even furtive.

Slaty-headed Parakeet *Psittacula himalayana.*
This and the similar, but slightly larger, Derbian or Lord
Derby's Parakeet *P. derbiana* need exactly the same
treatment as the others. They are beautifully colored
but rather more scarce than the other *Psittaculae*
shown.

Ring-necked Parakeet *Psittacula krameri.* Rose-ringed, Green or Bengal Parakeet, which includes two
well-known subspecies: the African *P.k. krameri* and
the illustrated Indian *P.k. manillensis.*
The best known of all parakeets, since it is not so large
as the Alexandrine it is more suitable for those with
restricted accommodation. It has a quiet demeanor, but
it is still wise to accommodate it apart from other
parakeets if breeding is the intention.

1 *Psittacula eupatria*
20–23½ in/
510–595 mm E
Afghanistan and West
Pakistan throughout
India to Indochina; Sri
Lanka; Andaman Is.
2 *P. cyanocephala*
13–14½ in/
330–370 mm India, N
West Pakistan, Nepal
and Bangladesh; Sri
Lanka
3 *P. alexandri (fasciata*
illustrated) 13–15 in/
330–380 mm ♀ has
bill wholly black N
India to Indochina,
north to S China and
south to Tenasserim
(the nominate race
occurs in Java and
Bali)
4 *P. himalayana*
15½–16 in/
395–405 mm A belt
from E Afghanistan to
the Gulf of Tangking
5 *P. krameri*
15–16½ in/
380–420 mm A belt
from Senegal across
Africa to Ethiopia;
India, W Burma

OLD WORLD PARAKEETS

PARROTS

African Gray Parrot *Psittacus erithacus*.

There is no denying the African Gray makes an excellent pet: intelligent, amusing and a first-rate talker, but how sad that more people do not make an effort to obtain a true pair (admittedly not always easy) and house them in a quiet aviary with a very deep nestbox or hollow tree-trunk. This is an exceptionally long-lived species, so there is plenty of time in which to find and establish a compatible pair. An aviary-bred youngster makes a better pet, and does not represent a drain on wild resources.

Meyer's Parrot *Poicephalus meyeri*. Brown Parrot.

This species can also make a delightful pet although it lacks the African Gray's phenomenal powers of mimicry. If given a sound aviary; a solid, well-primed nestbox and a varied seed and fruit diet, a well-mated pair can produce many healthy youngsters.

Senegal Parrot *Poicephalus senegalus*. Includes the nominate Yellow-bellied race *P.s. senegalus*. There are also two less-frequently-imported races.

They are generally reputed to be docile and friendly, although I have known some great biters and escapers! Provided they are allowed to settle down, true pairs of all forms should eventually breed well.

Blue-headed Parrot *Pionus menstruus*.

Members of the charming S. American genus *Pionus*, of which the Blue-headed and Maximilian's Parrot *P. maximiliani* are the most frequently seen, often take a while to settle down after importation. The Blue-headed needs similar care to the Amazons (see pages 163–4), likewise it makes an excellent pet if hand-reared — a fact which is largely responsible for the poor breeding histories of all *Pionus* parrots.

Red-capped Parrot *Pinopsitta pileata*.

Pileated Parrot.

This is a remarkably friendly and sociable bird, both towards its owner and its own kind. It has one of the most attractive reputations of all parrots: indulging in much mutual preening and rarely attempting to bite, even when handled. It requires only a small aviary, in which breeding might well be stimulated if *more* than a single pair are housed together.

1 *Psittacus erithacus*
13–13¾ in/
330–350 mm
Equatorial Africa from Atlantic coast and Gulf of Guinea islands to around Lake Victoria
2 *Poicephalus meyeri*
8¼–10 in/
210–255 mm Much of Africa's interior south of the Sahara
3 *P. senegalus*
9–10½ in/
230–265 mm A belt from Senegal east to Chad avoiding Gulf of Guinea north coast
4 *Pionus menstruus*
11–11½ in/
280–290 mm S Costa Rica to NW Peru, N Bolivia and C and E Brazil; Trinidad; avoids the high Andes
5 *Pinopsitta pileata*
8¾–9 in/220–230 mm
SE Brazil, SE Paraguay, NE Argentina

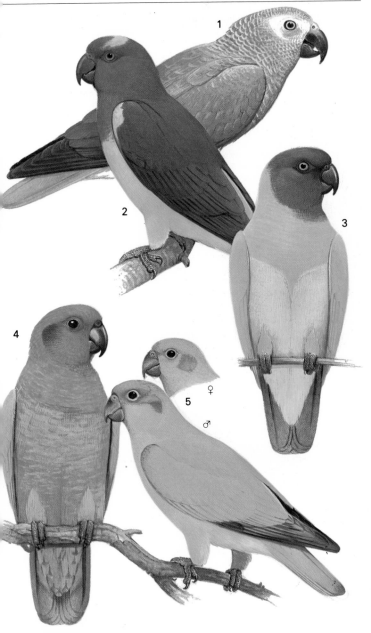

PARROTS

Hyacinthine Macaw *Anodorhynchus hyacinthinus*.
This magnificent bird is normally very gentle despite its
formidable beak. The few that do come on the market
are extremely expensive. It is rarely bred, and for the
best chance, the grounds of a large estate are needed,
where it may be kept at liberty.

Blue-and-Yellow Macaw *Ara ararauna*. Blue-and-
Gold or Yellow-breasted Macaw.
The most widely kept macaw; it has bred many times
and has hybridized with the following two species. All
macaws need a good varied diet, comprising seeds,
nuts, fruit and greenstuff. Many parrots, and in particular macaws, enjoy, and benefit from, a little meat occasionally.

Scarlet Macaw *Ara macao*. Red-and-Yellow or Red-
breasted Macaw.
After the Blue-and-Yellow, this is the best known of
the macaws. Because its temperament is less reliable it
is not so popular as a pet. It has bred many times and
apart from the preceding species, it has also hybridized
with the following two. It is particularly destructive to
woodwork, and this must be remembered when
aviaries for macaws are being designed.

Green-winged Macaw *Ara chloroptera*. Crimson,
Maroon, Red-and-Blue or Red-and-Green Macaw.
The Green-winged Macaw, which is sometimes confused with the Scarlet, is less frequently seen than
the other large macaws and is not often kept as a pet. It
is not bred very often but several hybrids have been
produced with the preceding two species. Macaws are
extremely hardy but do not like violent extremes of
weather, and are especially miserable in torrential rain
and direct sunshine. Shelters should be substantial
because they often double as nesting chambers.

Military Macaw *Ara militaris*.
Different races vary slightly in size and color. There is
disagreement whether the Grand Military or Great
Green Macaw *A. ambigua* (840 mm (33 in)) is a
distinct species or subspecies. They are only available
occasionally and bred rarely owing to the fact that few
true pairs are kept together.

1 *Anodorhynchus hyacinthinus* 34–40 in/ 865–1015 mm Brazil
2 *Ara ararauna* 29–35 in/ 735–890 mm N South America north to E Panama; Trinidad
3 *A. macao* 33–38 in/ 840–965 mm N South America north to Mexico; Trinidad
4 *A. chloroptera* 34–38 in/ 865–965 mm N South America north to E Panama
5 *A. militaris* 27–30 in/ 685–760 mm NW South America north to Mexico

PARROTS

Illiger's Macaw *Ara maracana*. Blue-winged Macaw. This "dainty" macaw is imported only infrequently which is a pity because it is a delightful bird in every respect: growing very tame and displaying considerable intelligence. Unfortunately it is very rarely bred, and little is known of its captive behavior.

Chestnut-fronted Macaw *Ara severa*. Severe Macaw. Another parrot which makes a wonderful pet to the detriment of its captive breeding record; however, it has been bred on several occasions, but quite often some misfortune has befallen either parents or chicks. It certainly needs serious attention.

Petz's Conure *Aratinga canicularis*. Half-moon Conure, Orange-fronted Conure or Parakeet.
Extremely popular as a pet in N. America, and rated even higher than the Budgerigar by many. If kept in a conducive environment it can be encouraged to breed, but for some reason such happy events are seldom, if ever, heard of east of the Atlantic. It displays much intelligence and is altogether a desirable subject worthy of a concerted captive-breeding effort.

Jenday Conure *Aratinga jandaya*. Jandaya or Yellow-headed Conure or Parakeet.
Considered by de Schauensee to be a subspecies of the rare and beautiful Sun Conure *A. solstitialis*. It is not exported in large numbers but is still fairly well known; it has bred regularly but is, nevertheless, in need of a sustained effort. All conures require good basic management; their main drawback is their lack of sexual dimorphism, which makes the selection of pairs a chancy matter.

Golden-crowned Conure *Aratinga aurea*. Peach-fronted Parakeet.
Not exported so regularly nowadays, it has never been favored as much in the USA as the next species. It has been bred occasionally and is a good choice for beginners, being typically hardy and very easy to feed — if conservative in taste.

Nanday Conure *Aratinga nenday*. Black-hooded (-masked, -headed) Conure or Parakeet.
For certain obscure reasons, many authors still persist in placing this in a genus (*Nandayus*) of its own. The fact that the Nanday has produced viable fertile hybrids when crossed with the Jenday Conure surely

1 *Ara maracana* 16½–17 in/ 420–430 mm Brazil south through Paraguay to NE Argentina
2 *A. severa* 18–20 in/ 455–510 mm E Panama to the Guianas and south through Brazil to N Bolivia
3 *Aratinga canicularis* 9½ in/240 mm Pacific coast of C America from Sinaloa, Mexico to W Costa Rica
4 *A. jandaya* 11½–12 in/ 290–305 mm E Brazil south of the Amazon
5 *A. aurea* 10–10½ in/ 255–265 mm Brazil south of the Amazon east to E Bolivia, N Paraguay and extreme NW Argentina

PARROTS

verifies its *Aratinga* status. In either event it is a regularly available and free-breeding species which requires conventional conure care.

Patagonian Conure *Cyanoliseus patagonus*. Burrowing Parrot. Includes the nominate race (the Lesser) and the Greater *C.p. byroni*.

These are large noisy and showy birds which are only suited to aviaries with much space. It is a communally nesting species which in the wild tunnels into cliffs and banks for as far as 122 cm (4 ft). It has bred in captivity, but needs an exceptionally tough nestbox or tree trunk, otherwise it helps to simulate their natural choice of site.

Quaker Parakeet *Myiopsitta monachus*. Monk or Gray-breasted Parakeet.

Another species best off in a zoo or large bird garden, the Quaker Parakeet is unique in building a large rambling nest. It is a highly adaptable, versatile bird which also makes a good pet but it is *very* destructive, so beware! In suitable localities, it makes an ideal liberty bird (a fact that is often discovered by accident!). There is a blue phase which possibly originated in Holland; a yellow mutant has also been recorded.

Red-bellied Conure *Pyrrhura frontalis*. Scaly-breasted or Maroon-bellied Conure.

The best known of all *Pyrrhura* parrots, this species has a free-breeding reputation. It offers considerable scope, nesting and living quite happily even in a colony; it has much in its favor and deserves an increasing popularity.

Sierra Parakeet *Bolborhynchus aymara*. Aymara or Gray-hooded Parakeet.

It is surprisingly quiet and worth serious consideration for this virtue alone! It has only recently come into prominence and is now earning a free-breeding and adaptable reputation; it often seems to like only sunflower seeds, but other types of food must be persevered with. It roosts all-year-round in its nestbox, as do many parrots.

1 *Aratinga nenday* 11½–13 in/ 290–330 mm SE Bolivia, Mato Grosso, Paraguay, N Argentina *(Text begins previous page.)*
2 *Cyanoliseus patagonus* (*bryoni* illustrated) 17–20 in/ 430–510 mm C Chile; N and C Argentina, occasionally Uruguay
3 *Myiopsitta monachus* 11½ in/ 290 mm C Bolivia; S Brazil south to C and E Argentina
4 *Pyrrhura frontalis* 10–11 in/ 255–280 mm SE Brazil, Uruguay, Paraguay, NE Argentina
5 *Bolborhynchus aymara* 7½–8 in/ 190–205 mm E slopes of Andes from C Bolivia to NW Argentina

PARROTS

Tovi Parakeet *Brotogeris jugularis*. Bee-bee Parrot;
Orange-chinned Parakeet.
This attractive species is suitable both as a pet and an
aviary breeding subject. It is widely available, but is
most popular in the USA. It deserves a wider following
since it is such an adaptable, peaceful species, of free-
breeding inclinations.

Orange-flanked Parakeet *Brotogeris pyrrhopterus*.
Gray-cheeked or Orange-winged Parakeet.
Readily available, it makes an excellent pet when
acquired as a young hand-reared bird. If kept for
breeding, it should be housed on its own. Some
individuals prove timid while others are quite the
opposite. It is a species hard to anticipate.

Tui Parakeet *Brotogeris sanctithomae*.
The Tui Parakeet has a similar demeanor to *B.
pyrrhopterus*, but is possibly a more consistent mixer,
being rather shy. It is regularly available at reasonable
cost and can be acquired as either a pet (preferably
hand-reared) or breeding stock (as which it has no
great reputation but plenty of promise).

Canary-winged Parakeet *Brotogeris versicolorus chirri*.
The also common White-winged race *B.v. versicolorus*
is often mistakenly called the Canary-winged but can
be identified by grayer coloring and a bluish area
around the eyes, apart from paler wings. Reasonably
hardy, as are the other *Brotogeris* species, much of the
above also applies here. Both races are in popular
demand both as gentle pets and serious breeding
stock. This race in particular makes an attractive show
in a lengthy aviary. Rather noisy, though, and not as yet
a really free breeder.

Black-headed Caique *Pionites melanocephala*. Includes the Pallid Caique *P.m. pallida*.
Caiques are small true parrots which need much the
same treatment as the Amazons overleaf, but are less
frequently available and more expensive. They can be
very noisy and inclined to spitefulness. Boiled maize is
highly beneficial, and a nectivorous-type food and
cracked walnuts are eagerly sought by most caiques.

1 *Brotogeris jugularis*
7 in/180 mm SW
Mexico to N Colombia
and N Venezuela
2 *B. pyrrhopterus*
7¾–8¼ in/
195–210 mm Pacific
coast of Ecuador just
into Peru
3 *B. sanctithomae*
(nominate race)
6½–7 in/
165–180 mm
(*takatsukasae* has a
yellow streak beneath
the eye) Amazon Basin
4 *B. versicolorus chirri*
8½–9 in/215–230 mm
S and E Brazil, N and E
Bolivia, Paraguay, N
Argentina
5 *Pionites
melanocephala* 9 in/
230 mm E Venezuela,
the Guianas and N
Brazil west to S
Colombia, E Ecuador
and NE Peru

PARROTS

Blue-fronted Amazon Parrot *Amazona aestiva.* Turquoise-fronted Parrot.
Regularly imported, it would probably make an excellent breeder were it not such a popular talker and comedian; it is to be hoped that more are kept for the former purpose to help atone for the many thousands which have lived unproductive solitary lives — victims of their own engaging personalities. Despite the temptation, a stranger should never attempt to touch an Amazon or any parrot — a good rule of thumb!

Orange-winged Amazon Parrot *Amazona amazonica.*
Frequently confused with the previous species, this smaller bird makes an equally good pet, despite its regular screaming, and frequently suffers the same "fate." Many Amazons eat only sunflower and hemp, but other foods should always be available and fruit, greenstuff and even meat and cheese should be offered *regularly.*

Salvin's Amazon Parrot *Amazona autumnalis salvini.*
The nominate race, the beautifully marked Yellow-cheeked or Red-lored Parrot, is commonest in America, and can be told by its scarlet forehead, lores and lower cheeks; the remainder of the head is mostly lilac except the upper cheek feathers which are orange-yellow with red bases. It is extremely noisy and appears very independently-minded, which on the whole probably makes it a better aviary subject than pet.

Yellow-fronted Amazon Parrot *Amazona ochrocephala.* Yellow-headed or Single Yellow-headed Parrot.
Besides this nominate race and the following two, there is a variety of other races. Rosemary Low probably quite rightly regards this as the best pet Amazon of all. So suitable is it that it is inexcusable that its propagation has been neglected, however it shows signs of much promise.

Panama Yellow-fronted Amazon Parrot *A.o. panamensis.*
Double Yellow-headed Amazon Parrot *A.o. oratrix.*
The second named is also called Levaillant's or Mexican Yellow-headed Amazon. Both these subspecies are well-known in the USA and have bred on several occasions. They are highly regarded as pets, and *A.o. panamensis* is commoner in Europe than even the nominate race.

1 *Amazona aestiva*
14–15 in/
355–380 mm Interior of Brazil south of the Amazon south to Paraguay and N Argentina
2 *A. amazonica*
12–13 in/
305–330 mm Colombia, Venezuela and the Guianas southeast through Brazil, E Ecuador, NE Peru and E Bolivia
3 *A. autumnalis salvini*
13¼–14 in/
335–355 mm Nicaragua to W Colombia and extreme NW Venezuela
4 *A. ochrocephala* (nominate race)
12–15 in/
305–380 mm (many races). C Mexico south to the Amazon and E Peru; Trinidad (ssp. *ochrocephala* occurs in Colombia, Venezuela and the Guianas south to the Amazon)
5 *A. o. panamensis*
12 in/305 mm W Panama to N Colombia
6 *A. o. oratrix* 15 in/
380 mm C Mexico to Belize

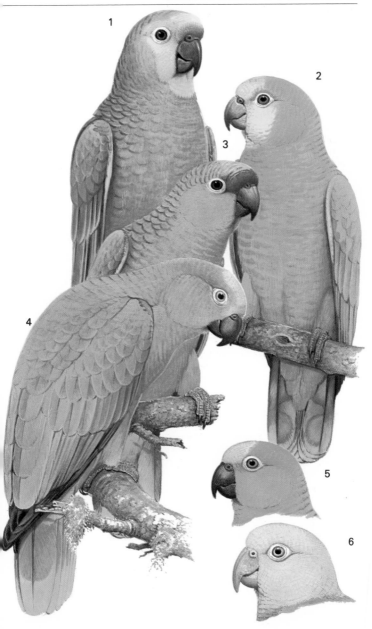

SOFTBILLS

CHAPTER 13: SOFTBILLS

The group of birds which in avicultural jargon is called "softbills" is still considered the least significant, despite its immense visual and scientific appeal. Such an understandable view casts no aspersions on their value as cage and aviary birds but simply on their rather more specialized requirements and supposed more delicate natures. A lot of nonsense is spoken and written about "delicate" and "frail" softbills. There is no such thing as a fragile wild animal — it is a contradiction of terms — all, in the confines of their own worlds, are tough and resilient; they have to be simply to survive. An animal becomes "delicate" only when jumped on from a great height by man or when transferred from its own environment to a strange one with no period of acclimatization.

We need look no further than this very group of birds to see appropriate examples of the inherent toughness of animals: the tiniest and most "delicate" of wrens and hummingbirds can thrive in conditions in which we would be hard pressed to survive one night; it is their world and they are integral parts of it. We have, regrettably, long since ceased to be a part of any natural world, and survive only through the services of technology. Aviculturally, therefore we should regard softbills — itself a pretty vague term — as birds requiring specialized attention. The literal definition of a softbill is usually held to be an avian eater of "soft" foods: this includes insectivores, frugivores, nectivores and invertebrate-feeders. This involves an astonishingly wide range of very different birds — in size, conceivably from cranes and flamingos down to hummingbirds; therefore the term is effectively restricted to cagebirds and further omits such birds as waders.

Typical softbills include tanagers, sunbirds, thrushes, mynahs, chats, flycatchers, toucans, hornbills, hummingbirds and starlings. Diets are a useful guide to categorizing cage and aviary birds, but with softbills they can be used only in the broadest of senses, and we must leave their peculiarities to the species-by-species notes. However, there is the question of live insect cultures, which are an invaluable aid to the successful maintenance of many softbilled birds.

The commonest cultures concern fruit-flies (*Drosophila*) and mealworms. Fruit-flies are by far the easiest to breed, requiring only a minimum of attention. If, in summer, a few over-ripe bananas are placed in a

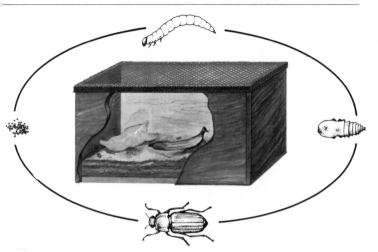

Mealworms are a staple food for many softbills. They can be bred quite easily in a home-made box as shown. The life cycle is indicated, it is the mealworm which is actually fed to the birds.

receptacle, the small brown-bodied flies will soon be in evidence. When a sufficient number are present and they have started to lay their eggs, the rudimentary culture can be removed to a warm room and developed so that a supply of live insects of the kind relished by all the smaller insectivores and nectivores is constantly available. Mealworms are more difficult, but by no means impossible, to breed: they demand conditions to be exactly right if they are to multiply in sufficient numbers to satisfy even the most humble collection of medium to large softbills. Mealworms are greatly favored by just about everything, and must be the most universally popular of all bird foods. Basically, a mealworm culture consists of alternating layers of bran and woolen material; moisture must be present, but strictly limited, if the culture is not to become stale and mouldy. The correct humidity is possibly best maintained by the regular provision of a few fresh banana skins, alternatively a piece of foam sponge may be laid on the culture, and periodically moistened. The mealworms develop into meal-beetles which lay microscopic eggs on the wool or foam, which in turn hatch into the tiny caterpillars so eagerly sought by all manner of birds. There are many different types of mealworm culture, and it seems to be a matter of luck, good judgment or flair in hitting on just the right conditions.

197

SOFTBILLS

Maggots (larvae of the blowfly) are equivalent to mealworms in food value but are not so popular although some birds, like the Hoopoe, can live almost exclusively on them in captivity. While still expensive, they are cheaper than bought mealworms, and serve well as the main source of live food for many of the larger softbills. In hot weather they can be bred without too much difficulty out-of-doors but it is a decidedly unpleasant and anti-social activity, recommended only to those possessing large and remote estates! The stench of putrefying meat is rare, distinctive and surprisingly far-carrying. And unless a spacious heated room can be put at its disposal, the culture will automatically die out in the winter. Some form of livefood is an essential element in a great many softbill diets, and a certain amount of local wildfood, such as ants' cocoons (commonly miscalled "ants' eggs"), can be collected without upsetting the local balance of nature. Other cultures can be set up, and those involving locusts and *Enchytraea* (white worms) are especially valuable. Tubifex, as used by aquarists, are favored by smaller insectivores; so are aphids and daphnia.

Complementing livefood, but not altogether replacing it, are the various insectile foods which one can either buy ready packaged or make oneself. For pet birds such as mynahs and small collections of half a dozen or so birds, it is as well to buy an appropriate commercial brand, but for medium to large collections, it is cheaper to buy the ingredients separately — blending regularly to ensure freshness. As with the brush-tongued parrot diets discussed in the preceding chapter, one can experiment endlessly with insectivorous mixtures, but I have great faith in the recipe set out below; and have seen it bring a gloss to the plumage and a sparkle to the eye of some pretty seedy birds. Moreover, it is not prohibitively expensive or difficult to concoct.

Although some manufacturers add dried insects (and you can do likewise), the main function of softfoods is not to imitate natural diets (which is impossible), but simply to ensure that all the birds' requirements are met in a palatable way. Of all softbills, the exclusively insectivorous are by far the most difficult to cater for, and are subjects only for the experienced aviculturists.

Fruit of many sorts is important to many softbills,

Insectivorous Food Mixture

Barley meal	453 g (16 oz)
Shrimp meal	283 g (10 oz)
Grass meal	142 g (5 oz)
Meat and bone meal	142 g (5 oz)
Fish meal	142 g (5 oz)
Soya bean flour	142 g (5 oz)
Liquid honey*	340 g (12 oz)
Mineral and vitamin powder	2 teaspoons

* Heated and used as the binding agent.

NB. It is very beneficial to squeeze in some finely diced apple *daily* when preparing.

while to a few, like toucans and turacos, it forms virtually their exclusive diet. It must always be of high quality, and you should offer only what you would yourself eat. However, be that as it may, it should still be possible to buy, particularly from wholesalers, partially damaged crates and boxes, or blemished wares, which would be difficult to place in a shop, and at *greatly* reduced prices. Contact your local greengrocer to similar effect. Economy is essential with a commodity as expensive as fruit; besides, it is a shame to see perfectly good fruit going to waste. There are very few fruits and vegetables that cannot be put to good use in a bird collection.

Birds probably vary as much in their preferences as do humans, and similarly it is not always wise to give them exactly what they want all the time. Bananas and grapes (mealworms, too, incidentally) will, given the chance, be consumed *ad infinitum* with lamentable consequences. The less popular and cheaper "hard" fruits, such as apples and pears, can be given as the bulk items for most run-of-the-mill softbills, with bananas, oranges, grapes, *soaked* sultanas and raisins and so on given in a supplementary capacity. I have found that the best method of presenting fruit to softbills is by dicing it with a sharp knife (slightly smaller than might seem necessary for each type of bird) and mixing the correct amounts together — thus, it is more difficult for the birds to pick and choose, while the juices of the favorite fruits tend to impregnate and make more attractive the less favored. Garnishing the finished fruit-salad can be the insectile mix, a few mealworms or whatever else is appropriate.

The majority of softbills — mynah birds, I'm afraid, included — are better suited to outside planted aviaries, which offer them ample space in which to fly around, a good selection of nesting-sites (hopefully, pairs, trios or groups will be housed together whenever possible) and access to sun, showers and fresh air. A well-landscaped, well-stocked aviary brings life to the most drab of gardens and seasons, and softbills are ideal inhabitants for they will not, as a rule, wreck it, and many are lively, handsome and accomplished songsters.

Mynah birds, the Shama, Pekin Robin and other popular softbilled cagebirds can be happily housed in restricted indoor cages, but most of those I have seen have an air of frustration about them. And it ought to be remembered that most of the larger softbills are considerably more messy in their habits than the majority of parrots or finches. Breeding in cages is not as feasible with softbills as it is with, say, Zebra Finches, so most housed in this way are condemned to barren lives. However, anyone already owning a pet mynah or committed to getting one need not worry unduly as to the bird's physical welfare — they are simple enough to feed, there being many specially prepared foods available. And the main problem is probably grossness, due to their enforced inactivity. Mynahs are naturally gregarious, and continually on the move through the dense forests of their Far Eastern homes.

It is not only in connexion with food that softbills vary considerably. And it is impossible to generalize about such matters as breeding and housing requirements, and general management techniques other than those outlined in Part I. A range of birds as wide as that covered between pages 206–47, which includes only representatives of the more common cage and aviary birds, incorporates a truly bewildering variety of behavior. Many species of softbills have evolved in a highly individual way and quite often bear only superficial resemblance to their closest relatives. For this reason, together with the sheer number of types involved, it is scarcely practicable to deal with these birds in the way possible for parrots, finches and Canaries. Therefore, one should refer to the species notes themselves and, obviously, to a specialist work if more detailed information is required.

The importance of specialization in all forms of animal husbandry cannot be overstressed, but it is even more true of a group like the softbilled birds. The broad-based zoological collection is on the decline, and taking its place is the smaller project devoted to just one or two aspects of the Animal Kingdom; hence we now have the invaluable specialist collections of waterfowl, parrots, pheasants, birds of prey and so on. The successes with the Canary and Budgerigar superbly illustrate the value of concentrating single-mindedly on but one objective. With softbills, as I have said, the situation is further complicated. I have in the past managed a collection supposedly concentrating on softbills, but even so have found myself torn between irreconcilable demands, due entirely to the enormous disparity of the birds covered by this rather vague definition. And I would strongly advise anyone who is sufficiently interested in softbills to decide on one particular family or group, and concentrate on this, willfully defying all diversions. I guarantee that such a policy will amply repay your devotion and not lack interest; it will both increase your enjoyment and the welfare of your birds. There are many groups of softbills which present themselves as reasonable subjects, and a fascinating spectacle they suggest. In furtherance of this somewhat progressive theory, the following subsections are devoted to those groups of softbills which are eminently suited to captivity and which are still, at the time of writing, fairly attainable. But the stringent exportation and importation laws now being instituted all over the world beg the immediate and concerted breeding of all wild birds at present in captivity.

PLOVERS

Although not usually accepted as bona fide softbills, plovers, especially those of the *Charadriidae* family (eg. the Blacksmith *Vanellus armatus* and Spur-winged *V. spinosus* Plovers and lapwings) demand, I think, a mention on account of their suitability and usefulness (utilizing ground-space) to aviculture. And, avi-culturally, they are closer to the softbills than any other group covered by this book. Their demands are few, providing that constant supplies of live food, small strips of lean meat and a good insectile mix are available. They do not require large expanses of water or flying-space, and are hardy once acclimatized.

SOFTBILLS

Breeding records are surprisingly good, with many beautiful eggs being produced. The nidifugous young are easy to rear, in a brooder if need be. The adults can be highly territorial, and it is best to keep only breeding pairs together.

TURACOS

Beautiful birds deserving the very best conditions and care. This comparatively small family of interesting frugivores would, I am sure, repay a specialist approach. Their exportation from Africa is likely to become very difficult and if the number being produced in aviaries is not increased significantly, only the White-cheeked Turaco is likely to be seen at all. In my experience, turacos are fairly co-operative and of a free-breeding inclination. They should be housed in aviaries which include a longish flight path and some tangles of branches where they can climb about.

CORACIIFORMES

Included in this cosmopolitan order are many wonderful birds, among the most interesting of all to serious softbill enthusiasts. Consider some of its members: kingfishers, motmots, bee-eaters, rollers, hoopoes and hornbills. Unfortunately, these birds are increasingly difficult and expensive to obtain, also to maintain. They are the province of the dedicated and wealthy, but have more potential to the serious breeder interested in contributing something of great importance both to aviculture and ornithology than virtually any other group of little-bred birds.

BULBULS

Only a very small percentage of the 118 species of bulbuls — an Old World family of mainly tropical birds — are seen frequently in collections: of these the Red-vented, Red-whiskered and White-cheeked *Pycnonotus leucogenys* are the commonest. Bulbuls are fine songsters, and easy to maintain in well-planted aviaries on fruit, some insects and an insectile mix. It is a family in need of specialist attention, and is neatly defined and of wide-ranging aesthetic and scientific appeal. Most, given cover and seclusion, should not present too many breeding problems. It is worth looking out for some of the infrequently seen bulbuls, such as the Chinese *P. sinensis* and the Brown-eared *Hypsipetes flavala*.

SOFTBILLS

THRUSHES

The large cosmopolitan family of thrushes and allies is less well-defined than the bulbuls' and consists of birds as dissimilar as the robin-chats, wheatears, shamas, ground-thrushes, Nightingale, morning-warblers, bluebirds, redstarts, stonechats, true thrushes and solitaires: a wonderful selection of visually beautiful, charming birds, which are, without doubt, the finest songsters of all.

Many members of this large family are frequently encountered in the aviaries of softbill enthusiasts, and a concerted breeding effort with free exchange of birds and ideas between like collections is needed so that these most typical of all songbirds can be bred much more consistently than they are at present. Most are omnivores with definite insectivorous or invertebrate preferences.

BABBLERS

Although this family is a little smaller (about 250 species) than the thrushes, it is poorly defined and incorporates some very different birds which, even with a knowledge of anatomy, are hard to recognize as close relatives. Amongst them are some well-known cagebirds: the Pekin Robin and Silver-eared Mesia, and some popular aviary subjects: the White-crested Laughing Thrush heading the list. Other babblers occasionally seen in captivity are the Red-headed Laughing Thrush, Common Babbler, scimitar-babblers, sibias, yuhinas and picathartes. They are individual in their ways: some being sociable and peaceful, while others are quarrelsome. Some, like the laughing thrushes are hardy enough not to be troubled by the coldest of temperate winters, while true babblers are happier if given extra heat. They are mostly fairly catholic in taste and present no dietary problems.

HUMMINGBIRDS

This highly distinctive and intensely absorbing family of tiny nectar-feeders is already generally considered to be the domain of the specialist, and indeed their requirements are so different from most others that only with specialist attention can they be successfully tackled, although their breeding is always likely to be problematical. There are over 300 species — all from the New World — and they vary considerably in personality, form and behavior. Much hardier than their appearance

SOFTBILLS

suggests, they are happy if allowed a certain amount of exposure to the elements all the year round.

The subject of hummingbird diets is always good for discussion, but I have most faith in Super Hydramin (a highly nutritious American human food) used in conjunction with sugar (or inverted sugar) and natural pollen. To this can be added various other supplements if desired.

SUNBIRDS WHITE-EYES AND HONEYCREEPERS

I have grouped these together simply because of their similar food preferences and management techniques. The white-eye family is surprisingly large, comprising some 79 species, and not at all like the other two physically but they (and the flower-peckers) are all nectar-feeders. It is a remarkably uniform family of small birds, characterized by a ring of white feathers around the eye. Very few are well known to aviculture.

Sunbirds — more obviously nectivorous than the white-eyes — are superficially very similar to the honeycreepers, which are in fact tanagers modified for a diet of nectar. (Do not confuse the "tanager-honeycreepers," with the quite separate Hawaiian honeycreepers.) These nectar-feeders require much the same treatment as hummingbirds but do not hover for their food, and need to have it in dishes or fountains accessible from the ground or a branch. They are also hardier than they appear but must be protected from prolonged bad weather, and are best housed in indoor pens with outside flights or tropical houses.

TANAGERS

An exceptionally interesting and beautiful family of some 233 South American species which are, by and large, ideal aviary birds deserving of specialist attention. Delicate during acclimatization but thereafter surprisingly hardy. Good mixers with their own kind and other birds in planted aviaries where they show off their lively personalities and vivid colors. Tanagers must have a good varied diet with plenty of soft fruit. Aviculturists considering specializing in tanagers should remember that, as a rule, more males than females are imported and that it might take a while before true pairs can be realized — but breeding prospects are ultimately good.

SOFTBILLS

STARLINGS

Prime avicultural subjects, the cosmopolitan starlings are hard to fault, being hardy, amusing, lively, colorful, gregarious and, most important of all, comparatively free breeders. Moreover, since they are all those things, they are an ideal choice for beginners. Their mischievous and inquisitive natures can lead to problems in mixed collections because, like those of the next section, they are enthusiastic egg-thieves. Outstanding examples are the various glossy starlings, Superb Starling, members of the *Sturnus* genus and, of course, many of the mynahs, including the famous Greater Hill Mynah. Incidentally, the strange oxpeckers *Buphagus* are also located here.

CROWS AND ALLIES

Although it is in some ways stretching a point to class the corvids as softbills, they are generally considered so. I am personally very fond of all these birds but the sombre black plumage of crows has earnt them few friends. True, they do have some unfortunate habits but then so do robins and thrushes if viewed from another angle. There is no doubting their worldwide success, and I would like nothing better than to set up a collection devoted solely to this marvellous family of over 100 species, which includes such beautiful, hardy, no-nonsense birds as the jays, magpies, treepies, nutcrackers and choughs, quite apart from the true crows themselves.

For successful breeding each pair must be given its own aviary, and this may deter some people, for they are not of course to be trusted with other birds including those of their own kind.

SOFTBILLS

Orange-breasted Green Pigeon *Treron bicincta*.
Fruit pigeons are not nearly so common in captivity as the more common seedeating pigeons, which is a pity because in confinement all they ask is plenty of fruit, together with some insect food and warm, well-planted quarters. The green pigeons are more frequently imported than the *Ptilinopus* fruit doves.

White-cheeked Turaco *Tauraco leucotis*.
At present more breeding successes have been recorded with the White-cheeked than any other of the African turacos, probably due to the fact that it is the commonest. One of the biggest problems encountered in rearing these chicks is their susceptibility to a rickets-like leg deformity, which needs massive doses of calcium to prevent/correct it. Turacos lay 2 white eggs which hatch into dark downy chicks after about 20 days.

Hartlaub's Turaco *Tauraco hartlaubi*. Blue-crested Turaco.
Another turaco which should breed given a fair chance. Acquiring a true pair with birds as expensive, sexually-alike and monogamous as turacos is a lottery; I have had the frustrating experience with both this species and the Schalow's *T. livingstonii schalowi* of many infertile eggs laid by right-thinking females while their "mates" stood around uninterestedly.

(Bohemian) Waxwing *Bombycilla garrulus*.
This widespread species, occurring on both sides of the Atlantic, is a popular subject. The American Cedar Waxwing *B. cedrorum* is very similar but slightly smaller; it lacks the white wing markings and has yellow undertail coverts. The remaining waxwing is the Japanese *B. japonica*, which has a pink-tipped tail and no wax-droplets on the wing. The active, gentle and sociable waxwings are best housed in mixed aviaries. They feed mainly on fruit and berries but young require many insects.

Blue-naped Mousebird *Colius macrourus*.
The 6 species of mousebirds or colies form a strange group of African birds, with a habit of scurrying about that has earned them their name. Highly gregarious outside the breeding season; always active, they are entertaining and easy to keep, and willing to breed. Their diet should include much fruit and insectivorous fare.

1 *Treron bicincta* 11–12 in/280–305 mm India to Taiwan, and south to Java ♀ lacks violet and orange breast bands, and has belly and thighs more yellow
2 *Tauraco leucotis* 15 in/380 mm Sudan to Somalia
3 *T. hartlaubi* 16 in/405 mm Highlands of Kenya and NE Tanzania
4 *Bombycilla garrulus* 7 in/180 mm North America and the Palearctic
5 *Colius macrourus* 14 in/355 mm (including tail) Trans Africa from Senegal to Somalia, and south to Tanzania

SOFTBILLS

White-breasted Kingfisher *Halcyon smyrnensis*. White-throated Kingfisher.

By no means are all kingfishers fish-eaters; in fact the majority are inland and upland birds, which live mainly on terrestrial fauna. These are probably a little easier to cater for in captivity than the true fish catchers, but most will live contentedly on livefood, strips of meat and fish etc (the latter placed in shallow dishes of water). Breeding is predictably rare but not impossible. They bathe by flying into pools.

Woodland Kingfisher *Halcyon senegalensis*.

Another vigorous *Halcyon* species, the Woodland should be treated as the above. Kingfishers are either "burrowers" or "tree-nesters;" this species bred at the Winged World in England, successfully rearing one youngster in an artificial earth bank.

Indian Roller *Coracias benghalensis*.

In my experience this species eats mostly livefood but it is also said to accept inanimate items. Hardy and active, all rollers must have roomy, high flights; they are hole-nesters and if a true pair can be obtained, they might breed, but it is unlikely that captive rollers will ever reproduce consistently.

Lilac-breasted Roller *Coracias caudata*.

I have seen this species cleverly hawking flying-ants in East Africa, while in captivity in England it has proved easy to keep on the usual livefood. However, rollers can become very quarrelsome, even in expansive aviaries, and it seems that, like many other specialist flyers, they are not ideally suited to aviculture — which is a pity.

Red-billed Hornbill *Tockus erythrorhynchus*.

The hornbills are a diverse family which appear mostly in zoos and bird gardens. The Red-billed is one of the small insectivorous species and can be easily managed in a roomy flight if protected from severe frosts and fed on live food, a little fruit and red meat, and insectile food. A true pair can be encouraged to start its interesting breeding cycle if a suitable nestbox and mud are provided.

1 *Halcyon smyrnensis* 11 in/280 mm Middle East to the Philippines
2 *H. senegalensis* 8 in/205 mm C Africa
3 *Coracias benghalensis* 13 in/330 mm Middle East to SW China
4 *C. caudata* 16 in/405 mm (including tail-plumes) Most of the southern third of Africa
5 *Tockus erythrorhynchus* 17–18 in/430–455 mm Trans Africa from Senegal to Somalia, and south to Tanzania ♀ slightly smaller bill.

SOFTBILLS

Coppersmith Barbet *Megalaima haemacephala*. Crimson-breasted Barbet.

Infrequently available, and with a reputation suggesting delicacy, the Coppersmith is more frugivorous than most barbets, but all do well on a mixture made up of 50 per cent insectile mix plus minced-meat and 25 per cent each of livefood and diced fruit. Barbets are not above using their strong beaks against other birds, or even their owners, when defending their nests.

Blue-throated Barbet *Megalaima asiatica*. Blue-cheeked Barbet.

Barbets are hardy, noisy, entertaining, omnivorous birds which mix well with other softbills. They like to excavate their own nesting and roosting holes in dead tree-trunks, but until this has been completed, they must be provided with nestboxes; if not given this facility in outside situations they often succumb. Most are perfectly willing to breed.

Toucan Barbet *Semnornis ramphastinus*.

This striking, robust neotropical species needs care similar to the above. The Toucan Barbet has such a strong, forceful character that it is best from every angle to provide it with separate roomy accommodation. The male can sometimes be told by the black stripe down its hind neck.

Lesser Golden-backed Woodpecker *Dinopium benghalense*. Black-rumped Goldenback.

Woodpeckers are subjects for the specialist, since they are argumentative, usually exclusively insectivorous, difficult to "meat-off" and incredibly destructive to *any* available wood! On the other hand, they are amusing, hardy and long-lived once established. The Golden-backed varieties are the most frequently available tropical species in Europe.

Lesser Green Broadbill *Calyptomena viridis*.

The 14 species of broadbills are typically omnivorous; however, this representative — the only one appearing regularly in softbill collections (and even so I have yet to see a female) — is mainly a fruit-eater, which to some extent explains its popularity. All broadbills are gentle and retiring — ideal for mixed collections. They are mainly Asian birds, but a few occur in Africa too.

1 *Megalaima haemacephala* 6–6¼ in/150–160 mm E Iran to SW China, and south to Indonesia
2 *M. asiatica* 9 in/ 230 mm India to S China
3 *Semnornis ramphastinus* 8½ in/ 215 mm The Andes of Colombia and Ecuador
4 *Dinopium benghalense* 11½ in/ 290 mm W Pakistan, India and W Burma ♀ has white spots on black crown, with red crest
5 *Calyptomena viridis* 7½ in/190 mm Jungles of SE Burma, S Thailand, E Malaysia and Indonesia ♀ much duller, lacks black neck spot and wing-markings

FRUGIVORES AND INSECTIVORES

211

SOFTBILLS

Toucans, aviculturally speaking, are of course immensely desirable, but they must be viewed with circumspection by those with less than zoos at their disposal. They are easy, if expensive, to look after and hardy, but need a purpose-designed aviary which takes into account their large size, poor flight and anti-social attitude to other birds. Only the toucanets are good mixers.

Toco Toucan *Ramphastos toco*.

Made famous by the advertising of a popular Irish brewery, the Toco Toucan is a definitive zoo-bird. It fetches a high price, and is sometimes beguilingly tame, when of course it becomes even more expensive. It needs a considerable amount and variety of good fruit, supplemented by an insectile mix and occasional slivers of meat or whole mice – which all toucans should be offered occasionally.

Sulfur-breasted Toucan *Ramphastos sulfuratus*. Keel-billed Toucan.

One of the toucans most regularly available, and therefore well-known to zoo or bird-garden visitors. A trio in a smallish aviary got on tolerably well and showed considerable nesting activity in both a nestbox and a wall cavity before Pasteurellosis struck them down. But all the indications are that the young are not difficult to rear.

Banded or Collared Aracari *Pteroglossus torquatus*.

Despite their reduced size, the aracaris are just as temperamental as their larger cousins, and need to be treated equally warily. Indeed they need similar consideration in most respects and are quite able to tolerate cold weather provided it is not accompanied by wind and rain.

Spot-billed Toucanet *Selenidera maculirostris*.
Emerald Toucanet *Aulacorhynchus prasinus prasinus*.

Both these toucanets, although not cogeners, need conventional toucan care, including good, dry, draughtproof winter night-quarters; if anything, the Spot-billed is the less hardy of the two. They are amongst the friendliest of all ramphastids and have even bred, notably at San Diego Zoo, USA and Walsrode Bird Park, Germany. Several races of *prasinus* exist which differ considerably in their bill and throat markings.

1 *Ramphastos toco* 20–25 in/ 510–635 mm Jungles of N & E Brazil, the Guianas, and south to Argentina and Paraguay
2 *R. sulfuratus* 18–22 in/ 455–560 mm S Mexico to Venezuela
3 *Pteroglossus torquatus* 15–16 in/ 380–405 mm S Mexico to Colombia and Venezuela
4 *Selenidera maculirostris* (nominate race) 10–13 in/ 255–330 mm NE Argentina to S Brazil
5 *Aulacorhynchus prasinus* (race *prasinus*) 13¼/335 mm High forests of Mexico
5a *A. p. caeruleogularis* 12¼ in/ 310 mm. Tropical highland forest of Veragua and Chiriqui.
5b *A. p. albibitta* 13 in/ 330 mm W & E slopes of Andes in Columbia.

1

2

3

♂ ♀

4

5

5 a   5 b

SOFTBILLS

Blue-winged Pitta *Pitta brachyura*. Indian or Bengal Pitta.

Pittas are primarily birds of the rainforest under-growth — rarely flying; therefore in captivity they need a moist earth floor with a carpet of leaf mould, plenty of thick cover in which, with luck, they might build their globular nests — and a few stout logs on which they can perch. Entirely insectivorous but not difficult to maintain; pittas are territorial and can be dangerous to other small birds when they venture to ground level.

Hooded Pitta *Pitta sordida*. Black-headed Pitta.

Requires the same care as other pittas with due regard taken of its terrestrial and territorial habits. Pittas progress by long leaps and should never be cramped for room.

Great Kiskadee *Pitangus sulphuratus*. Sulfury Tyrant; Derbian Flycatcher.

An active, robust and surprisingly free-breeding aviary inhabitant which, for safety's sake, demands one to itself as it becomes extremely pugnacious to other birds and even humans when nesting. The young are easy to rear, providing the adults have an omnivorous diet including fruit, strips of meat, livefood and a rich insectile mix. Kiskadees have many kingfisher-like habits and need a pool for bathing.

1 *Pitta brachyura* (*mollucensis*) 8 in/ 205 mm E India to SW China, and south to Indonesia
2 *P. sordida* 7½ in/ 190 mm Similar to *P. brachyura*, including New Guinea
3 *Pitangus sulphuratus* 9½ in/240 mm S Texas to Argentina

4 *Momotus momota*
15–17 in/
380–430 mm
(including tail) Mexico
to tropical South
America
5 *Upupa epops*
11–12 in/
280–305 mm (races
vary) Much of warmer
Old World, from Africa
to Borneo

Blue-crowned Motmot *Momotus momota.*

Large and potentially dangerous but not usually aggressive to other birds. Motmots, of which this is the most frequently available, like to tunnel, and for this reason should be housed on several feet of earth. Obviously this makes escape a real problem. This species has been bred successfully.

Hoopoe *Upupa epops.*

A familiar bird which although not widely available has proved to be a wonderful free-breeding subject for a planted aviary. Not difficult to keep given a constant supply of live maggots and mealworms – which should be mixed in a fortified insectile mixture with extra vitamins A and D. Hoopoes require a hole to nest in and this can be in either a nest-box or stone wall. The sexes are alike. No problems need be encountered rearing the young provided enough good food can be supplied.

215

SOFTBILLS

Red-vented Bulbul *Pycnonotus cafer*.
A first-rate subject for the young softbill enthusiast. Bulbuls are generally hardy and easy to keep but, like so many, delicate until acclimatized. The Asiatic species, such as the Red-vented, are more regularly available to S Europe than the African ones. All require a spacious planted aviary if they are to breed.

Red-whiskered Bulbul *Pycnonotus jocosus*. Red-eared (-cheeked) Bulbul.
Introduced into parts of the USA and Australia, the Red-whiskered Bulbul has displayed its adaptable nature. In aviaries bulbuls need an omnivorous diet with plenty of live and insectivorous-food and some fruit. They can be quarrelsome but are also active and amusing.

Golden-fronted Fruitsucker *Chloropsis aurifrons*. Golden-fronted Green Bulbul, Leafbird or Chloropsis.
More frugivorous but similar in other ways to the bulbuls. The liquid nature of its droppings together with its active behavior suggests a large planted aviary, but adequate shelter must be provided to ward off the effects of frost. It is a fine songster and an accomplished acrobat.

Hardwick's Fruitsucker *Chloropsis hardwickii*. Orange-bellied Leafbird or Chloropsis; Hardwick's Green Bulbul.
Requires the same care as the Golden-fronted and other *Chloropsis* species. It can be troublesome to smaller birds in a confined space. Apart from *Irena* (see below), the other genus of leafbirds — *Aegithina* — consists of 4 species of ioras, which are more insectivorous and not generally available (to aviculture).

Fairy Bluebird *Irena puella*.
The Fairy Bluebird has an enviable reputation for friendliness and non-aggression; unfortunately my experiences speak otherwise. I may have been unlucky but I have found them unreliable and prone to get into the most frightful scrapes. One pair had to be continually separated and reunited, the female being the worst offender. These problems apart, they are certainly lively, hardy and relatively easy to keep on a principally fruit diet.

1 *Pycnonotus cafer* 8 in/205 mm India to SW China (introduced Fiji)
2 *P. jocosus* 8 in/205 mm India to S China, and south to Malaysia (introduced USA, Australia and Mauritius)
3 *Chloropsis aurifrons* 7½ in/190 mm India to SW China, also Sumatra (not Malaysia)
4 *C. hardwickii* 7½ in/190 mm Highlands India to S China, and south to Malaysia ♀ has black replaced by green; moustachial stripe and orange belly paler
5 *Irena puella* 10 in/255 mm Forests India to SW China, and south to Indonesia (not C Thailand)

SOFTBILLS

Northern Mockingbird *Mimus polyglottos*. (American) Mockingbird.

Mockingbirds are thrush-like in many of their habits, being fine, territorial songsters, which feed on the ground. The Blue *Melanotis caerulescens* and Blue-and-White *M. hypoleucus* are much more colorful, and more popular with some for this reason: but like the Eastern Bluebird *Sialia sialis*, which was once common overseas they are now virtually unknown outside America.

(White-rumped) Shama *Copsychus malabaricus*.

Famous for its exceptional voice, hardy and agreeable – if territorially quarrelsome, like all chat-thrushes, which have some less hardy representatives, it requires insectivorous management.

Dhyal Bird *Copsychus saularis*. Dhyal (Thrush); Magpie Robin.

Almost as popular as the Shama, the Dhyal Bird also

1 *Mimus polyglottos*
10–10½ in/
255–265 mm S USA
and Mexico
2 *Copsychus
malabaricus* 11 in/
280 mm (♀ has tail
2 in/50 mm shorter)
Jungles India to SW
China, and south to
Indonesia ♀ much
duller
3 *C. saularis* 8½ in/
215 mm W Pakistan to
the Philippines, and
south to Indonesia
♀ duller: black replaced
by gray

218

INSECTIVORES

4 *Luscinia (Erithacus)
*calliope** 6 in/150 mm
Breeds over much of C
and E Palearctic;
winters from E
Pakistan to the
Philippines
5 *Cossypha heuglini*
8 in/205 mm Much of
CE and S Africa
excluding the Cape

requires similar care. Both can be wintered outside.
Breeding is a hectic affair, for which a large, well
planted aviary is desirable, if only to allow the hen some
breathing space.

**Siberian Rubythroat *Luscinia calliope*. Common Ruby-
throat.**
Small but aggressively inclined, this bush-robin is a
member of the same genus as the Nightingale *L.
megarhynchos*, but this lacks its vocal abilities. It is a
skulking, ground-loving bird, becoming active at dusk
when its croaky, frog-like, call-note is uttered.

White-browed Robin-chat *Cossypha heuglini*.
A typical small insectivore which is infrequently available. The robin-chats form an African genus which also
includes the Snowy-headed *C. niveicapilla* and Red-
capped *C. natalensis* species. Characterized by their
active and cheerful personalities: (they are more
suitable than most softbills for life in a roomy cage).

SOFTBILLS

Redstart *Phoenicurus phoenicurus*.
The 11 redstarts are part of the typical Palearctic avifauna, so there are no cold-weather problems, and in most other ways they are close enough to other trushes to present few difficulties.

Orange-headed Ground Thrush *Zoothera citrina*.
One of the more acquirable of the "exotic" thrushes, and an aviary bird much sought after for its peaceful and quiet nature (although it does not always approve of other small ground birds). It has a fine sustained song, and is as easy to maintain as a typical *Turdus* thrush (see below). It is essentially a terrestrial bird, and loves to pick over leaf mould etc. Two varieties are also seen: one lacks the wing-bar, the other (*Z.c. cyanotus*) has an orbital ring and other white facial markings.

Song Thrush *Turdus philomelos*.
A formidable and rightly famous songster. In captivity it breeds regularly, whereupon it seeks out thick cover. Livefood is essential to a growing family.

1 *Phoenicurus phoenicurus* 5½ in/ 140 mm Much of W and C Palearctic ♂ Summer plumage ♀ duller, lacks black and white facial markings but retains red tail
2 *Zoothera citrina* 8¼ in/215 mm W Pakistan to S China, and south to Indonesia ♀ has olive-brown upperparts

3 *Turdus philomelos*
9 in/230 mm Much of
W and C Palearctic;
winters south to N
Africa and the Near
East (introduced
Melbourne, Australia)
4 *T. merula* 10 in/
255 mm Europe, N
Africa and SW Asia
5 *Motacilla alba* (race
yarrellii (yarrellii
illustrated)) 7 in/
180 mm Much of
Eurasia and Iceland ♂
Summer plumage and
♀ have white throat
with black breast band

Blackbird *Turdus merula*.

The Eurasian Blackbird's song is even more enchanting than that of the superb Song Thrush. Care is very similar; but it is probably more territorial, although it does not object to the presence of dissimilar species. It requires a standard insectile mix with added fruit and live insects.

Pied Wagtail *Motacilla alba yarrellii*.

The Motacillidae family of wagtails, longclaws and pipits are ideal but sadly underestimated as aviary birds. Many of them would, given the chance, make attractive, free-breeding birds and better utilize the floors of many outside flights. The Pied Wagtail illustrated is the British race of the White Wagtail which occurs over much of the Palearctic Region. It needs insectivorous management, but is very territorial and pairs will often bicker and fight before establishing a breeding situation. A nestbox, open-fronted and raised off the ground, is a good stimulant.

4 ♂ ♀

5 ♂

SOFTBILLS

The large Timaliinae group (about 252 spp.) of babblers and wren-tits is allied to the Muscicapidae discussed on the previous two spreads. In their own number, they differ widely, but the larger ones are basically insectivorous, gregarious, hardy and well suited to aviculture. Many are pleasing songsters. Given the correct conditions breeding should be a distinct possibility but, as so often happens, the correct matching of pairs is a big obstacle.

Pekin Robin *Leiothrix lutea*.
Silver-eared Mesia *Leiothrix argentauris*.
The first-named of these two cogeners is so popular that many synonyms have been coined (including Red-billed Leiothrix, Pekin or Japanese Nightingale) by dealers in search of the exotic. The Pekin Robin is, I suppose, the world's most familiar softbill cagebird, but it is also a superb aviary bird, albeit an inveterate egg-thief. Both species need similar care and are surprisingly tough, they appreciate a small amount of seed in with their usual fare.

Black-headed Sibia *Heterophasia capistrata*.
A medium-sized cheerful bird which mixes well with equally-sized birds. It has refined insectivorous tastes but is nevertheless hardy, given a frost-proof shelter. Sexes are unfortunately alike — which impairs breeding prospects.

Red-headed Laughing Thrush *Garrulax erythrocephalus*.
White-crested Laughing Thrush *Garrulax leucolophus*.
The widespread *Garrulax* genus is sparsely represented in aviaries for reasons associated with availability, which is a shame. The White-crested Laughing Thrush is by far the best known: it is assertive, noisy, full of character, easy to keep (and, incidentally, loves ground-nuts) but dangerous to many other birds. The Red-headed is the complete opposite except that it too has an abundance of charm, is equally easy to keep and is long-lived.

Common Babbler *Turdoides caudatus*.
Song-babblers, such as this, are best thought of as insectivores with omnivorous leanings! They are good subjects for the novice softbill enthusiast. Usually sociable but some possess a mean streak.

1 *Leiothrix lutea* 6 in/150 mm W Himalayas to S China ♀ has throat and breast paler
2 *L. argentauris* 7 in/180 mm Himalayas to S China and Vietnam, and south to Sumatra ♀ duller
3 *Heterophasia capistrata* 10 in/255 mm India to SW China ♀ sometimes slightly smaller
4 *Garrulax erythrocephalus* 10½ in/265 mm W Himalayas to SW China, and south to Malaya
5 *G. leucolophus* 12 in/305 mm W Himalayas to SW China, and south to W Sumatra (not Malaya)
6 *Turdoides caudatus* 9 in/230 mm SE Iraq to India (not Sri Lanka)

1 ♂

2 ♂

3

4

5

6

SOFTBILLS

Yellow-collared Ixulus *Yuhina flavicollis*. Yellow-naped Yuhina.

Rarely available and expensive; birds of highly specialized insectivorous habits and requirements, such as this small relative of the babblers, are best left to the expert; who should have the facilities and flair to provide their not unreasonable requirements. In addition to small insects and soft fruits, a certain amount of nectar can also be offered.

Rufous-bellied Niltava *Niltava sundara*.

The most frequently imported of this genus. Niltavas are best avoided by those inexperienced in the intricacies of tropical flycatchers. I am a firm believer in fresh air, but obviously they cannot be expected to withstand the rigors of a hard winter unaided, and they must have snug overnight accommodation which includes artificially prolonged daylight. Outside, the problem of finding sufficient amounts of small live insects is eased, but their staple diet must be a wide variety of livefood (including blowflies), a fine insectile mix and a little nectar.

Verditer Flycatcher *Muscicapa thalassina*.

Rather more common than the foregoing, this attractive species requires similar care. All flycatchers must be allowed to bathe daily but since this often proves fatal in captivity — they can drown in as little as 25 mm (1 in) of water — extremely shallow amounts *must* only be given (12 mm ($\frac{1}{2}$ in)) in broad, gentlesided dishes; in small pens, they may be sprayed with tepid water from a fine mist spray.

Spotted Flycatcher *Muscicapa striata*.

This species, despite the fact that it will be more familiar to many readers, still requires the same sensitive handling as the two preceding Old World Flycatchers (Muscicapinae).

Black-throated Wattle-eye *Platysteira peltata*.

A lamentably rare subject, this member of the Monarch Flycatchers (Monarchinae) has a predictable reputation of "delicacy." However, given the same conditions as the previous species, this and the other monarchs can be long-lived and comparatively trouble-free: one specimen achieved the age of at least 11 years. The difficult acclimatization period is, however, fraught with danger, and it is obviously not the subject for a beginner.

1 *Yuhina flavicollis*
5$\frac{1}{4}$ in/135 mm
Himalayas and Burma to W China and Laos
2 *Niltava sundara*
6$\frac{1}{2}$ in/165 mm
Himalayas and Burma to W China
3 *Muscicapa thalassina* 6$\frac{1}{2}$ in/ 165 mm India to S China, and south to Sumatra and Borneo
4 *M. striata* 5$\frac{1}{2}$ in/ 140 mm Most of the Palearctic
5 *Platysteira peltata* 5 in/125 mm Angola and Zambia northeast to W Kenya

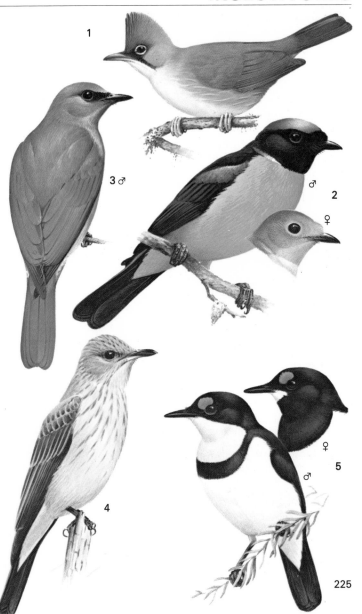

1

3 ♂

2 ♂

♀

4

♀

5

♂

SOFTBILLS

Great Tit *Parus major*.
A widespread and familiar species throughout much of the Old World which I have found to be incredibly energetic (if in a somewhat stereotyped routine). Perky, dainty and not at all difficult to maintain on livefood, seeds and a varied insectile mix. If a true pair can be obtained, there is no good reason why it should not prove extremely prolific.

Chestnut-bellied Nuthatch *Sitta castanea*. Chestnut-breasted Nuthatch.
Nuthatches are unusual aviary birds, and this species is the best known in captivity in Europe. Highly insectivorous, they must also be given ample opportunity to indulge their boundless energy — foraging on thick upright branches and cork bark. They are hardy but terribly difficult to breed.

Chestnut-flanked White-eye *Zosterops erythropleura*. Oriental White-eye *Zosterops palpebrosa*. Indian white-eye.
White-eyes are by far the best choice for those softbill enthusiasts wishing to progress on to nectivorous species, since they are the cheapest and reasonably hardy. Although firm in their preference for nectar, some people have maintained them on fruit and insects — but this combination is not to be recommended as a sole diet (however beneficial as a supplement); besides, nectar (see page 204) is so convenient. Well-mated white-eyes are usually more than willing to breed in thickly-planted tropical houses and conservatories, but the young seldom seem to survive. They are industrious and useful hunters of aphids and other plant pests.

Scarlet-backed Flowerpecker *Dicaeum cruentatum*.
Truly more delicate, the nectivorous flowerpeckers are better housed in an indoor, conservatory-style aviary or large cage, if a really good warm shed-annex is not available. Flowerpeckers are interesting birds for the more experienced keeper, and this species remains the most regularly available. A diet divided into finely-diced fruit before noon, and nectar afterwards has been proven successful. And it is possible for them to achieve worthwhile longevity.

1 *Parus major* 5½ in/ 140 mm Widespread throughout the Palearctic and Asia ♀ has less black on throat
2 *Sitta castanea* 5½ in/ 140 mm India and Burma to SW China and Vietnam ♀ has duller underparts
3 *Zosterops erythropleura* 4¾ in/ 120 mm E Asia: S China south to Cambodia
4 *Z. palpebrosa* 4¼ in/ 110 mm Afghanistan to S China, and south to Indonesia
5 *Dicaeum cruentatum* 3½ in/90 mm N India and Nepal to Hainan, and south to Sumatra and Borneo

SOFTBILLS

Hummingbirds in captivity, besides their remarkable visual appeal, are characterized by a pugnacious intolerance of other small birds, especially their own kind. Seldom can hummingbirds be mixed, even as pairs in huge, densely-planted flights. Many are "blusterers:" tough and argumentative on the surface but very prone to weakness if for any reason conditions are not quite right or if prevented from feeding for even a short while by a dominant companion. If mixing is to be attempted, it is important to provide well scattered feeding points — hanging some tubes in concealed sites. Hummingbirds consume more than their own weight in food daily, and their nectar must be supplemented by live fruit-flies etc. Bathing should be encouraged by daily spraying or moistened foliage. Their mastery of the air is so astonishing that they defy capture by net.

Streamertail *Trochilus polytmus*. (Long-tail) Doctor Bird.
Hummingbirds differ little in their individual requirements, but obviously a species such as this needs more than even a roomy cage if its glorious tail is not to become damaged or soiled. In any event, it is not seen at its best save in free flight.

Sparkling Violetear *Colibri coruscans*. Gould's Violet-ear.
A robust species — the most beautiful of the manageable *Colibri* violetears — it has been known to dominate even tanagers, forcing them to dive from bush to shrub at ground level. But, conversely, I have kept a pair which was very timid. It has been consistently bred at San Diego Zoo, Calif., USA.

Heavenly Sylph *Aglaicercus kingi*. Gould's Heavenly, Green- (Long-)tailed or Blue-throated Sylph.
A magnificent bird which, like the Streamertail, demands ample space. Members of this genus are comparatively easy to establish, unlike the visually similar trainbearers (*Lesbia*).

Ruby-topaz Hummingbird *Chrysolampis mosquitus*.
One of the commoner hummingbirds — quiet and reasonably tolerant — it is amongst those best suited to captivity but, like other South American animals, it could soon disappear entirely from foreign aviaries and the actual captive breeding of small nectivores is still firmly in its infancy.

1 *Trochilus polytmus* 10 in/255 mm (♀ lacks 6 in/150 mm tail-streamers) Jamaica
2 *Colibri coruscans* 5½ in/140 mm Colombia and Venezuela to N Argentine
3 *Aglaicercus kingi* 7½ in/190 mm The Andes from Venezuela to Bolivia
4 *Chrysolampis mosquitus* 3½ in/90 mm N and E South America

SOFTBILLS

Sunbirds, the Old World "equivalents" of the neo-tropical hummingbirds, call for similar but not identical care. Despite their larger size, they are no hardier, no more — or less — aggressive (although the injury they can occasion is proportional to their increased strength) and not much easier to breed. Some male sunbirds assume a female-like eclipse plumage out of the breeding season but usually sexual dimorphism is pronounced.

Scarlet-chested Sunbird *Nectarinia senegalensis.*
A large sunbird which needs color-food if the male is to retain his eye-catching pigments. Ultimately very long-lived, and prepared to breed, but as with other sunbirds the male becomes too antagonistic towards the female to make breeding likely, other than in a large well planted flight in which she can hide.

Tacazze Sunbird *Nectarinia tacazze.*
Lacking the variety of color, the Tacazze makes up for it by a stunning iridescence. I kept a pair in a tropical house for several years, where, after three, they regularly built nests and produced young but always failed to rear them for more than a week despite a seemingly perfect natural diet plus small spiders ad lib and fruitflies etc. Removal of the male at this crucial time ultimately led to a successful rearing.

Beautiful Sunbird *Nectarinia pulchella.*
A well-named species which needs standard care, but is prone to exceptionally difficult molts. Sunbirds appreciate some sweet fruit and this can be supplied as orange segments or half-grapes spiked on twigs. Like the hummingbirds, sunbirds are also "rain-bathers," but will use a fountain or wet foliage.

Variable Sunbird *Nectarinia venusta.*
The race illustrated is the Yellow-bellied (*N.v. falkensteini*). This charming little bird is common in E. Africa and reasonably priced abroad. There is a better chance of successfully mixing such "wedge-tailed" species than the more powerful "long-tails," such as the Scarlet-chested, Tacazze or Malachite Sunbirds (*N. famosa*), which are safest mixed with tanagers etc.

Van Hasselt's Sunbird *Nectarinia sperata.*
This Asiatic species is even smaller than the African Variable, and can be confidently mixed with similar small birds. Always provide a surplus of feeding stations.

1 *Nectarinia (Chalcomitra) senegalensis* 6 in/150 mm Much of Africa south of the Sahara Different races vary considerably
2 *N. tacazze* 9 in/230 mm (♀ lacks 3½ in/90 mm central tail-feathers) Highlands of E Africa
3 *N. pulchella* 6 in/150 mm (♀ lacks 1½ in/40 mm central tail-feathers) ♂ in breeding plumage A belt from Senegal to Ethiopia; in the east, north to C Sudan and south to S Tanzania
4 *N. (Cinnyris) venusta (falkensteini* illustrated) 4 in/100 mm ♂ in breeding plumage Much of C Africa, from Senegal to Ethiopia, south to Rhodesia Several races differ in their shades of yellow
5 *N. sperata* 4 in/100 mm E Pakistan and Burma to Philippines, and south to Indonesia

SOFTBILLS

Red-legged Honeycreeper *Cyanerpes cyaneus.* Yellow-winged Sugarbird or Honeycreeper; Blue Honeycreeper.

Honeycreepers have less dependence on nectar than hummingbirds and sunbirds but it still forms the staple element in their diet; preferably augmented by sweet fruit finely diced or simply laid open. They are slightly less tough than the sunbirds (and also less quarrelsome) and should not be made to withstand severe weather unaided, although they relish an outside flight during the day.

Purple Honeycreeper/Sugarbird *Cyanerpes caeruleus.* Yellow-legged Honeycreeper.

Care should be as for the above. The best accommodation is a well-planted indoor aviary with an outside one adjoining — into which the birds can go at will (although during bad weather it is advisable to shut them inside at night). They prove messy if confined in a small cage.

Blue Sugarbird/Dacnis *Dacnis cayana.* Black-throated or Turquoise Honeycreeper.

The shorter beak of this tubby little bird accurately indicates the increased importance of fruit and insects in its diet. All sugarbirds and other small nectivores require attention at least twice daily, and are therefore only suitable for people who can meet these demands.

Blue-crowned Chlorophonia *Chlorophonia occipitalis.* The most commonly exported of the chlorophonias, which are small but typical tanagers. They tend to be tricky to acclimatize, and need a very varied fruit diet, preferably inclusive of some nectar. This species chatters conversationally and is outstandingly attractive visually and behaviorally — being very active and far better suited to an aviary than cage. It is a rain-bather, sociable with other birds, and was first bred in Britain in 1971.

Violet Tanager/Euphonia *Euphonia violacea.* Violaceaus Euphonia.

Euphonias are small, gaily colored tanagers, in the wild they are believed to be the chief disseminators of the plant parasites, mistletoes (Loranthaceae): the seeds of which pass through the birds, enclosed in viscid sacs and adhere to other trees. In captivity they need a varied but also mainly frugivorous diet.

1 *Cyanerpes cyaneus* $4\frac{1}{2}$–5 in/115–130 mm S Mexico to Brazil and Bolivia; Cuba and Trinidad
2 *C. caeruleus* $3\frac{1}{4}$–$4\frac{1}{2}$ in/80–115 mm Guyana and Surinam
3 *Dacnis cayana* $4\frac{1}{2}$ in/ 115 mm S Mexico to Brazil; Trinidad and Tobago
4 *Chlorophonia occipitalis* $4\frac{1}{2}$–$5\frac{1}{2}$ in/ 115–140 mm S Mexico to W Panama ♀ lacks breast band, and has less yellow below A few races exist
5 *Euphonia violacea* $3\frac{3}{4}$–4 in/95–100 mm NE South America

SOFTBILLS

Blue-gray Tanager *Thraupis episcopus*. Blue or Silver-Blue Tanager.
This is one of the best known tanagers. Like the majority, both sexes sport colors of equal intensity. It is easy to maintain once established, and thrives on a varied fruit diet. Hardy and robust yet peaceful in collections of mixed tanagers, it does, however, have the reputation of disruptive nesting habits.

Blue-necked Tanager *Tangara cyanicollis*. Blue-headed Tanager.
All tanagers should be allowed to bathe in fresh, clean water at will; this is especially important during acclimatization. A varied diet, including sweet fruit, insectivorous and livefood, and grit is essential; bread and milk together with honey is beneficial and useful in tempting new arrivals on to a conventional diet.

Mrs Wilson's Tanager *Tangara larvata*. Masked or Golden-masked Tanager.
One of the most familiar and best studied of all tanagers. It is one of the hardiest of an otherwise unreliable group of birds, containing several species which have to be viewed circumspectly.

Superb Tanager *Tangara fastuosa*. Seven-colored Tanager.
One of the above mentioned rather fickle species which needs careful acclimatization by a highly experienced tanager enthusiast. Very prone to digestive disorders, and for this reason it is foolish to buy other than alert, bright-eyed, well-feathered birds. Once established, though, it should attain a good age of perhaps 10 years or more. It is rarely bred at present.

Silver-throated Tanager *Tangara icterocephala*.
This unusually colored species can be regarded as the equal of *T. larvata*, being generally trouble-free. The sexes are similar but the female is generally duller. Tanagers are not free-breeders but like to build their own nests high up in a bush or on an artificial base. The young are reared largely on live insects.

Spotted Emerald Tanager *Tangara guttata chrysophrys*. A subspecies of the Speckled Tanager.
Like the Superb this species can also be tricky to acclimatize, and is not the subject for a newcomer to softbills. Even acclimatized tanagers need good protection from adverse weather conditions.

1 *Thraupis episcopus* (*virens*) 6–7 in/ 150–180 mm Mexico to NW Peru, N Bolivia and the Amazon ♀ duller and tinged with green
2 *Tangara cyanicollis* 4¾–5½ in/ 120–140 mm S Peru, Bolivia; NW Venezuela, Colombia and Ecuador
3 *T. larvata* (*nigrocincta*) 5–5½ in/ 125–140 mm Mexico to NW South America (not El Salvador) ♀ possibly slightly duller
4 *T. fastuosa* 5½ in/140 mm E Brazil ♀ sometimes has golden rump a little duller
5 *T. icterocephala* 5½–5¾ in/ 140–145 mm Panama down W Andes to S Ecuador ♀ duller
6 *T. guttata* (race *chrysophrys* illustrated) 5 in/ 125 mm N South America ♀ more bluish, and lacks yellow on face

TANAGERS

1 ♂

2

3 ♂

4 ♂

5 ♂

6 ♂

235

SOFTBILLS

Black Tanager *Tachyphonus, rufus.*
Although a true tanager, like those on the preceding plate, the tougher-looking Black Tanager is definitely of a more robust constitution and also has a fairly consistent breeding record. It is extremely long-lived and thrives on a good varied omnivorous diet which should include some seeds and insects, the latter in abundance when breeding.

Shiny Cowbird *Molothrus bonariensis.* Silky, Glossy or Common Cowbird.
Cowbirds (there are five members of this genus plus the Giant Cowbird *Scaphidusa oryzivora)* can be conveniently thought of as cuckoo-aspirants. While they do sometimes make a half-hearted attempt at conventional breeding, this species illustrates a rather charming, bungling ineptitude when it comes to reproducing itself; it evidently succeeds tolerably well in the wild but I know of no captive breedings. Other cowbirds are becoming host-specific.

Troupial *Icterus icterus.* Common or Brazilian Hang-nest.
Highly omnivorous, the troupials (there are about 23 spp.) must be offered a wide variety of insectivorous food together with fruit and young mice etc. They are not aggressive, and should be given good frost-proof night-quarters.

Yellow-Headed Marshbird *Agelaius icterocephalus.*
Yellow-hooded Blackbird, Yellow Marsh Troupial.
Unfortunately the plainer colored females are rarely, if ever, imported, and so it is better to resist the temptation of buying just males. Marshbirds require similar care to the troupials with the addition of seed in their diet.

Military Starling *Sturnella loyca.* Long-tailed Mead-owlark; Patagonian Marsh Starling or Red-breasted Marshbird.
Confusion has surrounded the so-called Military Starling for some time but it is now generally held to be this member of the meadowlarks; other "military-starlings" include the Lesser Red-breasted Meadowlark *S. defilippi* and the Red-breasted Blackbird *Leistes militaris* – which is also seen in collections.
  They are attractive confiding birds requiring similar care to the foregoing, but on account of their larger size it is safest to mix them only with equally strong species.

1 *Tachyphonus rufus*
6½ in/165 mm
C America and Brazil
2 *Molothrus bonariensis* 7½ in/190 mm Colombia and Venezuela to Argentina
3 *Icterus icterus* 8¾–9½ in/220–240 mm C America, Colombia and Venezuela
4 *Agelaius icterocephalus* 7¼–7¾ in/185–195 mm Colombia and NE Peru to Trinidad and N Brazil ♀ has underparts yellowish and head olive-green
5 *Sturnella loyca* (*Pezites militaris*) 9½–10 in/240–255 mm S Argentina and Chile; ssp: Peru, NW Argentina and the Falklands ♀ has underparts rosy; upperbreast speckled gray; eyestripe and throat white

SOFTBILLS

Starlings are true omnivores, and easily maintained. Their main disadvantage is an aggressive demeanor when nesting; otherwise, they are bright, colorful and entertaining. They are inveterate bathers and most are confirmed hole-nesters.

Superb Spreo *Spreo superbus.* Superb or Spreo Starling.
A friendly, confiding bird which, if well acclimatized and provided with a comfortable shelter, can be wintered outside in most climates. It is amongst the easiest of softbills to breed but the young have tremendous appetites which take some satisfying. Hildebrandt's and Shelley's Starlings *S. hildebrandti* & *S. shelleyi* look similar but lack the white markings. Peters considers the latter to be a race of the former.

Green Glossy Starling *Lamprotornis chalybaeus.* Blue-eared or Green-winged Glossy Starling.
Also easy to maintain, as is the similar, but smaller, Lesser Blue-eared Glossy *L. chloropterus.* There are others that differ just a little in color while the Long-tailed Glossy Starling *L. caudatus* is also mainly green.

Purple Glossy Starling *Lamprotornis purpureus.*
A typical glossy starling, it needs good basic management. Frequently called the Purple-headed, and so is often confused with a similar, smaller species *(L. purpureiceps)* with the same common name.

Asian Green Starling *Aplonis panayensis.*
Until recently this species was seldom available. It is a gregarious bird that presents few problems, and is not too difficult to breed but, like the remainder of the family, it must have abundant insect-life when breeding.

Violet-backed Starling *Cinnyricinclus leucogaster.*
Amethyst or Plum-colored Starling.
Although it does well in an aviary, this starling is not so steady as many, or so hardy, and rarely breeds. It is certainly more insectivorous than the *Lamprotornis* species, and also much quieter and more peaceful. Some males show white on the outer tail feathers, these belong to the southern race, sometimes called Verreaux's Amethyst Starling *C. l. verreauxi.*

1 *Spreo superbus*
7–8¼ in/180–210 mm
E Africa: Ethiopia and Somalia south through Kenya to S Tanzania
2 *Lamprotornis (Lamprocolius) chalybaeus* 8–9 in/200–230 mm Much of Africa south of the Sahara ♀ usually smaller
3 *L. (Lamprocolius) purpureus* 8¼–10 in/210–255 mm W Africa to Sudan, Uganda and Kenya
4 *Aplonis panayensis* 7–8 in/180–205 mm NE India to Indonesia
5 *Cinnyricinclus leucogaster* 6½–7½ in/165–190 mm Much of Africa south of the Sahara; SW Arabia

SOFTBILLS

Rothschild's Starling *Leucospar rothschildi.* Rothschild's Grackle or Mynah.
A striking quarrelsome species which owes its current fame and popularity (reflected by a high price) to its precarious state in the wild. It has been found to be a reliable breeder and easy to keep — facts which have resulted in an increasing population and an insurance policy for the survival of the species.

Black-winged Starling *Sturnus melanopterus.*
Considerably smaller but still hardy, as are the other *Sturnus* starlings. It requires similar care to the glossy starling and being very willing to breed, entertaining and interesting to keep, it is a good choice for both novice and experienced softbill enthusiasts. Many Oriental starlings are referred to as mynahs.

Rosy-Pastor *Sturnus roseus.* Rose-colored Starling.
A nomadic, insectivorous and highly gregarious species which breeds only when conditions are most favorable, its single-brooded cycle is concentrated into a period as short as 30 days — in which time 5–6 eggs are laid, incubated and the young fledged.

Jerdon's Starling *Sturnus burmannicus.* Vinous-breasted Starling.
A gregarious ground-feeder, as are other starlings, the Jerdon's needs standard care. It is sufficiently hardy. Provided that they have good shelters, all starlings can be confidently wintered outside.

Malabar Mynah *Sturnus malabaricus.* Gray-headed, Chestnut-tailed or Ashy-headed Starling.
A hardy, amusing species which has the potential to be a free-breeder. It is possibly more arboreal than other starlings, and its diet should include plenty of fruit and insects. There are several other gray starlings such as the Daurian and Gray-backed Starlings *S. sturninus & S. sinensis,* which can create problems of identification (*sturninus* has a purplish back and white markings on the wing; *sinensis* has broad white shoulders on an otherwise black and gray plumage).

Pagoda Starling/Mynah *Sturnus pagodarum.* Brahminy Starling.
Friendly, amusing and free-breeding, the Pagoda Starling requires similar care to the remainder of this family and readily accepts a large nestbox, cramming it with any available material.

1 *Leucospar rothschildi* 11–13 in/ 280–330 mm Bali (rare) ♀ has shorter nuchal plumes
2 *Sturnus melanopterus* 8 in/ 205 mm Andaman and Nicobar Islands
3 *S. roseus* 8½ in/ 215 mm Middle East, occasionally invades E Europe
4 *S. burmannicus* 10 in/255 mm C Burma to Vietnam
5 *S. malabaricus* 7½–8 in/190–205 mm India to Indochina, and south to SW Thailand Plumage varies between races
6 *S. pagodarum* 8 in/ 205 mm Sri Lanka, India and north

SOFTBILLS

Mynah, or myna, is a substantive name for certain members of the starling family, and they are typical starlings in many of their habits.

Common Mynah *Acridotheres tristis.*
This species has been widely introduced into many areas of the Old World — where it generally flourishes in captivity, it lacks the great talking abilities of some others, and is therefore cheaper and more often bred by serious aviculturists. It has also been introduced into parts of the USA.

Bank Mynah *Acridotheres ginginianus.*
As with many mynahs, sexual dimorphism is virtually non-existent, and a group housed together in a spacious flight is the only sure way of providing conditions conducive to breeding. In the wild it likes to construct nesting holes in river banks. It is often maintained as a household pet.

Crested Mynah *Acridotheres cristatellus.*
Apart from more conventional nesting habits, this attractive but less frequently imported species needs much the same care as the above and other mynahs.

Greater Hill Mynah *Gracula religiosa intermedia.*
A ubiquitously kept pet which needs little introduction, there is a barrage of literature and facilities directed solely at its exploitation which has grown up simply because of its extraordinary powers of mimicry. It provides the sincere aviculturist interested in breeding with a splendid challenge; but it needs good, draught-proof winter/overnight accommodation, since it seems surprisingly reluctant to tolerate inclement weather, and generally manages to look exceedingly miserable.

Lesser Hill Mynah *Gracula religiosa indica.*
Javan Hill Mynah *Gracula religiosa religiosa.*
Both these birds are sought by discerning aviculturists; the first mentioned is also called the Southern Hill Mynah, and is the commoner of the two. They need much the same care as the foregoing and also require warm winter quarters.

1 *Acridotheres tristis*
9½–10 in/
240–255 mm
Afghanistan to SW China; Malaysia (introduced many places)
2 *A. ginginianus*
8½–9 in/215–230 mm Himalayas, N India and East Pakistan
3 *A. cristatellus* 10½ in/ 265 mm S China, Taiwan etc (introduced Vancouver, Canada)
4 *Gracula religiosa intermedia* 11½–12 in/ 290–305 mm Nepal, N India and Burma to SW China, and south to Thailand
5 *G. r. indica* 9–10 in/ 225–255 mm S and W India
6 *G. r. religiosa* 12½–15 in/ 320–380 mm S Burma, Malaysia and Indonesia

SOFTBILLS

Lanceolated Jay *Garrulus lanceolatus*. Eurasian Black-throated Jay.
Hardy and tough birds, which are also immensely attractive. One of the biggest problems concerning the breeding of such birds is the parents' habit of destroying their chicks; one's main chance often lies in supplying an abundance of *different* live food (insects to mice and chicks etc) when young are in the nest.

Eurasian Jay *Garrulus glandarius*.
Jays are marvellous aviary inhabitants which should be granted their own spacious outside accommodation. They are larger-than-life birds whose attraction is diminished by unnecessary competition. Temperate species such as this could not be easier to keep, eating more or less anything, and being especially fond of acorns. Hand-reared specimens become very tame and can display creditable powers of mimicry.

Pileated Jay *Cyanocorax affinis*.
(Mexican) Green Jay *Cyanocorax yncas*.
The first named is also called the Black-chested Jay. Both are somewhat less hardy than the Old World jays, and probably more insectivorous. Good, warm winter accommodation is essential. The green color of *C.*

1 *Garrulus lanceolatus* 12½ in/320 mm India and north
2 *G. glandarius* 13½ in/345 mm Much of the Palearctic
3 *Cyanocorax affinis* 14 in/355 mm Central and N South America
4 *C. yncas* 9½–11½ in/240–290 mm Texas to Honduras; highlands of N and W South America
5 *Cissa chinensis* 14–15 in/355–380 mm Himalayas to S China seaboard, and south to NW Borneo
6 *Pica pica* 18 in/455 mm Holarctic; India to S China seaboard (not Indonesia)

yncas, like that of the next species, often "fades" to blue if it is denied adequate shade from the sun's rays.

Hunting Cissa *Cissa chinensis*. Green Magpie.
In my experience, this species must be housed in a densely planted aviary, since it loves to skulk, and should be allowed to do so for the benefit of its health and plumage color. It proves to be hardy, graceful, extremely peaceful (for a magpie) and easy to feed, as are most omnivores. Unfortunately, its breeding record is not as good as its future promise.

Common Magpie *Pica pica*.
Of all the many beautiful magpies and treepies, I still count the widespread and common "ordinary" magpie amongst the most desirable. It is a hardy, mischievous species which tames readily. For obvious reasons it should not be mixed with other breeding birds.

All members of the Corvidae are intelligent and fond of unusual objects and have a pronounced hoarding instinct. In captivity, they will frequently store items such as nuts in nooks and crannies all over the place; this can lead inexperienced keepers into thinking that they are not offering enough food.

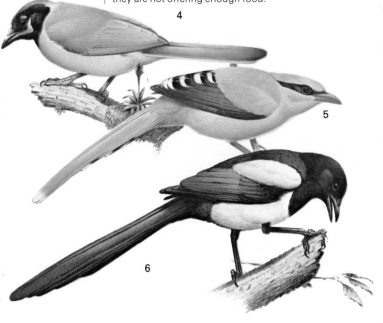

4

5

6

SOFTBILLS

Red-billed Blue Magpie *Urocissa erythrorhyncha.*
A very familiar and popular inmate of many zoos and bird gardens, although private aviculturists — who are able to devote a whole flight to a single pair of birds — have had significantly more breeding success. As so often happens with birds of this kind, though, the biggest threat to the chicks' lives is posed by the parent birds themselves.

Yellow-billed (Blue) Magpie *Urocissa flavirostris.*
Less common than the Red-billed but requiring the same treatment. Females can always be recognized by their grayish legs (those of males are dark red).

Indian Treepie *Dendrocitta vagabunda.* Wandering or Rufous Treepie.
Beautifully garbed in subtle shades of tan and gray, it has one of the most delightful calls of all non-songsters: a melodious warbling and bubbling trill. I have nearly bred this species several times but adverse factors of one sort or another have always triumphed. One chick was reared successfully at Waddesdon in England in 1974 mainly on mealworms and locusts, although mice etc. would greatly increase the chances of success.

Azure-winged Magpie *Cyanopica cyanus.*
This delightfully colored bird is most pleasing in habits, manner and temperament. Some pairs have proved most prolific, but in any event it is a delightful bird.

Chough *Pyrrhocorax pyrrhocorax.*
The Chough is quite prepared to breed providing a true pair is housed in an adequate aviary. The provision of lambs' wool and woody heatherstems is an invaluable aid in bringing to a satisfactory conclusion the lengthy nest-building behaviour. It is declining in the wild, and consistent captive breeding would be of tremendous importance.

Jackdaw *Corvus monedula.*
A familiar bird over much of the Palearctic Region and south into Asia, the disarming Jackdaw has a special place in the hearts of many people. It tames readily, being easy to hand-rear. An altogether appropriate subject for the beginner. An old wives' tale would have us believe that to split a Jackdaw's tongue will make it talk; some Jackdaws will mimic a few words naturally, and there is no need to attempt such cruel and drastic measures.

1 *Urocissa erythrorhyncha* 25–26 in/ 635–660 mm (including 18 in/ 455 mm tail) Himalayas to Hainan
2 *U. flavirostris* 24–25 in/ 610–635 mm (including 18 in/ 455 mm tail) Himalayas to SW China ♂ above blue, below pale yellow, legs red; ♀ dark green-blue, legs gray
3 *Dendrocitta vagabunda* 17–18 in/430–460 mm (including 9 in/ 230 mm tail) India to Laos and S Vietnam
4 *Cyanopica cyanus* 13 in/330 mm Spain; E China and Japan
5 *Pyrrhocorax pyrrhocorax* 15 in/ 380 mm Scattered mountains and cliffs from W Europe and N Africa to S and C Asia
6 *Corvus monedula* 13 in/330 mm Much of the Palearctic

GLOSSARY

Albino A mutation in which all dark pigments are missing.

Brood-parasitic A bird which has its eggs hatched and reared by another species.

Buff A type of feathering on Canaries in which the feathers have white edges (see also *Yellow*).

Cap The top of a bird's head, notably applied to Lizard Canaries.

Cere The bare patch above the beak of some birds, notably some parrots.

Chromosomes Minute rod-like bodies which carry an animal's genes.

Clear An egg which is infertile or cagebirds which lack any dark feathers.

Cline A strain or line of animals evolving in relative isolation.

Clutch All the eggs laid in one breeding attempt.

Color-food A red coloring agent mixed into food to enhance natural color.

Cogener A member of the same genus as another.

Consort The plain-headed mate of a crested (Corona) Gloster Canary.

Conspecific Members of the same species.

Corona See *Consort*.

Crepuscular Active at twilight.

Crestbred Non-crested Canaries bred from one crested parent.

Crop The expanded part of the oesophagus in which food is stored and partially digested.

Cross-breeding The mating of an animal of one species to that of another (see also *Mule* and *Hybrid*).

Cryptic color Plumage coloration which aids camouflage.

Dilute A plumage color that is paler than normal.

Display An animal's behavior calculated to impress and win a mate.

Dominant A distinguishing characteristic carried by a bird's genes which is dominant over other genes (see *Recessive*).

Double-brooded A bird which breeds twice per year.

Double buffing The mating of two buff-feathered Canaries.

Double character A bird which has received two quantities of the same color character from its parents.

Double yellowing The mating of two yellow-feathered Canaries.

Flighted A cagebird over one year old which has molted its nest feathers (see *Unflighted*).

Foul feathers The few light-colored feathers on an otherwise dark bird.

Frosted See *Buff*.

Frugivore A fruit-eater.

Genes The part of the chromosome which carries the inheritable characters of an animal.

Gregarious Animals which group together.

Grizzled The overall impression given by the mixture of dark and light color on the same feather.

Hardbill A vague term usually applied to small birds (finches) which feed by cracking open seeds.

Host-specific A brood-parasitic bird which lays its eggs in the nest of only one other species (see *Brood-Parasitic* and *Parasite*).

Hybrid The offspring resulting from the mating of two different species (see also *Mule*).

Ideal The "perfect" bird when applied to exhibition stock.

Inbreeding The mating of animals which are of close blood relationship.

Insectile or **Insectivorous** food A mixture concocted to replace an insectivore's natural food.

Insectivore An insect-eater.

Jonque An old term for yellow (*qv*).

Lethal Gene One that kills a chick before it hatches.

Mealy See *Buff*.

Melanistic An animal with extra dark pigmentation.

Metabolic rate The speed at which an animal burns up and utilizes its food.

Monogamous An animal which mates for life (see also *Polygamous*).

Monotypic The sole member of its genus.

Mule Offspring of a Canary crossbred with another species.

Mutation A sudden chromosomal divergence from normal.

Nectivore A nectar-eater.

Neotropical Originating in the tropics of the New World.

Nest feathers A chick's first feathers.

Nidifugous Active soon after hatching.

Normal Usually applied to the wild type (*qv*).

Omnivore An animal feeding on many different kinds of food.

Pan-tropical Occurring in all tropical countries.

Parasite Applied to birds, a species which lays its eggs in the nests of another (see also *Brood-parasitic* and *Host-specific*)

Plainhead A Canary with no head crest.

Polygamous An animal which has more than one mate (see also *Monogamous*).

Psittacine Any parrot or parrot-like bird.

Recessive A characteristic carried by a bird's genes which has no visible effect (see *Dominant*).

Self Just one color.

Sex-linked Recessive

BIBLIOGRAPHY

characters carried by the sex chromosome (see Chapter 10).

Sexual dimorphism The difference in plumage between the sexes of the same species.

Single-brooded A bird which breeds once per year.

Single-character A bird which has received only one color character in its genetic make-up.

Softbill A vague term usually applied to any medium to small bird which feeds on fruit, insects or invertebrates.

Splitting The color-breeding of birds in which one color character is dominant and the other recessive (see Chapter 10).

Stance A bird's posture.

Strain See *Cline.*

Stereotyped behavior Habitual or ritualized mannerisms.

Taxonomy The scientific classification of animals.

Ticked A contrasting small mark on a bird's plumage.

Tours The repertoires of Song Canaries.

Type-breed The "official" visual form of a kind of cagebird as set down for exhibition purposes (see *Wild Type*).

Unflighted A current year bred cagebird which still has its nest feathers.

Wild Type The form of a cagebird as it is found in the wild.

Yellow or **Jonque** A type of Canary feather which is shorter and lacks the white edge of a buff *(qv)* feather.

Principal References and Further Reading

Austin, O. L., & Singer, A., *Birds of the World*, Hamlyn, London, 1965

Avicultural Magazine, various articles

Bates, H., & Busenbark, R., *Finches and Softbilled Birds*, T.F.H. Publications, Neptune City, N.J., USA, 1970

Bond, J., *Birds of the West Indies*, Collins, London, 1971

Cage & Aviary Birds, weekly journal, various articles

Campbell, B., *The Dictionary of Birds in Colour*, Michael Joseph, London, 1974

De Schauensee, R.M., *A Guide to the Birds of South America*, Livingston, Wynnewood, Pa., USA, 1970

Forshaw, J.M., & Cooper, W.T., *Parrots of the World*, Doubleday, Garden City, N.Y., 1973

Glenister, A.G., *The Birds of the Malay Peninsular*, Oxford University Press, paperback edn., 1971

Gruson, E.S., *Checklist of the Birds of the World*, Collins, London, 1976

Hollom, P.A.D., *The Popular Handbook of British Birds*, H.F. & G. Witherby, London, 1965

King, B.F., Dickinson, E.C., & Woodcock, M.W., *A Field Guide to the Birds of South-East Asia*, Collins, London, 1976

Land, H. C., *Birds of Guatemala*, Livingstone, Wynnewood, Pa., USA. 1970

Low, R., *Parrots of South America*, John Gifford, London, 1972

Lynch, G., *Canaries in Colour*, Blandford, London, 1976

MacDonald, J.D., *Birds of Australia*, H.F. & G. Witherby, London, 1973

Mackworth-Praed, C. W., & Grant, C. H. B., *African Handbook of Birds*, 6 vols., Longman, London, 1960–1970

Restall, R.L., *Finches and other Seedeating Birds*, Faber & Faber, London, 1975

Robins, C.S., Bruun, B., Zim, H.S., & Singer, A., *Birds of North America*, Golden Press, N.Y., 1966

Rogers, C.H., *Budgerigars*, John Gifford, London, 1975

Rogers, C.H., *Encyclopedia of Cage & Aviary Birds*, Pelham Books, London, 1975

Rogers, C.H., *Zebra Finches*, K&R Books, Leicester, England, 1975

Roots, C., *Softbilled Birds*, John Gifford, London, 1970

Rutgers, A., *Budgerigars in Colour*, Blandford, London, 1976

Rutgers, A., *The Handbook of Foreign Birds*, 2 vols., Blandford, London, 1977

Smythes, B.E., & Hughes, A.M., *The Birds of Burma*, Oliver & Boyd, Edinburgh and London, 1953

Walker, G.B.R., Avon, D., & Tilford, T., *Coloured Canaries*, Blandford, London, 1976

Watmough, W., *The Cult of the Budgerigar*, "Cage Birds," London, 1960

Whistler, H., *Popular Handbook of Indian Birds*, Oliver & Boyd, Edinburgh and London, 1963

Williams, J.G., *A Field Guide to the Birds of East and Central Africa*, Collins, London, 1963

Woolham, F., Avon, D., & Tilford, T., *Aviary Birds in Colour*, Blandford, London, 1974

Yealland, J.J., *Cage Birds in Colour*, H.F. & G. Witherby, London, 1971

INDEX

Figures in **bold** type indicate illustrations

Acanthis 122–3
Acridotheres 242–3
Aegithina 216
Agapornis **176–8**
Agelaius 236–7
Aglaicercus 228–9
Aidemosyne 134–5
Alisterus 168–9
Amadina 146–7
Amandava 132–3
Amazona 194–5
Anodorhynchus 186–7
anti-biotics 41
Aplonis 238–9
Aprosmictus 168–9
Apus 18
Ara **186–9**
Aratinga 163, **188–91**
Archaeopteryx 8–9
Aulacorhynchus 212–3
Avadavat, Green 132–3,
    Red 132–3
babblers 39, 203, 222–3
Babbler, Common 203,
    222–3
banding **44–5**
Barbet, Blue-cheeked
    210–1, Blue-throated
    210–1, Coppersmith
    210–1, Crimson-
    breasted 210–1, Toucan
    210–1
Barnardius 159
bee-eaters 202
Bengalese (see Finch,
    Bengalese)
Bird, Dhyal 218–9, Doctor
    228–9, Indigo 148,
    Long-tail Doctor 228–9,
    Paddy 146–7, Temple
    146–7
birds of prey 10, 201
Bishop, Black-winged Red
    154–5, Crimson-
    crowned 154–5, Golden
    152–3, Orange 154, Red
    154–5, Yellow
    (- crowned) 152–3,
    Zanzibar Red 154
Blackbird **221**, Red-
    breasted 236–7, Yellow-
    hooded 236–7
Bluebill, Red-headed
    124–5
Bluebird, Eastern 218,
    Fairy 216–7
bluebirds 203
Bobwhite **109**
Boblorhynchus 163,
    190–1
Bombycilla 206–7
Brambling 118–9
Broadbill, Lesser Green
    210–1
Brotogeris 163–5, 192–3
Budgerigar 14, 16–18,
    20–3, 26–7, 32, 35, 40,
    47, 56–7, **59**, **74–96**, 98,
    101, 146, 156–9, 174,
    188, 201, Albino **81**,
    Blue Series **77**, **79**,
    Clear-flighted **89**,
    Clearwing **85**, Crested
    93, Dominant Pied **87**,
    89, Dutch Pied **87**,
    Graywing **85**, **87**, Green
    75, **79**, Lacewing **81**,
    Lutino **81**, Opaline **81**,
    83, **85**, **87**, Recessive
    Pied **89**, Red-eyed **81**
Bulbul, Brown-eared 202,
    Chinese 202, Golden-
    fronted Green 216–7,
    Hardwick's Green
    216–7, Red-cheeked
    (- eared) 216–7, Red-
    vented **111**, Reed
    110–1, Varied 116–7,
    Versicolor 116–7,
Bullfinch 102, 122–3
Bunting 98, 101–2,
    110–3, **116–7**, Black-
    headed **111**, Common
    111, Cinnamon-
    breasted (Rock) **110**,
    Golden-breasted **110**–1,
    Indigo 116–7, Lazuli
    116–7, Leclancher's
    116–7, Nonpareil
    116–7, Orange-breasted
    116–7, Painted 116–7,
    Rainbow 116–7, Red-
    headed **111**, Reed
    110–1, Varied 116–**7**,
    Versicolor 116–**7**,
    Yellow **111**
Buphagus 205
Buttonquail 100
Cacatua 166–7
Caique, Black-headed
    192–3, Pallid 192
Calyptomena 210–1
Canary 13–4, 18, 20–2,
    26–7, 40, 47, **60–74**, 76,
    84, 95, 102–3, 118,
    200–1, Belgian 62, **69**,
    Black-headed 118–**9**,
    Border **61**–2, Crested
    64, **67**–8, Cumberland
    Fancy 62, Fife **61**, 64,
    Frilled **63**–5, Gloster 18,
    63, 65, Icterine 118–**9**,
    Ino 65, **71**, Lancashire
    62–3, 66, Lizard 62,
    65–6, London **65–6**,
    Malinois 68, New Color
    66, **71**, Norwich 62,
    67–8, Red Factor 60,
    62, 68, **71**, Roller (see
    Canary, Song), Scotch
    Fancy 68–**9**, Song 20–1,
    62, 68, 70, **73**, Spanish
    Timbrado 68, White-
    ground 70, **73**, Yellow-
    eye 118–**9**, Yellow-
    fronted 118–**9**,
    Yorkshire **69**–70
Cardinal 15, 98, 101,
    114–5, Dominican
    114–5, Green 102,
    114–5, Pope 114–**5**,
    Pygmy 112–3, Red
    114–5, Red-colored
    114–5, Red-crested
    102, 114–5, Scarlet
    114–5, Virginian 101,
    114–5, Yellow 114–**5**,
    Yellow-billed 114–**5**
Cardinal-grosbeak 101,
    114–7
Cardinalis 114–5
Carduelis 12, 14, 120–**1**
carnivores 9, 34
Carpodacus 122–3
catching birds 42–3
Chaffinch 118–**9**
Chalcophaps 104–5
Charadriidae 201

chat-thrushes 218–**9**
chats 196
Chloebia 138–**9**
Chloris 16
Chlorophonia, Blue-
crowned 232–**3**
Chlorophonia 232–**3**
Chloropsis, Golden-fronted
216–**7**, Orange-bellied
216–**7**
Chloropsis 216–**7**
Chough 205, 246–**7**
Chrysolampis 228–**9**
Cinnyricinclus 238–**9**
Cissa, Hunting 244–**5**
Cissa 244–**5**
classification 11–**2**
Coccothraustes 122–**3**
Cockatiel 158–**9**, 174–**5**
Cockatoo 20, 157, 159,
166–8, Black **166–8**, **167**, Great
White 166–**7**, Greater
Sulfur-crested 166–**7**,
Leadbeater's 166–**7**,
Lesser Sulfur-crested
166, Major Mitchell's
166–**7**, Moluccan
166–**7**, Palm 166–**8**,
167, Pink 166–**7**, Rose-
breasted 166–**7**, Rose-
crested 166–**7**, Roseate
166–**7**, Salmon-crested
166–**7**, Umbrella 166–**7**,
White-crested 166–**7**
Colibri 228–**9**
Colin, Virginian 109
Colinus **109**
Colius 206–**7**
Columba 12
Columbina 97, 106–**7**
Condor, Andean 18
Conure 157, **188–91**.
Black-hooded
(-headed, -masked) 188,
190–**1**, Golden-
crowned 188–**9**, Half-
moon 188–**9**, Jandaya
188–**9**, Jenday 188–**9**,
Maroon-bellied 190–**1**,
Nanday 188, 190–**1**,
Orange-fronted 188–**9**,
Patagonian 190–**1**,

Peach-fronted 188–**9**,
Petz's 188–**9**, Red-
bellied 190–**1**, Scaly-
breasted 190–**1**, Sun
188, Yellow-headed
188–**9**
Conuropsis 18
Copsychus 21, **218–9**
Coracias 208–**9**
Coraciiformes 202
Cordon-bleu, Blue-
breasted 128–**9**, Blue-
capped 128–**9**, Blue-
headed 128–**9**, Red-
cheeked 128–**9**, 148,
Violet-eared 128–**9**, 148
corvids 39, 244–**7**
Corvus 246–**7**
Cossypha **219**
Coturnix 100, 106, **108**
Cowbird, Giant 236, Shiny
236–**7**, Silky 236–**7**
Crossbill Common 122–**3**,
Red 122–**3**, Spruce
122–**3**
crows 205
Cut-throat 146–**7**
Cyanerpes 232–**3**
Cyanocorax 244–**5**
Cyanoliseus 190–**1**
Cyanopica 246–**7**

Dacnis, Blue 232–**3**
Dacnis 232–**3**
Dendeocitta 246–**7**
Dicaeum 226–**7**
diet 9–10, 22, 34–40, 42,
82, 96–8
Dinopium 210–**1**
Dodo 18
Dove 35, 96–9, 104–**7**,
Barbary 14, 97–8,
104–**5**, Barred 104–**5**,
Barred Ground 104–**5**,
Blue-spotted Wood
106–**7**, Cape 97, 106–**7**,
Collared 104, Croaking
Ground 106–**7**,
Diamond 21, 97–8,
106–**7**, Domestic
104–**5**, Dwarf Turtle
106–**7**, Emerald 104–**5**,
Emerald-spotted 106,

Green-winged 104–**5**,
Ground 106–**7**, Java 14,
97, 104, Laughing
104–**5**, Long-tailed
106–**7**, Masked 106–**7**,
Mourning 98, Namaqua
97, 106–**7**, necklace
104–**5**, Palm 104–**5**,
Peaceful 104–**5**, Pigmy
106, Red Collared 98,
106–**7** Red Turtle
106–**7**, Rock 12, Ringed
Turtle 104–**5**, Ruddy
Ground 97, 106–**7**,
Spotted 104–**5**,
Talpacoti 97, 106–**7**,
Tambourine 106, Zebra
104–**5**
doves, wood 97, 106–**7**
ducks (see waterfowl)
Dyal 218–**9**

Eagle 10
Eclectus 168–**9**
Ectopistes 18
Elanus 54
Emberiza **110–1**
Emberizidae 101–2, 114–7
Emblema 134–**5**
Eolophus 166–**7**
Erythrura 138–**9**
Estrilda **130–3**
Estrildidae 101–2, 130–3
Euphonia 232–**3**
Euphonia, Violaceous
232–**3**, Violet 232–**3**
Euplectes **152–5**
Eurypyga 11

falcons 19
Finch 15–6, 26, 28, 34–5,
39–40, 42, 49, 95–6, 98,
101–3, 200, Alario
118–**9**, Angolian
Singing 118–**9**, Aurora
124–**5**, Banded 136–**7**,
Bengalese 23, 49, 95–6,
102, 136, 140–**1**,
Bicheno's 136–**7**,
Black-crested 112–**3**,
Black-ringed 137,
Black-tailed Lavender
127, Black-throated

251

INDEX

136, Cherry 134–5, Chestnut-breasted 142–3, Crimson 112–3, Cuban 112–3, Cuban Olive 112–3, Diadem 134–5, Double-bar 136–7, Gouldian 138–9, Gray Singing 118–9, Green Singing 102, 118–9, Lady Gould's 138–9, Lavender **127**, Lined 112–3, Maja 142–3, Mascot 142–3, Melba 124–**5**, 148, Melodious 112–3, Modest 134–5, Nutmeg 142–3, Olive 112–3, Owl (-faced) 136–**7**, Parson **136**, Plain-colored 134–5, Plum-headed 134–5, Purple-breasted 138–9, Purple-crowned 112–3, Red-headed 146–**7**, Red-tailed **137**, Ribbon 146–**7**, Rufous-tailed **137**, Saffron 112–3, Society (see Bengalese), Spice 142–3, Spot-sided 134–5, Star **137**, Steel 148–**9**, Strawberry 132, Striated 142–3, Tiger 132–3, Zebra 18, 20, 23, 95–6, 102, **134–6**, 140, 200
Firefinch 126, African **127**, Blue-billed **127**, Common **126–7**, Dark **127**, Red-billed **126–7**, Senegal **126–7**
Firetail, Diamond 134–5
Flower-pecker 204, 226–**7**, Scarlet-backed 226–**7**
Flycatcher, Derbian 214–**5**, Spotted 224–**5**, Verditer 224–**5**
Flycatchers 15, 34, 196, 224–**5**, Monarch 224–**5**, Old World 224–**5**
Forpus 163, **178–9**
Fringilla 118–**9**

252

Fringillidae 101–**2**
frugivores 9, 15, 34, 38, 196–247
Fruitsucker, Golden-fronted 216–**7**, Hardwick's 216–**7**
Galah 166–**7**
Gallus 13
Garrulax 222–**3**
Garrulus 244–**5**
genetics **88–92**
Geopelia 21, 97–8, **104–7**
Goldfinch 66, 101, 118, 120–**1**
goldfinches 102, 120–1
Grackle, Rothschild's 240–**1**
Gracula 21, 242–**3**
Grassfinch, Long-tailed **136**, Masked **137**, Heck's 136
Grassquit, Melodious 112–3, Yellow-faced 112–3
Greenfinch 16, 120–**1**
greenfinches 102, 120–1
Grenadier, Crimson 154–**5**, Purple 128–**9**, 148, Red 154–**3**, Scarlet 154–**5**
Grosbeak, Scarlet 102, 122–**3**
ground-thrushes **203**
Gubernatrix 114–**5**
Halcyon 208–**9**
Hangnest, Brazilian 236–**7**, Common 236–7
hardbills (see seedeaters)
Hawfinch 102, Black-headed 122–3, Black-tailed 122–3, Chinese 122–3, Japanese 122
hemipodes 100
herons 10
Heterophasia 222–**3**
Hirundo 18
Honeycreeper 204, 232–**3**, Black-throated 232–3, Blue 232–3, Purple 232–3, Red-legged 232–3, Turquoise 232–3, Yellow-legged 232–3, Yellow-winged 232–3

honeycreepers, Hawaiian 204
Hoopoe 198, 202, **215**
Hornbill 196, 202, 208–**9**, Red-billed 208–**9**
Hummingbird 15, 30, 35, 39, 196, 203–4, 228–**9**, Bee 7, Ruby-topaz 228–**9**
Hypargos 124–**5**
Icterus 236–**7**
insectivores 9, 34–5, 38–**9**, 196–247
ioras 216
Irena 216–**7**
Ixulus, Yellow-collared 224–**5**
Jackdaw 246–**7**
Jay 22, 41, 205, 244–**5**, Black-chested 244–**5**, Eurasian 244–**5**, Eurasian Black-throated 244–**5**, Green 244–**5**, Lanceolated 244–**5**, Mexican 244–**5**, Pileated 244–**5**,
Jungle Fowl, Red 13
Kingfisher 34, 202, 208–**9**, White-breasted 208–**9**, White-throated 208–**9**, Woodland 208–**9**
Kiskadee, Great 214–**5**
Kite, Black-shouldered 54
Lagonosticta 126–**7**
Lamprotornis 238–**9**
lapwings 201
Lark, Scribbling **111**
Leafbird, Golden-fronted 216–**7**, Orange-bellied 216–**7**
Leiothrix, *Red-billed* 222–**3**
Leiothrix 21, 222–**3**
Leistes 236
Lesbia 228
Leucospar 240–**1**
Lily-trotter 10
Linnet 14, 66, 102, 118, 122–**3**
livefood 40, 52, **196–8**
Lonchura 18, **140–5**
loons 10
Lophortyx 109

INDEX

Lophospingus 112–3
Loriculus **179**
Lorikeet 39, 160–2,
    180–**1**, Blue Mountain
    180–**1**, Blue-bellied
    180–**1**, Ornate 180–**1**,
    Ornamental 180–**1**,
    Rainbow 162, 180–**1**,
    Swainson's 180–**1**
Lorius 161, 180–**1**
Lory 160–2, 180–**1**,
    Chattering 162, 180–**1**,
    Jobi 180, King 168–**9**,
    Purple-naped 180–**1**,
    Red 168–**9**
Lovebird 20, 35, 98, 157,
    160, **176–8**, Abyssinian
    176–**7**, Black-winged
    176–**7**, Fisoher's 176–**7**,
    Gray-headed **178**,
    Madagascar **178**,
    Masked 176–**7**, Peach-
    faced 176–**7**, Red-faced
    176–**7**, Rosy-faced
    176–**7**
Loxia 122–3
Luscinia **219**

Macaw, 20, 27–8, 156–7,
    162, **186–9**, Blue-and-
    Gold 186–**7**, Blue-and-
    Yellow 186–**7**, Blue-
    winged 188–**9**,
    Chestnut-fronted
    188–**9**, Crimson 186–**7**,
    Grand Military 186,
    Great Green 186, Green-
    winged 186–**7**,
    Hyacinthine 186–**7**,
    Illiger's 188–**9**, Maroon
    186–**7**, Military 186–**7**,
    Red-and-Blue 186–**7**,
    Red-and-Green 186–**7**,
    Red-and-Yellow 186–**7**,
    Red-breasted 186–**7**,
    Scarlet 186–**7**, Severe
    188–**9**, Yellow-breasted
    186–**7**
Magpie 22, 41, 205,
    244–7, Azure-winged
    246–**7**, Common 244–**5**,
    Green 244–**5**, Red-
    billed 246–**7**, Yellow-

billed 246–**7**
Mandingoa 124–**5**
    Mannikin 102–3
    140–7, Black-and-
    White 144–**5**, Black-
    breasted 144–**5**, Black-
    headed 142, 144–**5**,
    Blue-billed 144–**5**,
    Bronze (-winged)
    144–**5**, Chestnut-
    breasted 142–**3**,
    Fernando Po 144–**5**,
    Gray-headed 140–**1**,
    Magpie 144–**5**, Nutmeg
    142–**3**, Pale-headed
    142–**3**, Rice 146–**7**,
    Rufous-backed 144–**5**,
    Striated 142–**3**, Three-
    colored 142–**3**, Tri-
    colored 142–**4**, White-
    headed 142–**3**, White-
    rumped (-backed)
    142–**3**
Marshbird, Red-breasted
    236–**7**, Yellow-headed
    236–**7**
Meadowlark, Lesser Red-
    breasted 236, Long-
    tailed 236–**7**
Megalaima 210–**1**
Mellisuga 7
Mesia, Silver-eared 203,
    222–**3**
Micropsitta 156
Mimus **218**
Mockingbird, American
    218, Blue 218, Blue-
    and-White 218,
    Northern **218**
Molothrus 236–**7**
Momotus **215**
morning-warblers 203
Motacilla **221**
Motmot 202, 215, Blue-
    crowned **215**
Mousebird, Blue-naped
    206–**7**
mules 60, **73**
Munia, Black-headed 142,
    144–**5**, Chestnut
    (- bellied) 144–**5**, Javan

White-headed 142,
    Long-tailed 138–**9**, Red
    132–**3**, Sharp-tailed 18,
    Spotted 142–**3**, Tri-
    colored 142–**3**, White-
    headed 142–**3**, White
    rumped (-backed)
    142–**3**, White-throated
    140–**1**
Muscicapa 224–**5**
Muscicapidae 222
Myiopsitta 190–**1**
Myna(h) 21, 25, 196, 200,
    240–3, Bank 242–**3**,
    Common 242–**3**,
    Crested 242–**3**, Greater
    Hill 21, 25, 74, 94, 205,
    242–**3**, Javan Hill
    242–**3**, Lesser Hill
    242–**3**, Malabar 240–**1**,
    Pagoda 240–**1**,
    Rothschild's 240–**1**,
    Southern Hill 242–**3**
Nandayus 188
Nectarinia 230–**1**
nectivores 9, 15, 34, 38,
    160–2, 180–**1**, 196,
    203–4, 226–33
Neophema 159, 174–**5**
Nightingale 203, 219,
    Japanese 222–**3**, Pekin
    222–**3**, Virginian 114–**5**
Niltava 224–**5**
Niltava, Rufous-bellied
    224–**5**
Nonpareil, Pin-tailed
    138–**9**
Nun, Black-headed
    144–**5**, Tri-colored
    142–**3**, White-headed
    142–**3**
nutcrackers 205
Nuthatch, Chestnut-
    bellied (-breasted)
    226–**7**
Nymphicus 174–**5**

Oena 97, 106–**7**
omnivores 9, 22, 38–9,
    196–247
Ortygospiza 124, **126–7**
Ostrich 7
oxpeckers 205

253

INDEX

Padda 20, 146–7
Parakeet 28, 157, 162–3,
168–9, 182–3, **188–93**,
Adelaide 168–9,
Alexandrine 182–3,
Australian King 168–9,
Aymara 190–1, Banded
182–3, Barraband
172–3, Beautiful 174–5,
Bengal 182–3, Black-
hooded (-masked, -
headed) 188, 190–1,
Black-tailed 170–1,
Blood-rumped 172–3,
Blossom-headed 182,
Blue-banded Grass
174–5, Blue-vented
174–5, Blue-winged
Grass 174–5, Bourke's
174–5, Canary-winged
192–3, Carolina 18,
Chestnut-shouldered
174–5, Crimson-winged
168–9, Derbian 182,
Elegant Grass 174,
Gray-breasted 190–1,
Gray-cheeked 192–3,
Green 182–3, Large
Indian 182–3, Lord
Derby's 182, Lineolated
163, Malabar 162,
Many-colored 172–3,
Monk 190–1,
Moustached 182–3,
Mulga 172–3, Orange-
chinned 192–3, Orange-
flanked 192–3, Orange-
fronted 188–9, Orange-
winged 192–3, Peach-
fronted 188–9,
Pennant's 168–9, Pink-
bellied 174–5, Plum-
headed 182–3, Prince of
Wales 172–3, Princess
(Alexandra) 172–3,
Quaker 163, 190–1,.
Queen Alexandra
172–3, Red-backed
172–3, Red-breasted
182–3, Red-rumped
160, 172–3, Ring-
necked 13, 162, 182–3,
Rock Pebbler 170–1,

Rock Peplar 170–1,
Rose-ringed 162,
182–3, Scarlet-chested
(-breasted) 174–5,
Sierra 163, 190–1,
Slaty-headed 182–3,
Splendid Grass 174–5,
Stanley 170–1, Tovi
192–3, Tui 192–3,
Turquoisine Grass
174–5, Varied 172–3,
White-winged 192,
Yellow-headed 188–9,
Yellow-rumped 170–1
parakeets, grass 159,
174–5
Paroaria 114–5
Parrot 14, 16, 21, 26–9,
32–5, 39–40, 42, 44, 46,
57–8, **156–95**, 200–1,
Amazon 20, 157, 163–6,
194–5, Blue-headed
164, 184–5, Blue-
fronted Amazon 194–5,
Bourke's 174–5, Brown
184–5, Burrowing
190–1, Double Yellow-
headed 194–5, Eclectus
168–9, Levaillant's
194–5, Maximilian's
184, Mexican Yellow-
headed 194–5, Meyer's
184–5, Orange-winged
194–5, Panama Yellow-
fronted 194–5, Pileated
184–5, Red-capped
164, 184–5, Red-lored
194, red-winged 168–9,
Regent 170–1, Rose Hill
170–1, Salvin's 194–5,
Senegal 184–5, Single
Yellow-headed 194–5,
Superb 172–3, Temple
168–9, Turquoise-
fronted 194–5, Yellow-
cheeked 194, Yellow-
fronted 194–5, Yellow-
headed 194–5
Parrotfinch 102, 138–9
Blue-headed 138–9,
Pin-tailed 138–9, Red-
headed 138–9
Parrotlet 157, 160, 163,

178–9, Blue-crowned
179, Blue-rumped
178–9, Celestial **178**,
Lesson's **178**, Mexican
178–9, Pacific **178**,
Turquoise-rumped
178–9, Vernal **179**
parrots, pygmy 156
Parus 226–7
Passer 150–1
Passerina 116–7
pelicans 10
pests 46, 58
Petronia, Yellow-throated
150–1
Petronia 150–1
pheasants 35, 51, 98, 201
Phoenicurus **220**
Pica 244–5
picathartes 203
Pigeon 12–3, 19, 34–6,
51, 96–9, Orange-
breasted Green 206–7,
Passenger 18
pigeons, fruit 206
Pinopsitta 164, 184–5
Pionites 192–3
Pionus 164, 184–5
Pitangus 214–5
Pitta, Bengal **214**, Black-
headed **214**, Blue-
winged **214**, Hooded
214, Indian **214**
Pitta **214**
plants 32, 38, 80
Platycercus 159, **168–71**
Platysteira 224–5
Ploceidae 103, 152–3
Ploceus 152–3
Plover 201–2, Blacksmith
201, Spurwinged 201
Poephila 18, **134–7**
Poicephalus 184–5
Polytelis 159, **170–3**
predators, 29, 86
Probosciger 166, **169**
Psephotus 159, 172–3
Psittacula 13, 162, 182–3
Psittacus 20, 184–5
Pteroglossus 212–3
Ptilinopus 206
Pycnonotus 202, 216–7
Pyrrhocorax 246–7

INDEX

Pyrrhura 163, 190–1
Pyrrhula 16, 122–3
Pytilia 124–5
Pytilia, Green-winged
124–**5**, Red-winged
124–**5**
Quail 34–5, 96, 99–101,
108–9, Blue (see
Painted), Blue-breasted
(see Painted) Bobwhite
109, Button (see
Painted), Californian
109, Chinese painted
(see Painted), Common
108, Harlequin, 100,
108, Japanese 100, **108**,
King (see Painted),
Painted 100, 106, **108**
Quail-finch, (West
African) 124, **126**
quarantine 41
Quelea 150–1
Quelea, Red-billed 150–1,
Red-headed 150–1
Ramphastos 212–3
Raphus 18
Redpoll 102, 122–3
Redrump 172–3
Redstart 203, **220**,
Common **220**
Rhodospingus 112–3
Ricebird 142–3, 146–7
Ringdove, Blonde 104–5
Ringing **44–5**
Ringneck, Alexandrine
182–3
Robin, Magpie 218–9,
Pekin 21–2, 200, 203,
222–3
Robin-chat 203, 219,
Red-capped 219,
Snowy-headed 219,
White-browed **219**
robins 205
Roller 202, 208–9, Lilac-
breasted 208-9
Rosefinch, Common
122–3, Indian 102, 122–3
Rosella, Adelaide 168–9,
Blue 170–1, Common
170–1, Crimson 168–**9**,
Eastern 170–1, Golden-
mantled 170, Mealy

170–1, Pale-headed
170, Pennant's 168–**9**,
Red 170–1, Stanley
170–1, Western 170–1,
Yellow 168–**71**, Yellow-
cheeked 170–1
Rubythroat, Common **219**,
Siberian **219**
Ruficauda **137**
Scaphidusa 236
scimitar-babblers 203
Seedeater, Lined 112–3,
White-rumped 118–**9**,
Yellow-rumped 118
seedeaters 9, 16, 22, 28,
34, 51, 95–**155**
seeds 35–8
Selenidera 212–3
Semnornis 210–1
Serin 118–9, Yellow-
rumped 118
Serinus 13, 18–**9**
Shama (White-rumped)
21, 200, 203, **218–9**
Sibia, 203, Black-headed
222–3
Sicalis 112–3
Silverbill, African 140–1,
Gray-headed 140–1,
Indian 140–1, Pearl-
headed 140–1
Sitta 226–7
softbills 9, 16, 22, 28, 34,
38, 51, 95–**155**
Sparrow, Arabian Golden
150, Diamond 134–**5**,
Java 20, 146–7,
(Sudan) Golden 150–1,
Yellow 150–1, Yellow-
throated 150–1
sparrows, American 101
Spermestes 144
Spermophaga 124–5
Spicebird 142–3
Sporophila 112–3
Sporopipes 150–1
Spreo 238–9
Spreo, Superb 238–9
Starling 34, 98, 196, 205,
236–43, Amethyst
238–9, Ashy-headed
240–1, Asian 238–9,
Black-winged 240–1,

Blue-eared 238–9,
Brahminy 240–1,
Chestnut-tailed 240–1,
Daurian 240, Gray-
backed 240, Gray-
headed 240–1, Green
Glossy 238–9, Green-
winged 238–9,
Hildebrandt's 238,
Jerdon's 240–1, Lesser
Blue-eared 238, Long-
tailed Glossy 238,
Military 236–7, Pagoda
240–1, Patagonian
Marsh 236–7, Plum-
colored 238–9, Purple-
headed 238–9, Purple-
headed 238–9, Rose-
colored 240–1,
Rothschild's 240–1,
Shelley's 238, Spreo
238–9, Superb 205,
238–9, Verreaux's
Amethyst 238, Vinous-
breasted 240–1, Violet-
backed 238–9,
stonechats 203
Streamertail 228–9
Streptopelia 14, **104–7**
Struthio 7
Sturnella 236–7
Sturnus 205, 240–1
Sugarbird, Blue 232–3,
Purple 232–3, Yellow-
winged 232–3
Sunbird 15, 39, 196, 204,
230–1, Beautiful 230–1,
Malachite 230, Scarlet-
chested 230–1, Tacazze
230–1, Van Hasselt's
230–1, Variable 230–1,
Yellow-bellied 230–1
Sunbittern 11
Swallow, Barn 18
Swift 18
Sylph, Blue-throated
228–9, Gould's
Heavenly 228–9, Green-
tailed 228–9, Heavenly
228–9, Long-tailed
228–9
Tachyphonus 236–7
Tanager 15, 196, 204,
232–7, Black 236–7,

255

INDEX

Blue 234–5, Blue-gray
234–5, Blue-headed
234–5, Blue-necked
234–5, Golden-masked
234–5, Masked 234–5,
Mrs. Wilson's 234–5,
Seven-colored 234–5,
Silver-blue 234–5,
Silver-throated 234–5,
Speckled 234, Spotted
Emerald 234–5, Superb
234–5, Violet 232–3
Tangara 234–5
Tauraco 206–7
Thraupis 234–5
Thrush 39, 196, 203, 205,
Dyal 218–9, Orange-
headed Ground 220,
Red-headed Laughing
203, 222–3, Song
220–1, White-crested
Laughing 203, 222–3
Tiaris 112–3
Timiliinae 222–3
Tit, Great 226–7
Tockus 208–9
Toucan 34, 38, 196, 199,
212–3, Keel-billed
212–3, Sulfur-breasted
212–3, Toco 212–3
Toucanet 212–3, Emerald
212–3, Spot-billed
212–3
Treepie 205, 246–7, Indian
246–7, Rufous 246–7,
Wandering 246–7
Treron 206–7
Trichoglossus 161, 180–1
Trochilus 228–9
Troupial 236–7, Yellow
Marsh 236–7
Turaco 38, 199, 202,
206–7, Hartlaub's
206–7, Schalow's 206,
White-cheeked 202,
206–7
Turdoides 222–3
Turdus **220–1**
Turtur 106–7
Twinspot, Green 124–5,
Peter's 124–5
Upupa 215
Uraeginthus 128–9

Urocissa 246–7
Vidua 148–9
Viduinae 103
viduines 127
Violetear, Gould's 228–9,
Sparkling 228–9
Vultur 18
waders 10, 33, 196
Wagtail 221, Pied **221**,
White 221
waterfowl 19, 35, 51, 201
Wattle-eye, Black-
throated 224–5
Waxbill 98, 101–3, 110,
124–47, Black-cheeked
130–1, Black-crowned
130–1, Black-headed
130, Blue-headed
128–9, Bluish **127**,
Common 130–1,
Crimson-faced 124–5,
Crimson-rumped 130–1,
Dufresne's 132–3,
Golden-breasted 132–3,
Gray **127**, 130–1,
Grenadier 128–9,
Lavender **127**, Orange-
breasted 132–3,
Orange-cheeked 132–3,
148, Pink-cheeked
130–1, Red 132–3,
Red-cheeked 130–1,
Red-eared 130–1, 132,
148, Red-winged
124–5, Rosy-rumped
130–1, Ruddy **127**,
130–1, St. Helena
130–1, 148, Senegal
130–1, Sundevall's
130–1, Violet-eared
128–9, Yellow-billed
132–3, Zebra 132–3
Waxwing, American Cedar
206, (Bohemian)
206–7, Japanese 206
Weaver, 101–**3**, **150–5**,
Baya 152–3, Black-
headed 152–3,
Crimson-crowned
154–5, Grenadier
154–5, Half-masked
152–3, Masked 152–3,
Napoleon 152–4,

Orange 154, Red-billed
150–1, Red-headed
150–1, Rufous-necked
152–3, Scaly-crowned
150–1, Scaly-fronted
150–1, Southern
Masked 152, Speckle-
fronted 150–1, Spotted-
backed 152–3, Taha
152–3, V-marked
152–3, Village 152–**3**,
Vitelline (Masked)
152–3
wheatears 203
White-eye 204, 226–7,
Chestnut-flanked
226–7, Indian 226–7,
Oriental 226–7
Whydah 101–3, 148–9,
154–5, Broad-tailed
Paradise 148, Fischer's
148–9, Gold-backed
154–5, Jackson's 154,
Long-tailed 154–5,
Paradise 148–9,
Pintailed 148–9, Queen
148–9, Red-collared
154–5, Red-naped
154–5, Shaft-tailed
148–9, Steel-blue 148,
Straw-tailed 148–9,
Yellow-backed 154–5,
Yellow-mantled 154–5,
Widow-bird, gold-backed
154–5, Long-tailed
154–5, Red-collared
154–5, Red-naped
154–5, Shaft-tailed
148–9, Yellow-backed
154–5, Yellow-mantled
154–5
Woodpecker 10, 210–1,
Black-rumped 210–1,
Lesser Golden-backed
210–1
wren-tits 222
Yellowhammer 111
Yuhina 224–5
Yuhina 203, 224–**5**,
Yellow-naped 224–5
Zenaida 98
Zoothera 220
Zosterops 226–7